FANTASTIC FACTS

First published in 2017 by Miles Kelly Publishing Ltd
Harding's Barn, Bardfield End Green, Thaxted, Essex, CM6 3PX, UK

2 4 6 8 10 9 7 5 3 1

Publishing Director Belinda Gallagher
Creative Director Jo Cowan
Editorial Director Rosie Neave
Senior Editor Fran Bromage
Designer Simon Lee
Image Manager Liberty Newton
Indexer Marie Lorimer
Production Elizabeth Collins, Caroline Kelly
Reprographics Stephan Davis, Jennifer Cozens, Thom Allaway
Assets Lorraine King

ISBN 978-1-78617-332-4

Printed in China

British Library Cataloguing-in-Publication Data
A catalogue record for this book is available from the British Library

Made with paper from a sustainable forest

www.mileskelly.net

FANTASTIC FACTS

Miles
Kelly

Contents

EARTH AND SPACE

SCIENCE

PREHISTORIC LIFE

THE ANIMAL WORLD

HISTORY

EARTH AND SPACE

1 Space is all around the Earth, high above the air. Here on the Earth's surface we are surrounded by air. If you go upwards, up a mountain or in an aircraft, the air grows thinner until there is none at all. Space officially begins 100 kilometres up from sea level. It is mostly empty, but there are many exciting things such as planets, stars and galaxies. People who travel in space are called astronauts.

▶ In space, astronauts wear spacesuits to go outside a space station or a spacecraft as it circles the Earth. Much farther away are planets, stars and galaxies.

Our life-giving star

2 The Sun is our nearest star. It does not look like other stars because it is so much closer to us. Most stars are so far away they look like points of light in the sky. The Sun is not solid like the Earth, but is a giant ball of superhot gases, so hot that they glow like the flames of a bonfire.

◀ The Sun's hot, glowing gas is always on the move, bubbling up to the surface and sinking back down again.

3 Very little could live on Earth without the Sun. Deep in its centre the Sun is constantly making energy that keeps its gases hot and glowing. This energy works its way to the surface where it escapes as heat and light. Without it, the Earth would be cold and dark with hardly any life at all.

4 The Sun is often spotty. Sunspots appear on the surface, some wider than the Earth. They look dark because they are cooler than the rest of the Sun. Solar flares – explosions of energy – suddenly shoot out from the Sun. The Sun also throws huge loops of gas called prominences out into space.

5 When the Moon hides the Sun there is a solar eclipse. Every so often, the Sun, Moon and Earth line up in space so that the Moon comes directly between the Earth and the Sun. This stops the sunlight from reaching a small area on Earth. This area grows dark and cold, as if night has come early.

▶ When there is an eclipse, we can see the corona (glowing gas) around the Sun.

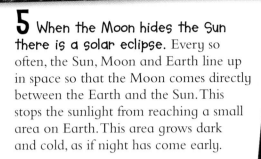

Sun

I DON'T BELIEVE IT!
The surface of the Sun is nearly 60 times hotter than boiling water. It is so hot it would melt a spacecraft flying near it.

Moon

Total eclipse

▲ When the Moon casts a shadow on the Earth, there is a solar eclipse.

Earth

Shadow of eclipse

A family of planets

NEPTUNE

SATURN

URANUS

JUPITER

6 The Sun is surrounded by a family of circling planets called the Solar System. This family is held together by an invisible force called gravity, which pulls things towards each other. It is the same force that pulls us down to the ground and stops us from floating away. The Sun's gravity pulls on the planets and keeps them circling around it.

▲ ▶ The eight planets are all different. Mercury, nearest the Sun, is small and hot. Then Venus, Earth and Mars are rocky and cooler. Beyond them Jupiter, Saturn, Uranus and Neptune are large and cold.

Asteroid belt

7 The Earth is one of eight planets in the Sun's family. They all circle the Sun at different distances from it. The four planets nearest to the Sun are all balls of rock. The next four planets are much bigger and are made of gas and liquid.

8 Moons circle the planets, travelling with them round the Sun. Earth has one moon. It circles the Earth while the Earth circles round the Sun. Mars has two tiny moons, but Mercury and Venus have none at all. There are large families of moons, like miniature solar systems, around all the large gas planets.

I DON'T BELIEVE IT!
If the Sun was the size of a large beach ball, the Earth would be as small as a pea, and the Moon would look like a pinhead.

SUN

MARS

Earth's moon

EARTH

VENUS

MERCURY

9 There are millions of smaller members in the Sun's family. Some are tiny specks of dust speeding through space between the planets. Larger chunks of rock, many as large as mountains, are called asteroids. Comets come from the edge of the Solar System, skimming past the Sun before they disappear again.

The Earth's neighbours

10 Venus and Mars are the nearest planets to the Earth. Venus is closer to the Sun than the Earth while Mars is farther away. Each takes a different amount of time to circle the Sun and we call this its year. A year on Venus is 225 days, on Earth 365 days and on Mars 687 days.

▲ All we can see of Venus from space are the tops of its clouds. They take just four days to race right around the planet.

11 Venus is the hottest planet. It is hotter than Mercury, although Mercury is closer to the Sun and gets more of the Sun's heat. Heat builds up on Venus because it is completely covered by clouds that trap the heat, like the glass in a greenhouse.

12 Venus has poisonous clouds with drops of acid that would burn your skin. They are not like clouds on Earth, which are made of droplets of water. These thick clouds do not let much sunshine reach the surface of Venus.

▼ Under its clouds, Venus has hundreds of volcanoes, large and small, all over its surface. We do not know if any of them are still erupting.

Radio aerial

Solar panel

Camera

▲ *Mariner 9* was the first space probe to circle another planet. Since that time more than 30 other crafts have travelled to Mars and several have soft-landed, including four rovers.

13 Winds on Mars whip up huge dust storms that can cover the whole planet. Mars is very dry, like a desert, and covered in red dust. When a space probe called *Mariner 9* arrived there in 1971, the whole planet was hidden by dust clouds.

14 Mars has the largest volcano in the Solar System. It is called Olympus Mons and is three times as high as Mount Everest, the tallest mountain on Earth. Olympus Mons is an old volcano and it has not erupted for millions of years.

PLANET-SPOTTING

See if you can spot Venus in the night sky. It is often the first bright 'star' to appear in the evening, just above where the Sun has set. Because of this we sometimes call it the 'evening star'.

Olympus Mons

15 There are plans to send astronauts to Mars but the journey would take six months or more. The astronauts would have to take with them everything they need for the journey there and back and for their stay on Mars.

Valles Marineris

◄ An enormous valley seems to cut Mars in half. It is called Valles Marineris. To the left is a row of three huge volcanoes and beyond them you can see the largest volcano, Olympus Mons.

Comets, asteroids and meteors

16 **There are probably billions of tiny comets at the edge of the Solar System.** They circle the Sun far beyond Neptune and even Pluto. Sometimes one is disturbed and moves inwards towards the Sun, looping around it before going back to where it came from. Some comets come back to the Sun regularly, such as Halley's comet, which returns every 76 years.

17 A comet is often called a dirty snowball because it is made of dust and ice mixed together. Heat from the Sun melts some of the ice. This makes dust and gas stream away from the comet, forming a huge tail that glows in the sunlight.

▲ The solid part of a comet is hidden inside a huge, glowing cloud that stretches into a long tail.

18 **Comet tails always point away from the Sun.** Although it looks bright, a comet's tail is extremely thin so it is blown outwards, away from the Sun. When the comet moves away from the Sun, its tail goes in front of it.

19 **Asteroids are chunks of rock that failed to stick together to make a planet.** Most of them circle the Sun between Mars and Jupiter where there would be room for another planet. There are millions of asteroids, some the size of a car, and others as big as mountains.

ASTEROIDS

Asteroids travel in a ring around the Sun. This ring is called the asteroid belt and can be found between Mars and Jupiter.

20 **Meteors are sometimes called shooting stars.** They are not really stars, just streaks of light that flash across the night sky. Meteors are made when pebbles racing through space at high speed hit the top of the air above the Earth. The pebble gets so hot it burns up. We see it as a glowing streak for a few seconds.

▼ At certain times of year there are meteor showers, when you can see more shooting stars than usual.

QUIZ

1. Which way does a comet tail always point?

2. What is another name for a meteor?

3. Where is the asteroid belt?

Answers:
1. Away from the Sun
2. Shooting star
3. Between Mars and Jupiter

17

A star is born

21 **Stars are born in clouds of dust and gas called nebulae.** Astronomers can see these clouds as shining patches in the night sky, or dark patches against the distant stars. These clouds shrink as gravity pulls the dust and gas together. At the centre, the gas gets hotter and hotter until a new star is born.

22 **Stars begin their lives when they start making energy.** When the dust and gas pulls tightly together it gets very hot. Finally it gets so hot in the middle that it can start making energy. The energy makes the star shine, giving out heat and light like the Sun.

KEY

1 Clumps of gas in this nebula start to shrink into the tight round balls that will become stars.

2 The gas spirals round as it is pulled inwards. Any left over gas and dust may form planets around the new star.

3 Deep in its centre, the new star starts making energy, but it is still hidden by the cloud of dust and gas.

4 The dust and gas are blown away and we can see the star shining. Maybe it has a family of planets like the Sun.

23 Young stars often stay together in clusters. When they start to shine they light up the nebula, making it glow with bright colours. Then the starlight blows away the remains of the cloud and we can see a group of new stars, called a star cluster.

This cluster of young stars, with many stars of different colours and sizes, will gradually drift apart, breaking up the cluster.

QUIZ

1. What is a nebula?
2. How long has the Sun been shining?
3. What colour are large hot stars?
4. What is a group of new young stars called?

Answers:
1. A cloud of dust and gas in space 2. About 4.5 billion years 3. Bluish-white 4. Star cluster

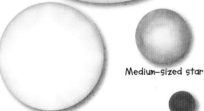

Large white star

Medium-sized star

Small red star

24 Smaller stars live much longer than huge stars. Stars use up their gas to make energy, and the largest stars use up their gas much faster than smaller stars. The Sun is about halfway through its life. It has been shining for about 4.5 billion years and will go on shining for another 4.5 billion years.

At the end of its life a red giant star threw out this glowing cloud of gas.

25 Large stars are very hot and white, smaller stars are cooler and redder. A large star can make energy faster and get much hotter than a smaller star. This gives them a very bright, bluish-white colour. Smaller stars are cooler. This makes them look red and shine less brightly. Ordinary in-between stars like our Sun look yellow.

Billions of galaxies

26 **The Sun is part of a huge family of stars called the Milky Way Galaxy.** There are billions of other stars in our Galaxy, as many as the grains of sand on a beach. We call it the Milky Way because it looks like a very faint band of light in the night sky, as though someone has spilt some milk across space.

▲ This huge spiral galaxy contains billions of stars. Our Milky Way Galaxy would look like this if we could see it from above.

27 **Curling arms give some galaxies their spiral shape.** The Milky Way has arms made of bright stars and glowing clouds of gas that curl round into a spiral shape. Some galaxies, called elliptical galaxies, have a round shape like a squashed ball. Other galaxies have no particular shape.

I DON'T BELIEVE IT!
If you could fit the Milky Way onto these two pages, the Sun would be so tiny, you could not see it.

28 There are billions of galaxies outside the Milky Way. Some are larger than the Milky Way and many are smaller, but they all have more stars than you can count. The galaxies tend to stay together in groups called clusters.

29 There is no bump when galaxies collide. A galaxy is mostly empty space between the stars. But when galaxies get very close they can pull each other out of shape. Sometimes they look as if they have grown a huge tail stretching out into space, or their shape may change into a ring of glowing stars.

A CLUSTER OF GALAXIES

Astronomers have nicknamed this interesting cluster of galaxies the 'Bullet Cluster'. It is made up of two colliding groups of galaxies.

▲ These two galaxies are so close that each has pulled a long tail of bright stars from the other.

▼ From left to right these are spiral, irregular, and elliptical galaxies, and a spiral galaxy with a bar across the middle.

Looking into space

30 People have imagined they can see the outlines of people and animals in the star patterns in the sky. These patterns are called constellations. Hundreds of years ago astronomers named the constellations to help them find their way around the skies.

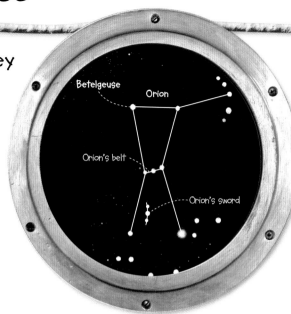

◀ The constellation Scorpius (in the Southern Hemisphere) is easy to recognize because it looks like a scorpion with a curved tail.

▲ The constellation Orion (shown here in the Northern Hemisphere) is one of the most recognizable in the night sky.

31 Astronomers use huge telescopes to see much more than we can see with just our eyes. Telescopes make things look bigger and nearer. They also show faint, glowing clouds of gas, and distant stars and galaxies.

▲ Mauna Kea observatory is situated on the summit of Mauna Kea on the US island of Hawaii. Telescopes are usually located high up, far from towns and cities so that they have a clear view of the skies.

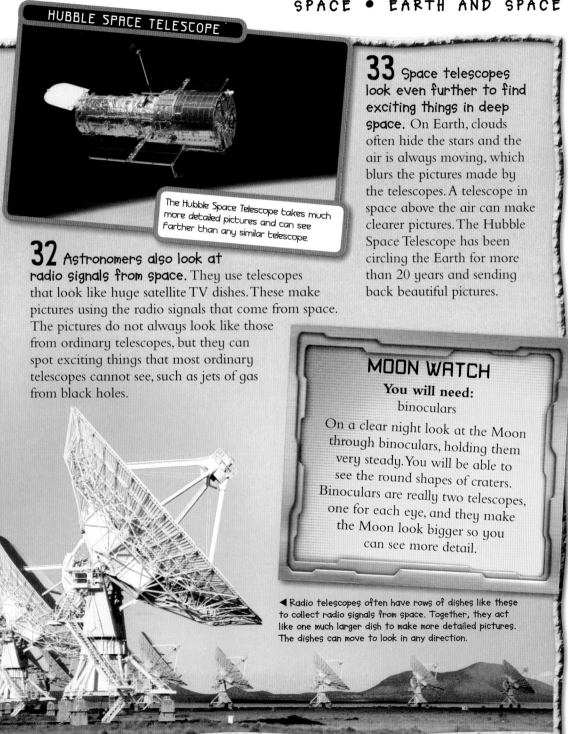

HUBBLE SPACE TELESCOPE

The Hubble Space Telescope takes much more detailed pictures and can see farther than any similar telescope.

33 Space telescopes look even further to find exciting things in deep space. On Earth, clouds often hide the stars and the air is always moving, which blurs the pictures made by the telescopes. A telescope in space above the air can make clearer pictures. The Hubble Space Telescope has been circling the Earth for more than 20 years and sending back beautiful pictures.

32 Astronomers also look at radio signals from space. They use telescopes that look like huge satellite TV dishes. These make pictures using the radio signals that come from space. The pictures do not always look like those from ordinary telescopes, but they can spot exciting things that most ordinary telescopes cannot see, such as jets of gas from black holes.

MOON WATCH

You will need:
binoculars

On a clear night look at the Moon through binoculars, holding them very steady. You will be able to see the round shapes of craters. Binoculars are really two telescopes, one for each eye, and they make the Moon look bigger so you can see more detail.

◀ Radio telescopes often have rows of dishes like these to collect radio signals from space. Together, they act like one much larger dish to make more detailed pictures. The dishes can move to look in any direction.

23

Flying in space

34 A rocket must travel nearly 40 times faster than a jumbo jet to blast into space. Slower than that, and gravity will pull it back to Earth. Rockets are powered by burning fuel, which makes hot gases. These gases rush out of the engines, shooting the rocket upwards.

◄ Each stage fires its engine to make the rocket go faster and faster until it puts the satellite into space.

Second stage
This needs less power and fuel to keep it going

Fuel tank

Oxidizer tank

First stage
This uses its fuel and then falls away, otherwise it would be 'dead weight'

Rocket engine

This shuttle was blasted into space by three rocket engines and two huge booster rockets.

35 A single rocket is usually not powerful enough to launch a satellite or spacecraft. So most have two or three stages, which are really separate rockets mounted on top of each other, each with its own engines. When the first stage has used up its fuel it drops away, and the second stage starts. Finally the third stage takes over to go into space.

36 **Some launchers have boosters.** These are extra rockets fixed to the main one. Most boosters burn solid fuel, like giant firework rockets. They fall away when the fuel has burnt up. Some drift down on parachutes into the sea, to be used again.

The shuttle puts down its wheels and lands on the runway. A parachute and speed brakes bring the shuttle to a standstill.

◀ On 8 July, 2011, space shuttle *Atlantis* took off from Florida, USA on the final mission of the 30-year space shuttle programme.

37 **The space shuttles were re-usable spaceplanes.** The first was launched in 1981 and there were more than 130 missions. The shuttle took off straight up like a rocket, carrying a load of up to 24 tonnes. To land it swooped down to glide onto a runway.

25

Robot explorers

38 Robot spacecraft called probes have explored all the planets. Probes take close-up pictures and measurements, and send the data back to scientists on Earth. Some probes circle planets taking pictures. For a really close-up look, a probe can land on the surface.

39 In 1976, two Viking spacecraft landed on Mars to look for life. They scooped up some dust and tested it to see if any tiny creatures lived on Mars. They did not find any signs of life and their pictures showed only a dry, red, dusty desert.

Cameras

Power supply

▶ *Voyager 2* gave us close-up pictures of four different planets.

Radio dish sends messages to Earth

40 Two Voyager probes left Earth in 1977 to visit the gas giant planets. They reached Jupiter in 1979, flying past and on to Saturn. *Voyager 2* then went on to visit Uranus in 1986 and Neptune in 1989. They sent back thousands of close-up pictures of each planet and its moons and rings as they flew past. They also discovered new rings and many new moons around the giant planets. Both Voyagers are now leaving the Solar System and will send back information about space between the stars until 2020.

◀ The Viking landers took soil samples from Mars, but found no signs of life.

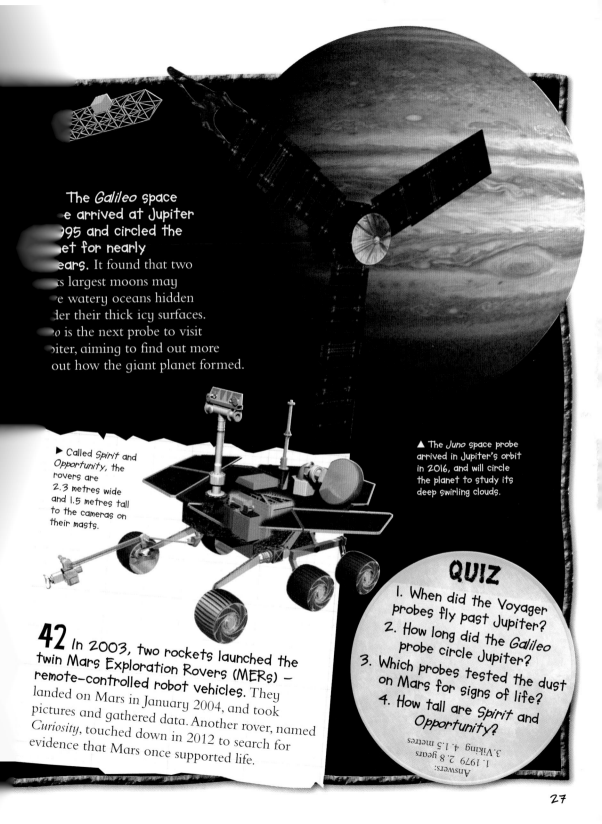

The *Galileo* space ...e arrived at Jupiter ...995 and circled the ...et for nearly ...ears. It found that two ...s largest moons may ...e watery oceans hidden ...der their thick icy surfaces. ...o is the next probe to visit ...piter, aiming to find out more ...out how the giant planet formed.

► Called *Spirit* and *Opportunity*, the rovers are 2.3 metres wide and 1.5 metres tall to the cameras on their masts.

▲ The *Juno* space probe arrived in Jupiter's orbit in 2016, and will circle the planet to study its deep swirling clouds.

42 In 2003, two rockets launched the twin Mars Exploration Rovers (MERs) – remote-controlled robot vehicles. They landed on Mars in January 2004, and took pictures and gathered data. Another rover, named *Curiosity*, touched down in 2012 to search for evidence that Mars once supported life.

QUIZ

1. When did the Voyager probes fly past Jupiter?
2. How long did the *Galileo* probe circle Jupiter?
3. Which probes tested the dust on Mars for signs of life?
4. How tall are *Spirit* and *Opportunity*?

Answers:
1. 1979 2. 8 years
3. Viking 4. 1.5 metres

Where did Earth come from?

43 **The Earth came from a cloud in space.**
Scientists think the Earth formed from a huge cloud of gas and dust around 4500 million years ago. A star near the cloud exploded, making the cloud spin. As the cloud spun around, gases gathered at its centre and formed the Sun. Dust whizzed around the Sun and stuck together to form lumps of rock. In time the rocks crashed into each other to make the planets. The Earth is one of these planets.

(5) The Earth was made up of one large piece of land, now split into seven chunks known as continents

▶ Clouds of gas and dust are made by the remains of old stars that have exploded or simply stopped shining. It is here that new stars and their planets form.

(1) Cloud starts to spin

(4) Volcanoes erupt, releasing gases, helping to form the first atmosphere

(3) The Earth begins to cool and a hard shell forms

(2) Dust gathers into lumps of rock which form a small planet

44 At first the Earth was very hot. As the rocks crashed together they warmed each other up. Later, as the Earth formed, the rocks inside it melted. The new Earth was a ball of liquid rock with a thin, solid shell.

45 Huge numbers of large rocks called meteorites crashed into the Earth. They made round hollows on the surface. These hollows are called craters. The Moon was hit with rocks at the same time. Look at the Moon with binoculars – you can see the craters that were made long ago.

▶ The Moon was also hit by rocks in space, and these made huge craters, and mountain ranges up to 5000 metres high.

▶ Erupting volcanoes and fierce storms helped form the atmosphere and oceans. These provided energy that was needed for life on Earth to begin.

46 The oceans and seas formed as the Earth cooled down. Volcanoes erupted, letting out steam, gases and rocks from inside the Earth. As the Earth cooled, the steam changed to water droplets and made clouds. As the Earth cooled further, rain fell from the clouds. It rained for millions of years to make the seas and oceans.

I DON'T BELIEVE IT!
Millions of rocks crash into Earth as it speeds through space. Some larger ones may reach the ground as meteorites.

Night and day

47 **The Earth is like a huge spinning top.** It continues to spin because it was formed from a spinning cloud of gas and dust. It does not spin straight up like a top but leans a little to one side. The Earth takes 24 hours to spin around once. We call this period of time a day.

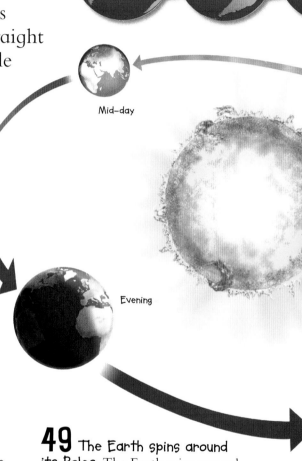

Mid-day

Evening

48 **The Earth's spinning makes day and night.** Each part of the Earth spins towards the Sun, and then away from it every day. When a part of the Earth is facing the Sun it is day-time there. When that part is facing away from the Sun it is night-time. Is the Earth facing the Sun or facing away from it where you are?

North

◀ If you were in space and looked at the Earth from the side, it would appear to move from left to right. If you looked down on Earth from the North Pole, it would seem to be moving anticlockwise.

South

49 **The Earth spins around its Poles.** The Earth spins around two points on its surface. They are at opposite ends of the Earth. One is on top of the Earth. It is called the North Pole. The other is at the bottom of the Earth. It is called the South Pole. The North and South Poles are so cold, they are covered by ice and snow.

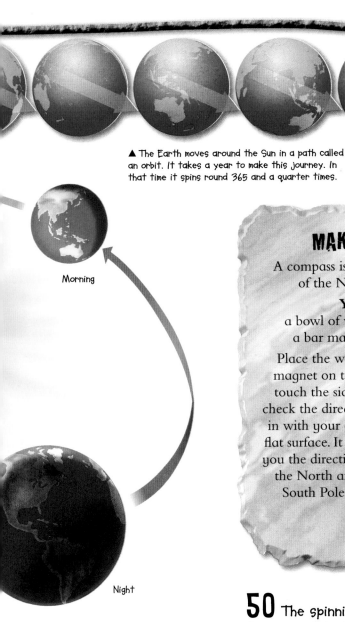

▲ The Earth moves around the Sun in a path called an orbit. It takes a year to make this journey. In that time it spins round 365 and a quarter times.

Morning

Night

▲ As one part of the Earth turns into sunlight, another part turns into darkness. It is morning when a part turns into sunlight, and evening when it turns into darkness.

MAKE A COMPASS

A compass is used to find the direction of the North and South Poles.

You will need:

a bowl of water   a piece of wood
a bar magnet   a real compass

Place the wood in the water with the magnet on top. Make sure they do not touch the sides. When the wood is still, check the direction the magnet is pointing in with your compass, by placing it on a flat surface. It will tell you the direction of the North and South Poles.

50 The spinning Earth acts like a magnet. At the centre of the Earth is liquid iron. As the Earth spins, it makes the iron behave like a magnet with a North and South Pole. These act on the magnet in a compass to make the needle point to the North and South Poles.

The four seasons

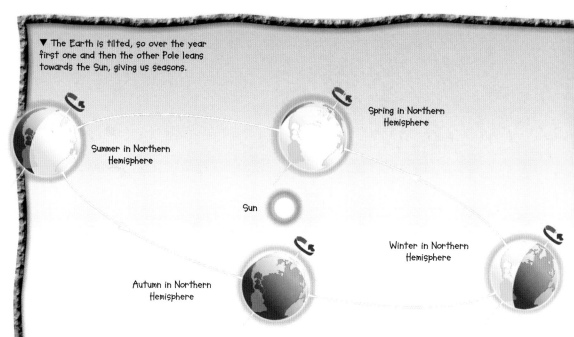

▼ The Earth is tilted, so over the year first one and then the other Pole leans towards the Sun, giving us seasons.

Spring in Northern Hemisphere

Summer in Northern Hemisphere

Sun

Winter in Northern Hemisphere

Autumn in Northern Hemisphere

51 **The reason for the seasons lies in space.** Our planet Earth plots a path through space that takes it around the Sun. This path, or orbit, takes one year. In June, for example, the North Pole leans towards the Sun. The Sun heats the northern half of Earth and there is summer.

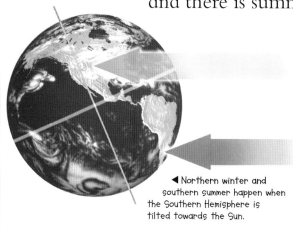

◄ Northern winter and southern summer happen when the Southern Hemisphere is tilted towards the Sun.

52 When it is summer in Argentina, it is winter in Canada. In December, the South Pole leans towards the Sun. Places in the southern half of the world, such as Argentina, have summer. At the same time, places in the northern half, such as Canada, have winter.

53 A day can last 21 hours!
Night and day happen because
Earth is spinning as it circles the
Sun. At the height of summer, places
near the North Pole are so tilted
towards the Sun that it is light
almost all day long. In Stockholm,
Sweden, Midsummer's Eve lasts
21 hours because the Sun
disappears below the horizon for
only three hours.

▲ At the North Pole, the Sun never disappears below the horizon at Midsummer's Day.

▼ Deciduous trees like these lose their leaves in autumn, but evergreens keep their leaves all year round.

I DON'T BELIEVE IT!

When the Sun shines all day in the far north, there is 24-hour night in the far south.

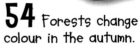

54 Forests change
colour in the autumn.
Autumn comes between
summer and winter. Trees
prepare for the cold winter
months ahead by losing their
leaves. First, though, they suck
back the precious green
chlorophyll, or dye, in their
leaves, making them turn
glorious shades of red, orange
and brown.

Inside the Earth

55 There are different layers inside the Earth. There is a thin, rocky crust on the surface, a solid middle called the mantle and a centre called the core. The outer core is liquid but the inner part of the core is solid metal.

56 At the centre of the Earth is a huge metal ball called the inner core. It is 2500 kilometres wide and is made mainly from iron, with some nickel. The ball has an incredible temperature of around 7000°C – hot enough to make the metals melt. However, they stay solid because the other layers of the Earth push down heavily on them.

57 Around the centre of the Earth flows a hot, liquid layer of iron and nickel. This layer is the outer core and is about 2200 kilometres thick. As the Earth spins, the inner and outer core move at different speeds.

58 The largest layer is called the mantle. It is around 2900 kilometres thick. It lies between the core and the crust. The mantle is made of soft, hot rock. In the upper mantle, near the crust, the rock moves more slowly.

Crust

Atmosphere

Mantle
4500°C

Outer core
5000°C

Inner core
7000°C

◄ The internal structure of the Earth. The centre of the Earth – the inner core – is solid even though it is intensely hot. This is because it is under extreme pressure.

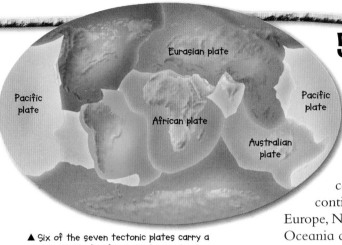

Eurasian plate

Pacific plate

Pacific plate

African plate

Australian plate

▲ Six of the seven tectonic plates carry a continent. The Pacific plate does not.

59 The crust is divided into huge slabs of rock called tectonic plates. The plates all have both land and seas on top of them except for the Pacific plate, which is just covered by water. The large areas of land on the plates are called continents. There are seven continents in total – Africa, Asia, Europe, North America, South America, Oceania and Antarctica.

60 The Earth's surface is covered by crust. Land is made of continental crust between 20 and 70 kilometres thick. Most of this is made from a rock called granite. The ocean bed is made of oceanic crust about eight kilometres thick. It is made mainly from a rock called basalt.

▼ The Great Rift Valley in Kenya is part of a huge system of rift valleys. It is the result of tectonic plates moving apart, causing the Earth's crust to separate.

61 Very, very slowly, the continents are moving. Slow-flowing mantle under the crust moves the tectonic plates across the Earth's surface. As the plates move, so do the continents. In some places, the plates push into each other. In others, they move apart. North America is moving 3 centimetres away from Europe every year!

Massive mountains

62 **The Earth is covered with a thick layer of rock, or 'crust'.** In some places, sections of crust have squeezed together, forcing their way upwards to make mountains. Mountains often form in a long line or group, called a mountain range. High up, it is cold and windy. This means that the tops of mountains are very icy, snowy and stormy.

Mount Everest
8848 metres
(Asia)

Mount Kilimanjaro
5895 metres
(Africa)

Mount Cook 3754 metres (Oceania)

63 **Mount Everest is the world's highest mountain.** It's on the border between Nepal and China, in the Himalayas mountain range. It is about 8848 metres high. The first people to climb to the top of Everest were Edmund Hillary and Tenzing Norgay, on 29 May, 1953.

▼ Mount Everest is so high that climbers have to climb it over several days, stopping at camps along the way.

64 **The highest mountain on Earth isn't the hardest to climb.** Another peak, K2, is much tougher for mountaineers. At 8611 metres, it's the world's second-highest mountain. Its steep slopes and swirling storms make it incredibly dangerous. Fewer than 300 people have ever climbed it, and over 65 have died in the attempt.

▲ Edmund Hillary (left) and Tenzing Norgay, photographed in 1953, the year they became the first to climb Mount Everest. Hillary died in 2008.

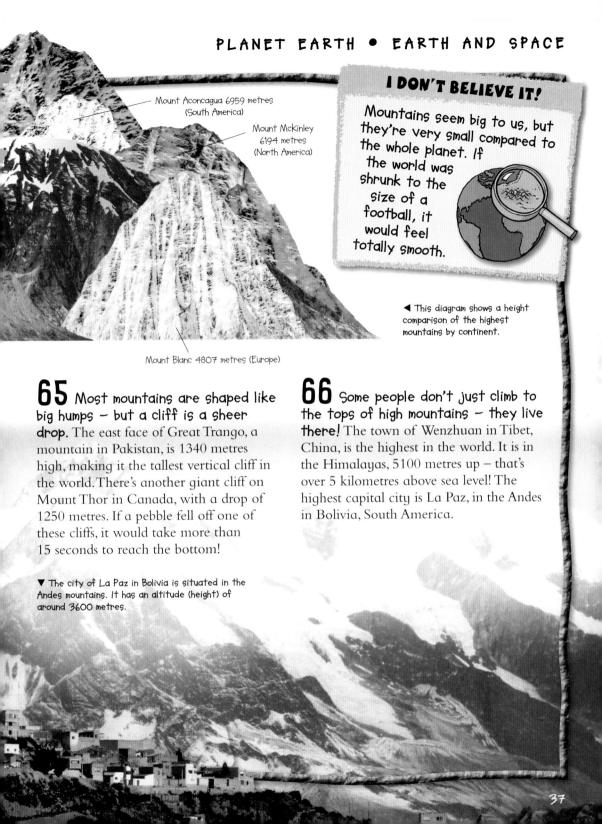

Mount Aconcagua 6959 metres
(South America)

Mount Mckinley
6194 metres
(North America)

Mount Blanc 4807 metres (Europe)

I DON'T BELIEVE IT!

Mountains seem big to us, but they're very small compared to the whole planet. If the world was shrunk to the size of a football, it would feel totally smooth.

◄ This diagram shows a height comparison of the highest mountains by continent.

65 Most mountains are shaped like big humps – but a cliff is a sheer drop. The east face of Great Trango, a mountain in Pakistan, is 1340 metres high, making it the tallest vertical cliff in the world. There's another giant cliff on Mount Thor in Canada, with a drop of 1250 metres. If a pebble fell off one of these cliffs, it would take more than 15 seconds to reach the bottom!

▼ The city of La Paz in Bolivia is situated in the Andes mountains. It has an altitude (height) of around 3600 metres.

66 Some people don't just climb to the tops of high mountains – they live there! The town of Wenzhuan in Tibet, China, is the highest in the world. It is in the Himalayas, 5100 metres up – that's over 5 kilometres above sea level! The highest capital city is La Paz, in the Andes in Bolivia, South America.

Hot volcanoes

67 **Volcanoes happen because the Earth is hot inside.** The surface is cool, but it gets hotter the deeper you go into the Earth. Under the crust, magma is under so much pressure that it is almost solid. Sometimes the pressure is released by the shifting of the crust and the magma melts. Then it can bubble up through the cracks in the crust as volcanoes.

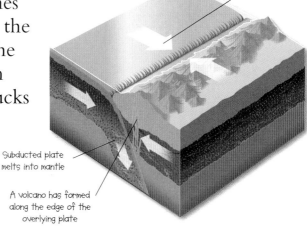

▼ Here, an oceanic plate dips below a continental plate. The thinner oceanic plate is pushed down into the mantle.

Plates move together

Subducted plate melts into mantle

A volcano has formed along the edge of the overlying plate

I DON'T BELIEVE IT!

Tectonic plates move at about the same speed as your fingernails grow. That is just a few centimetres each year.

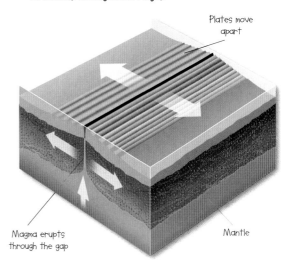

▼ Constructive boundaries often occur in the middle of oceans, forming ocean ridges.

Plates move apart

Magma erupts through the gap

Mantle

68 **The Earth's crust is cracked into giant pieces called tectonic plates.** There are about 60 plates, and the seven largest are thousands of kilometres across. Tectonic plates move slowly across the Earth's surface. This movement, called continental drift, has caused the continents to move apart over millions of years.

69 About 250 million years ago there was just one continent, known as Pangaea. The movement of tectonics plates broke Pangaea apart and moved the land around to form the continents we recognize today.

70 Most volcanoes erupt along plate boundaries. These are the cracks separating tectonic plates. On a world map of plate boundaries (below) you can see there are often rows of volcanoes along boundaries.

71 Volcanoes also happen at 'hot spots'. These are places where especially hot magma being driven upwards in the mantle, burns through the middle of a plate to form volcanoes. The most famous hot-spot volcanoes are those of the Hawaiian islands.

▼ Most active volcanoes occur along the 'Ring of Fire' (tinted red). Five volcanoes from around the world are highlighted on the map below.

Hawaii, Pacific Ocean

Mount Rainier, North America

Mount Bromo, Asia

EURASIAN PLATE

RING OF FIRE

NORTH AMERICAN PLATE

AFRICAN PLATE

PACIFIC PLATE

INDO AUSTRALIAN PLATE

SOUTH AMERICAN PLATE

ANTARCTIC PLATE

Arenal, South America

Mount Kilimanjaro, Africa

Parts of a volcano

72 **Material erupted from a volcano can build up to form a mountain.** Beneath the surface is a system of pipes and chambers that supply the volcano with magma from below the crust.

73 **A magma chamber is a store of molten rock under a volcano.** As magma moves through cracks in the Earth's crust, it collects in huge reservoirs underground. Magma chambers are usually 1–10 kilometres underground. Some volcanoes have several magma chambers.

74 **Magma rises up through a conduit.** This is a giant pipe that leads from the magma chamber to the surface. Usually there is one main conduit that leads to the summit of a volcano. The hole at the top of the conduit is called a vent. There are often side vents on a volcano's slopes that have branched off the main conduit.

Vent

Side vent

Conduit

Upper magma chamber

◀ The mountain on the surface is only the tip of a volcano. Chambers and pipes deep underground store and feed magma to the volcano.

Deep magma chamber

Mantle

A **composite volcano** (also known as a stratovolcano) has steep sides built up of layers of lava and ash.

A **shield volcano** has a low, wide shape, with gently sloping sides.

▶ Volcanoes come in different shapes and sizes. Here are three common examples.

A **caldera** is a huge crater left after an old eruption. New cones often grow again inside.

75 A crater can form around the vent of a volcano. As magma is blasted out during an eruption, the material forms a rim around the top of the vent. Sometimes several vents may be erupting into the same crater. A crater can fill with lava during an eruption. When this forms a pool it is known as a lava lake.

▼ Crater Lake in Oregon, USA. It formed in the caldera of Mount Mazama and is around 9 kilometres across.

76 Lakes can form in the craters of dormant (inactive) volcanoes. When a volcano stops erupting and cools down, its crater can slowly fill with rain water, creating a lake. Crater lakes also form in calderas — huge craters that form when a volcano collapses into its empty magma chamber.

QUIZ

Which of these are parts of a volcano?
1. Conduit
2. Bed chamber
3. Side vent
4. Ventricle
5. Crater

Answers:
Only 1, 3 and 5 are parts of a volcano

Lava

◄ A slow-moving lava flow engulfs a road. A person could walk away from a lava flow like this without any danger.

78 A lava flow is a river of lava. Thin, runny lava can flow downhill at speeds up to 100 kilometres an hour. Lava flows follow the natural contours of the land. They can reach many kilometres from the volcano before the lava cools and stops. Lava often spreads out to form lava fields.

77 Lava is liquid rock ejected from a volcano. Some lava is very runny and flows downhill quickly. Another type is thick and gooey and flows very slowly. The temperature, consistency and thickness of lava affect the way it is erupted.

▼ Sometimes lava keeps flowing below the surface through a 'lava tunnel', under a solidified crust.

TRUE OR FALSE?

1. Aa lava is fast flowing.
2. Igneous rock is made when lava cools down.
3. A shortcrust bomb is made from lava.

Answers:
1. False – aa lava is thick, slow-moving lava
2. True – all igneous rocks are formed when magma, lava or ash cools
3. False – but a breadcrust bomb is

79 When lava or magma cools, it forms rock. This kind of rock is called igneous rock. Basalt – a dark-coloured rock – is one common type of igneous rock. Over time, lava flows build up on top of each other forming deep layers of igneous rock.

The front of the lava flow is steep

▲ Slow-flowing lava with a jagged surface is called aa lava.

Lava has a smooth, folded surface

80 Pahoehoe and aa are the two main types of lava. Thick lava that flows slowly cools to form jagged blocks. This is called aa (say ah) lava. Fast-flowing, runny lava cools to form rock with a smooth surface. This is called pahoehoe (say pa-hoey-hoey) lava.

▲ Fast-flowing lava, called pahoehoe lava, cools to form smooth, rope-like rock.

Pele's tears

▶ Pele's tears are tiny lava bombs often produced in Hawaiian eruptions.

Breadcrust bomb

Spindle bomb

81 A volcanic bomb is a flying lump of lava. Lumps of lava, usually bigger than the size of a fist, are thrown upwards by jets of gas from the vent during an eruption. Sometimes the outside of a bomb solidifies while it is in the air and splits open when it lands. This is called a breadcrust bomb. If the bomb is still soft when it lands, the bomb splats like a cowpat.

Cowpat bomb

Ribbon bomb

◀ Lumps of lava blasted into the air by a volcano form different shapes in the air.

Hot springs and fountains

82 **There are natural hot baths and showers all over the world.** You might think water outdoors is cold, but in some places, water meets hot rock under the ground and gets heated up. It sometimes even boils. The hot water can then make a lake or spring – or even shoot out of the ground like a fountain, forming a geyser.

▲ A mudpot, like this one in Myvatn Geothermal Area in Iceland, is a pool of hot, bubbling mud. Some mudpots are boiling hot. Others bubble as hot gases burst up through them.

83 **Besides geysers, the Earth's hot water can form amazing thermal (hot) springs and pools.** They often occur in places where there are lots of volcanoes, such as New Zealand and Japan. Some thermal pools are famous for their beautiful colours. These are caused by millions of bacteria (tiny living things) that live in the very hot water.

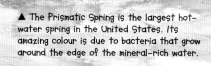

▲ The Prismatic Spring is the largest hot-water spring in the United States. Its amazing colour is due to bacteria that grow around the edge of the mineral-rich water.

84 You shouldn't stand too close to a geyser – even if nothing's happening! A geyser is a hole in the ground that suddenly shoots out hot water and steam. Under the hole there is a water-filled chamber. Hot rock beneath it heats the water until it rises back to the surface and erupts in a giant jet of water and steam.

85 Old Faithful is one of the world's most famous geysers. Found in Yellowstone National Park USA, it gets its name because it erupts on average once every 94 minutes. Its jet of steam and water can reach 55 metres high – as high as a 15-storey building.

▶ Strokkur (Icelandic for 'churn') is a geyser in Iceland. It erupts regularly, every 5–10 minutes, and can shoot water up to 25 metres in the air.

86 Soap helps geysers to erupt. People discovered this when they tried to use hot water pools and geysers to wash their clothes in. Soap disturbs the cold water in the chamber, helping the hot water to burst through.

I DON'T BELIEVE IT!

Japanese macaque monkeys use thermal springs as hot baths! They live in the mountains of Japan where winters are very cold. They climb into the natural hot pools to keep themselves warm.

▼ When rainwater seeps into the earth, it can be heated by hot rocks underground before rising back up to the surface as hot springs, pools and geysers.

Rainfall adds to groundwater

Geyser

Hot spring

Cold water travels down

Water is heated by hot rocks

Heated water starts to move upwards

Heat from Earth's interior

The rock cycle

87 Rocks and minerals form our planet, so they are all around us. Minerals are the building blocks of rocks. They are formed inorganically, meaning no living thing helps to create them. Rocks are aggregates (combinations) of particles from one or more minerals. Rocks and minerals make up much of the Earth and we couldn't live without them. We use them for building, cleaning, art – we even eat them.

▲ Millions of people live near active volcanoes. The soil is rich in minerals for farming.

▶ The rock cycle is the long, slow journey of rocks down from the surface and then up again. Rocks are often changed during this process.

88 All rock goes through a cycle over millions of years. During the rock cycle, rocks form deep in the Earth, move and sometimes change, go up to the surface and eventually return below the ground. There are three kinds of rock – igneous, sedimentary and metamorphic. They form in different ways and have different features.

Weathering of rocks at surface

Erosion and transport

Laying down of sediment

Burial and becoming more compact under pressure

SEDIMENTARY ROCK

Deep burial and metamorphism (changing structure

89 Rocks can go around the cycle in lots of ways. Igneous rocks were once molten (liquid), and have hardened beneath or above the surface. Metamorphic rock forms when rock is changed by heat, pressure or a combination of the two. Sedimentary rocks are formed when sediment – small particles of rock – becomes buried.

I DON'T BELIEVE IT!

The outer rock layer of the Earth is made of seven main segments (plates). Over time, these plates have moved across the surface of the Earth at a rate of between 5 and 15 centimetres a year, creating volcanoes, mountains and oceans.

90 Exposed rock is eroded (worn away) over time. This is a process in which tiny pieces (particles) of rock are loosened and transported as a result of gravity, wind, water or ice. Gradually these particles may become buried under more rock particles, forming sediment. If the sediment is buried deep enough to reach the mantle it will be heated by magma (hot molten rock), which may melt or bake it. Uplift and erosion can then expose them again.

IGNEOUS ROCK

Magma forms crystals as it cools

METAMORPHIC ROCK

Melting to form magma

The rock that changes

91 Metamorphic rock is rock that has been changed by heat or pressure (or both) into a new form deep underground. Pressure from movement of the Earth's crust, the weight of the rocks above and heat from magma cause metamorphic changes. Most of these happen at temperatures of 200–500°C. The rock does not melt – that would make igneous rock – but it is altered.

92 The appearance and texture of rock changes as a result of heat and pressure. Crystals break down and form, and a rock's chemical structure can change as its minerals react together. If the change is made under pressure, the rock crystals grow flat and form layers. If shale is compressed it forms slate.

▼ Slate forms when fine clay settles in layers and is then compressed and heated.

① Bands of shale form solid layers

Shale

② Movement creates curves

Slate

▼ Part of a slate landscape on Valencia Island off the coast of Ireland. This useful rock has been quarried and mined for thousands of years.

93 Sometimes rocks don't stop changing. For example, over centuries shale becomes slate, which looks the same as shale but is far harder and is more likely to split into sheets. However, if slate is then heated and squeezed it will be transformed again into phyllite, then schist and finally gneiss. This is the incredibly hard rock that forms the Alps.

I DON'T BELIEVE IT!
Gneiss found in northern Canada is the world's oldest rock. It was created under the volcanoes that made the first landmasses around four billion years ago.

▼ The Alps is a long mountain range stretching from east to west across Europe, formed about 40–20 million years ago.

94 Eclogite is one of the rarest, but most interesting, metamorphic rocks. It is full of crystals and minerals so it is very coarse-grained. Eclogite is green and often studded with red garnets, and sometimes even diamonds. It forms deep in the Earth's mantle, reaching the surface through volcanoes.

▼ No other rock contains as many interesting crystals and minerals as eclogite, which is formed by extremely high pressures and temperatures.

What are minerals?

95 Minerals are natural substances that form crystals. There are over 4000 different minerals but only about 30 are found all over the world. Quartz and feldspar are two of the most common types of mineral.

▼ Crystal shapes are set by the arrangement of atoms and molecules inside the mineral.

Cubic

Tetragonal

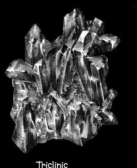

Orthorhombic

Monoclinic

96 A mineral is a chemical compound (a combination of two or more substances) or element (a single fundamental substance). Rocks are made from minerals. Limestone is made mainly of the mineral calcite (calcium carbonate), and granite contains quartz, mica and feldspar.

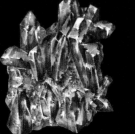

Hexagonal

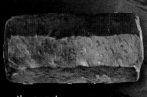

Triclinic

Trigonal

97 Minerals form crystals. They can do this in several ways. Some are formed as hot molten magma cools. Others come from water (the white powder left when water evaporates is a mineral deposit). Crystals can also be formed when minerals are altered by heat or pressure.

98 Crystals have seven basic shapes. Some just look like a jumble of different surfaces and angles. They have flat, often shiny faces and sharp edges.

99 The tiny grains you can see in most rocks are actually minerals, often forced together. Large crystals form in cracks and holes in rocks, where they have space to grow. The deeper the rock, the longer it generally takes to reach the surface, and the more time the crystal has to grow.

100 Some minerals are so valuable that they are mined. This might mean scraping them from the ground, or blowing up the rocks that hold them. Minerals buried deep underground are reached by drilling down and digging tunnels. People have mined minerals for thousands of years.

▼ Miners have to follow the direction of the mineral-rich band in the seam of rock.

Forming waterways

101 **A river can start from a spring.** This is where water flows from the ground. Rain soaks through the ground, and gushes out from the side of a hill. The trickle of water that flows from a spring is called a stream. Many streams join to make a river.

102 **A river changes as it flows to the sea.** Rivers begin in hills and mountains. They are narrow and flow quickly there. When the river flows through flatter land it becomes wider and slow-moving. It makes loops called meanders that may separate and form oxbow lakes. The point where the river meets the sea is the river mouth. This may be a wide channel called an estuary or a group of sandy islands called a delta.

◀ Waterfalls may only be a few centimetres high, or come crashing over a cliff with a massive drop. Angel Falls in Venezuela form the highest falls in the world. One of the drops is an amazing 807 metres.

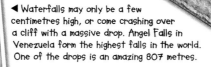

103 **Water wears rocks down to make a waterfall.** When a river flows from a layer of hard rock onto softer rock, it wears the softer rock down. The rocks and pebbles in the water grind the soft rock away to make a cliff face. At the bottom of the waterfall they make a deep pool called a plunge pool.

◀ High in the mountains, streams join to form the headwater of a river. From here the river flows through the mountains, then more slowly across the plains to the sea.

104 Lakes often form in hollows in the ground. The hollows may be left when glaciers melt or plates in the Earth's crust move apart. Some lakes form when a landslide makes a dam across a river.

▲ A landslide has fallen into the river and blocked the flow of water to make a lake.

105 A lake can form in the crater of a volcano. A few have also formed in craters left by meteorites that hit Earth long ago.

▼ This lake was formed in a volcanic crater.

106 Some lake water can be brightly coloured. The colours are made by tiny organisms called algae or by minerals dissolved in the water.

◀ Most lakes are blue but some are green, pink, red or even white. The Laguna Colorado in Chile is red due to tiny organisms (creatures) that live in the water.

Rivers and waterfalls

107 **The Earth is laced with thousands of rivers.** Rivers are channels of water that flow towards the sea. They allow the rain that falls on the land to drain away. Rivers also provide people and animals with drinking water and a place to wash, swim and fish. A waterfall is a place where a river flows over a rocky ledge and pours down to a lower level.

108 **The world's longest river is the Nile, in Africa.** It starts in the area near Lake Victoria and flows north to Egypt, where it opens into the Mediterranean Sea. The journey covers nearly 6700 kilometres, and about 3470 cubic metres of water flows out of the Nile every second. The Nile provides water, a transport route, and fishing for millions of people. If it wasn't for the Nile, the civilization of ancient Egypt could not have existed.

109 **Although the Nile is the longest river, the Amazon is the biggest.** The Amazon flows from west to east across South America, and empties into the Atlantic Ocean. It carries 58 times as much water as the Nile, and about 200,000 cubic metres flow out of it each second. In some places, the Amazon is an amazing 60 kilometres wide.

◀ This aerial photo of the River Amazon shows how it twists and loops as it flows through the Amazon rainforest in South America.

▶ At Angel Falls, the world's highest waterfall, the water spreads out into a misty spray as it plunges down the cliff.

◀ Part of the Grand Canyon, with the Colorado River visible at the bottom of a deep gorge.

110 Angel Falls in Venezuela is the world's highest waterfall, spilling over a drop 979 metres high. It flows off the side of a very high, flat-topped mountain. Although it's the world's highest waterfall, it's not the biggest. Many waterfalls are much wider and carry more water – including Niagara Falls in North America and Victoria Falls in Africa.

111 Rivers can cut through solid rock. Over thousands of years, as a river flows, it wears away the rock around it. If the stone is quite soft, the river can carve a deep, steep-sided valley, or gorge. The Grand Canyon in Arizona, USA, is a massive gorge cut by the Colorado River. It is about 450 kilometres long, and in areas it is up to 29 kilometres wide and 1.8 kilometres deep.

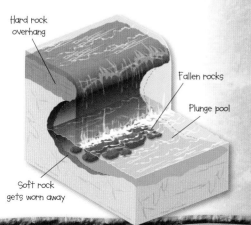

Hard rock overhang

Fallen rocks

Plunge pool

Soft rock gets worn away

◀ A waterfall forms where a river flows from hard rock onto softer rock. The softer rock is worn away faster, while the overhanging ledge of hard rock gradually crumbles away. Over time, the waterfall retreats, or moves upstream.

Dry deserts

112 Deserts occur in places where it's hard for rain to reach. Most rain comes from clouds that form over the sea and blow onto the land. If there's a big mountain range, the clouds never reach the other side and so an area called a rain shadow desert forms. Deserts also form in the middle of continents. The land there is so far from the sea, rain clouds rarely reach it.

▲ The Namib Desert in the southwest of Africa contains some of the biggest sand dunes in the world.

113 The world's biggest desert used to be a swamp! The Sahara takes up most of northern Africa. It is made up of 9 million square kilometres of dry sand, pebbles and boulders. There are some oases too, where freshwater springs flow out of the ground. Animal bones and objects left by ancient peoples show that around 6000 years ago, the Sahara was green and swampy. Lots of hippos, crocodiles and humans lived there.

▼ These sand piles show the relative sizes of the world's biggest deserts.

Sahara 9,269,000 km²

Australian deserts 3,800,000 km²

Arabian Desert 1,300,000 km²

Gobi Desert 1,040,000 km²

Kalahari Desert 520,000 km²

114 Deserts aren't always hot. The hottest temperature ever recorded was 57.8°C in Libya. However, deserts can be cold, too. The average temperature in the Atacama Desert, South America is only about 10°C. In the Gobi Desert in Asia, winter temperatures can drop to −40°C. All deserts can be cold at night, as there are no clouds to stop heat escaping.

▲ Desert roses aren't plants. They occur when desert minerals, such as gypsum, combine with sand to form crystals.

▶ Sand dunes form in different shapes and patterns, depending on the type of wind and sand in the desert. The blue arrows indicate the wind direction.

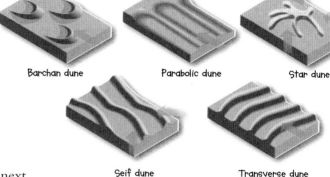

Barchan dune

Parabolic dune

Star dune

Seif dune

Transverse dune

115 The world's driest desert is the Aatacama Desert in Chile, South America. This desert is right next to the sea! It formed because in South America, rain clouds blow from east to west. They drop their rain on the Amazon rainforest, but cannot get past the Andes mountains. On the other side of the Andes, next to the Pacific Ocean, is the Atacama Desert. It is so dry that people who died there 9000 years ago have been preserved as mummies.

116 Even in dry deserts, there is water if you know where to look. Desert plants, such as cactuses store water in their stems, leaves or spines. When rain does fall, it seeps into the ground and stays there. Desert people and animals chew desert plants or dig into the ground to find enough water.

▶ An oasis is a freshwater spring in a desert. Oases form when water stored deep underground meets a barrier of rock that it can't soak through, and rises to the desert surface.

Fantastic forests

117 There are three main kinds of forest. They are coniferous, temperate and tropical forests. Each grow in different regions of the world, depending on the climate.

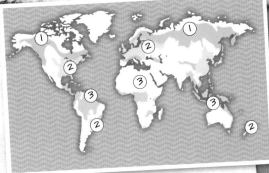

▲ This map shows the major areas of forest in the world:
① Coniferous forest
② Temperate forest
③ Tropical forest

118 Coniferous trees form huge forests around the northern part of the planet. They have long, green, needle–like leaves covered in a waxy coating. These trees stay in leaf throughout the year. In winter, the waxy surface helps snow slide off the leaves so that sunlight can reach them to keep them alive. Coniferous trees produce seeds in cones.

◀ Squirrels can open seed cones from coniferous trees in just a few seconds.

119 Most trees in temperate forests have flat, broad leaves and need large amounts of water to keep them alive. In winter, the trees cannot get enough water from the frozen ground, so they lose their leaves and grow new ones in spring. Deer, rabbits, foxes and mice live on the woodland floor while squirrels, woodpeckers and owls live in the trees.

▲ A jaguar stalks through a dense tropical forest in Belize.

▲ The Hoh temperate rainforest in Washington state, USA, is home to elks, bears and cougars.

120 Large numbers of trees grow close together in a tropical forest. They have broad, evergreen leaves and branches that almost touch. These form a leafy roof over the forest called a canopy. It rains almost every day in a tropical rainforest. The vegetation is so thick, it can take a raindrop ten minutes to reach the ground. Three-quarters of all known animal and plant species live in rainforests. They include huge spiders, brightly coloured frogs and jungle cats.

QUIZ

1. What are the three main kinds of forest?
2. Which types of tree produce seeds in cones?
3. In which kind of forest would you find brightly coloured frogs?

Answers:
1. Coniferous, temperate and tropical 2. Coniferous trees 3. Tropical rainforest

What is a rainforest?

121 Rainforests are places where lots of rain falls every year — usually more than 2000 millimetres. They are filled with enormous, broad-leaved trees and a bewildering collection of living things. Rainforests usually grow in warm, steamy parts of the world.

122 Trees provide habitats (homes) for millions of rainforest animals and plants. Much of the wildlife in these forests cannot survive anywhere else — just one of the reasons why people want to make sure rainforests are kept safe.

Toco toucan

123 Of all the different habitats found on Earth, rainforests have the biggest range of living things. They are home to more than 80 percent of all insects and a single rainforest in South America has 18,000 different types of plants. The word 'biodiversity' is used to describe the range of living things that live in one habitat.

Tapir

Queen Alexandra's birdwing butterfly

124 Rainforests have four main layers. The bottom layers are the dark, dank forest floor and understorey, where the shortest plants live. Here, bugs, frogs, fungi and many other living things thrive. The middle layer is the forest canopy and the top layer is the emergent layer. This is where the tallest trees poke up above a blanket of green leaves. The trees are home to vines, mosses, monkeys, lizards, snakes, insects and thousands of species (types) of bird.

CANOPY

◄ Most animals and plants live in the rainforest canopy layer. The understorey is very gloomy because not much sunlight reaches it.

I DON'T BELIEVE IT!
People who live in rainforests can build their entire homes from plant materials. Walls are made from palm stems or bamboo and leaves can be woven to make roofs and floors.

UNDERSTOREY

Red-eyed tree frog

FOREST FLOOR

125 Rainforests are home to people as well as animals and plants. Many tribes (groups of people) live in these dense, green forests around the world, finding food, medicines and shelter amongst the trees. Some of them still follow a traditional lifestyle, hunting animals and gathering plants for food.

The ends of the Earth

126 The Earth is round, but it has two 'ends' — the North Pole and the South Pole. The Earth is constantly spinning around an imaginary line called the axis. At the ends of this axis are the poles. Here, it is always cold, because the poles are so far from the Sun.

North Pole

ARCTIC REGION

ANTARCTIC REGION

Axis

South Pole

▲ The position of the poles means they receive little heat from the Sun.

127 At the North Pole, the average temperature is −20°C. At the South pole, it's much colder — about −50°C. It's hard for humans to survive in this cold. Water droplets in your breath would freeze on your face. If you were to touch something made of metal with your bare hand, it would freeze onto your skin and stick there.

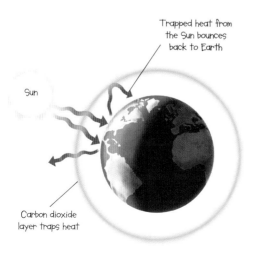

Trapped heat from the Sun bounces back to Earth

Sun

Carbon dioxide layer traps heat

128 The area around the North Pole is called the Arctic. Parts of Europe, Asia and North America reach into the Arctic, but most of it is actually the Arctic Ocean. Many animals live in the Arctic. Polar bears and seals live on the ice and Arctic foxes, Arctic hares and snowy owls live on the land. The sea around the pole is mainly frozen. Scientists have found the ice is melting because of global warming. This is happening because pollution in the air is trapping heat close to the Earth, making it warm up.

◀ Pollution in the form of carbon dioxide gas traps heat from the Sun, making the Earth warm up. This is one reason that the polar ice is melting.

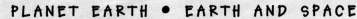

▲ There are several different species (types) of penguins living in Antarctica. These emperor penguins and their chicks are the largest species.

129 The Antarctic is mostly made up of a huge continent, called **Antarctica.** Much of it is covered in a layer of solid ice up to 4.7 kilometres thick. The Antarctic is colder than the Arctic because its thick ice and mountains make it very high, and the air is colder higher up. Because Antarctica is so big, the seas around it cannot warm it very much. Little wildlife lives here, but it is home to lots of penguins.

I DON'T BELIEVE IT!

Explorers at the poles sometimes lose body parts. If they let their fingers, toes or nose get too cold, they can get frostbite. Blood stops flowing to these parts, and they can turn black and fall off.

130 Explorers didn't make it to the poles until the 20th century. US explorer Robert Peary and his team reached the North Pole in 1909. Soon afterwards, two explorers raced to reach the South Pole. Norwegian Roald Amundsen arrived first, in December 1911. British explorer Robert Scott arrived one month later – but he and his men died on their way home.

◀ There are no towns or cities in Antarctica as it's so cold, but people do go there to explore and to study nature. They sometimes use snowmobiles to travel around on the snow and ice.

Glaciers and icebergs

131 About two percent of the water in the world is permanently frozen as ice. The ice is found at the chilly polar regions, and on high mountains where the air is freezing cold. On steep slopes, the ice creeps downhill, like a very slow river. This kind of ice 'river' is called a glacier. On high mountains, glaciers flow downhill until they reach warmer air and start to melt. At the poles, many glaciers flow into the sea.

▼ Instead of melting on the way down a mountain, this glacier in Prince William Sound, Alaska is flowing into a fjord.

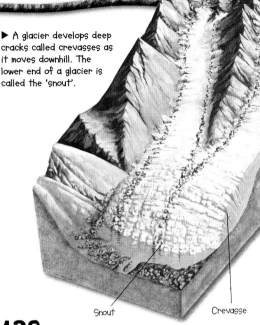

▶ A glacier develops deep cracks called crevasses as it moves downhill. The lower end of a glacier is called the 'snout'.

Snout

Crevasse

132 One of the world's biggest glaciers, not including the ice at the poles, is the Siachen Glacier in the Himalayas. It is 78 kilometres long and, in places, its ice is over 100 metres thick. India and Pakistan fought a war over who the glacier belongs to starting in 1984 and ending with a ceasefire in 2003. It has been home to hundreds of soldiers for more than 30 years.

133 Glaciers have shaped the Earth.

As a glacier flows down a mountain, the heavy ice pushes and scrapes at the soil and rocks. This carves a huge, U-shaped valley, known as a glacial valley. 20,000 years ago, when the Earth was in an Ice Age, glaciers covered much more of the land than they do now. Since then, many have melted, revealing their glacial valleys.

135 Icebergs exist because of glaciers.

At the poles, glaciers flow downhill to the sea. There, the ice is slowly pushed out into the water, where it starts to float. Every so often, a large chunk of the glacier breaks off and floats away into the sea. This is an iceberg and it drifts until it melts.

134 Icebergs are a problem for ships.

As an iceberg floats, only about one-tenth of it sticks up out of the sea. The rest is below the surface. Many icebergs have odd, lumpy shapes. This means that a ship can bump into the underwater part of an iceberg, even if the part above water looks far away. Icebergs have damaged and sunk many ships, including the famous ocean liner *Titanic* in 1912.

▼ These penguins are on an iceberg in the Southern Ocean, close to Antarctica. A huge mass of ice can be seen below the water's surface.

MAKE AN ICEBERG

You will need:

plastic container   clear bowl   water

1. Fill the container with water and put it in the freezer.
2. When frozen, remove your 'iceberg' from the container.
3. Fill the clear bowl with water and place your iceberg in it.
4. Look through the side to see how much of your iceberg is underwater, and what shape it makes.

Amazing oceans

136 About 70 percent of the Earth's surface is covered by ocean. The oceans cover about 361 million square kilometres and they are all connected. The average depth of the ocean is 3750 metres. Over 90 percent of the Earth's species (types) of living things live in the oceans.

▶ The *Trieste*, which made the deepest deep-sea dive ever in 1960, was made of a large tank full of gasoline to give buoyancy, with a small round passenger chamber fixed underneath.

137 The deepest point in all the world's oceans is called Challenger Deep. It is in the Mariana Trench in the Pacific Ocean and is 10,923 metres deep – almost 11 kilometres. A tower of 3500 elephants, one on top of the next, could stand in it without touching the surface. In 1960, two explorers, Jacques Piccard and Don Walsh, visited the bottom of Challenger Deep in a diving vessel called *Trieste*.

138 If you were sitting at the bottom of the deep ocean, you'd be squashed flat. At great depths, the weight of all the water above presses from all sides. At the bottom of Challenger Deep, the water pressure is more than 1000 times stronger than at the surface. It's cold, too – only just above freezing point. People can only go there inside specially built diving machines with thick walls that can resist the pressure and cold.

Oceanic crust

Deep-sea trench

Ocean ridge

Underwater volcano

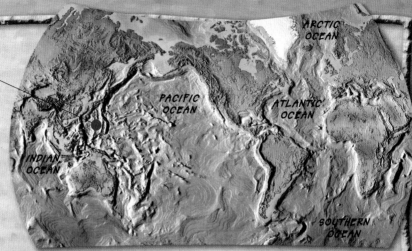

Challenger Deep

ARCTIC OCEAN

PACIFIC OCEAN

ATLANTIC OCEAN

INDIAN OCEAN

SOUTHERN OCEAN

▶ This map shows the ridges, trenches, plains and mountains within the world's oceans, as well as those on land.

139 One of the world's most extreme environments is found under the sea. Within hydrothermal vents, incredibly hot water bubbles out from inside the Earth at temperatures of up to 400°C. Around the hot vents live unusual creatures such as giant tubeworms and sea spiders, and tiny bacteria that feed on the minerals dissolved in the hot water. Hydrothermal vents were only discovered in 1977.

▼ A cross-section of the seabed. It usually slopes gently away from the shore, then drops steeply down to a flat plain.

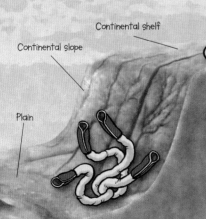

Continental shelf

Continental slope

Plain

140 Sea level – the height of the sea – is about the same all over the world. It changes over time, as the Earth's temperature varies. About 20,000 years ago, during the Ice Age, the sea level was 130 metres lower than it is now. At the moment, the sea level is rising because global warming is making ice melt at the poles.

TRUE OR FALSE?

1. Challenger Deep is deeper than Mount Everest is tall.
2. The water at the bottom of the sea is always very cold.
3. Sea creatures bigger than blue whales could exist.

Answers:
1. True – Everest is only 8848 m high 2. False – the water can be hot around hydrothermal vents 3. True – the sea is so big, it could contain species unknown to science

67

Tides and shores

141 Almost all seashores have tides, which affect the way the land is worn away. Tides alter the amount of time that a particular patch of the shore is underwater or exposed to the air, so they also affect coastal habitats and wildlife.

142 Tides are caused by the pulling power or gravity of the Moon and Sun, and the daily spinning of the Earth. A high tide occurs about 12.5 hours after the previous high tide, with low tides midway between.

Moon

Spinning Earth

Tidal bulge

◀ The Moon's gravity pulls the sea into 'bulges' on the near and opposite sides, where it is high tide. Inbetween is low tide. As the Earth spins daily, the 'bulge' travels around the planet.

I DON'T BELIEVE IT!

The tidal range is the difference in height between high and low tide. In the Bay of Fundy in Canada it is 17 metres, and in parts of the Mediterranean Sea it is less than 0.3 metres.

143 Spring tides are extra-high – the water level rises more than normal. They happen when the Moon and Sun are in line with the Earth, adding their gravities together every 14 days (two weeks). Neap tides are extra-low, when the Sun and Moon are at right angles, so their pulling strengths partly cancel each other out. A neap tide occurs seven days after a spring tide.

▼ At new Moon and full Moon, the Sun, Moon and Earth are in a straight line, causing spring tides. At the first and last quarters of the Moon, the Sun and Moon are not aligned, so neap tides occur.

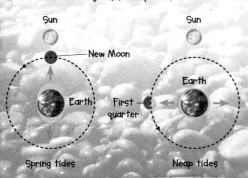
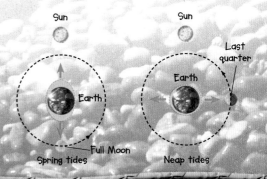

Sun
Sun
Sun
Sun

New Moon

Last quarter

Earth
Earth
Earth

Earth
First quarter

Full Moon

Spring tides
Neap tides
Spring tides
Neap tides

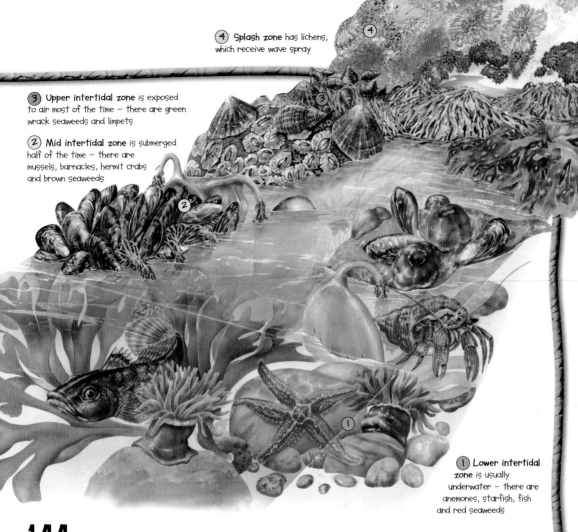

④ **Splash zone** has lichens, which receive wave spray

③ **Upper intertidal zone** is exposed to air most of the time – there are green wrack seaweeds and limpets

② **Mid intertidal zone** is submerged half of the time – there are mussels, barnacles, hermit crabs and brown seaweeds

① **Lower intertidal zone** is usually underwater – there are anemones, starfish, fish and red seaweeds

▲ The amount of time underwater determines which animals and plants live along a rocky shore.

144 Tides produce 'zones' along seashores, from the high tide zone to the low tide zone. Different seaweeds and animals are adapted to each zone.

145 Ocean currents affect the seashore. A current flowing towards the shore can bring particles of sediment to add to the land. A current flowing away sweeps sediment out to sea. Currents also alter the direction and power of waves.

146 If a wind blows waves at an angle onto a beach, each wave carries particles of sand upwards and sideways. When they recede, the particles roll back. Particles gradually zigzag along the shore – a process called longshore drift. Groynes built into the sea help to control it, so beaches don't wash away.

Extreme earthquakes

147 **An earthquake happens when the Earth's crust moves suddenly.** The crust trembles, cracks, or lurches up and down. Earthquakes can be disastrous. They make houses fall down, tear roads apart and destroy bridges. They can also cause tsunamis.

Fault line

Focus

Shock waves

▶ Earthquakes often happen when two tectonic plates slip and grind against each other. The focus is the point where the plates suddenly move.

148 **Earthquakes happen because the Earth's crust is like a jigsaw.** It is made up of several huge pieces called tectonic plates. The plates fit together quite neatly, covering the Earth. However they can squeeze and push against each other. Sometimes, this pushing makes the plates slip and move suddenly, causing an earthquake.

▼ The San Andreas fault in California USA is a crack in the Earth's crust where two tectonic plates join. It has been the scene of several major earthquakes.

▼ Earthquakes waves travel through and across the ground in four different ways.

(1) Primary waves stretch then squeeze the ground

(2) Secondary waves shake the ground from side to side

(3) Raleigh waves move in ripples up and down across the surface

(4) Love waves travel across the surface moving the ground from side to side

▶ Damage caused by an earthquake in Kobe, Japan, 1995. It measured 7.2 on the Richter Scale and killed more than 6000 people.

149 Earthquakes can flatten whole cities and kill thousands. One of the deadliest earthquakes ever hit the city of Tangshan, China in 1976. Most of the city's buildings were destroyed, and at least 240,000 people died. In 2003, an earthquake destroyed the ancient city of Bam in Iran. Over 70 percent of its buildings fell down and around 30,000 people were killed.

150 Scientists measure earthquakes using the Richter scale. It records the amount of energy that an earthquake releases. The biggest quakes are not always the most dangerous – it depends where they happen. In a big city, a quake measuring 4 or 5 on the scale could do more damage than a quake measuring 8 or 9 in the countryside.

151 There are things you can do to stay safer during an earthquake. For example, if you are outside, you should keep away from buildings and power lines. If you are indoors, you should shelter under a strong table. Some places also have quake-proof buildings.

I DON'T BELIEVE IT!

Since ancient times, people have noticed animals behaving strangely just before earthquakes. Dogs and cats can get agitated, and herds of cattle have been known to run away.

▼ As there are a lot of earthquakes in Japan, school children regularly practise what to do if an earthquake strikes.

Terrifying tsunamis

152 **A tsunami is a giant wave, or series of waves.** Tsunamis form when a large amount of water in a sea or lake is moved suddenly. This sets up a circular wave, a bit like the ripples you see when you throw a pebble into a pond. The wave then zooms outwards until it hits land.

▶ A tsunami begins as fast-travelling waves far out at sea. As they approach land, the waves slow down, but become much taller.

As the tall tsunami reaches shallow water, it surges forward onto the shore

153 **When a tsunami hits, it can smash the coast to smithereens.** Out in the ocean, tsunami waves are very long, low and fast-moving. However as a tsunami moves into shallow water, the wave slows down. All the water in it piles up, forming a powerful wall of water, often between 10 and 30 metres high. As it crashes onto the shore, it can flood towns, tear up trees and sweep away cars, buildings and people.

▼ A tsunami wave crashes onto the promenade on Ao Nang Beach, Thailand in 2004. The power and speed of a tsunami can easily sweep away cars and even entire buildings.

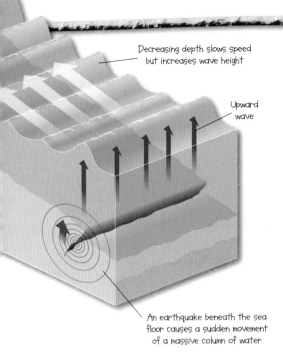

Decreasing depth slows speed but increases wave height

Upward wave

An earthquake beneath the sea floor causes a sudden movement of a massive column of water

155 The tallest tsunami was higher than a skyscraper.
It occurred at Lituya Bay, in Alaska, USA, in 1958. An earthquake triggered a landslide, and rock and soil plunged into the sea. A giant tsunami, over 500 metres high, zoomed down the bay. Luckily, there were no towns there, but the wave stripped the coast of trees. A giant tsunami such as this is sometimes called a mega tsunami.

154 Most tsunamis are caused by earthquakes under the sea. A section of seabed shifts suddenly and the water above it is jolted upwards. Tsunamis can also happen when a landslide or volcanic eruption throws a large amount of rock into the sea, pushing the water aside. This happened when Krakatau, a volcano in Indonesia, erupted in 1883. The tsunamis it caused killed 36,000 people.

156 A tsunami in the Indian Ocean in 2004 was the deadliest ever recorded. It was caused by a huge undersea earthquake near the coast of Indonesia. Tsunami waves spread across the ocean and swamped coasts in Indonesia, Thailand, Sri Lanka, India and the Maldive Islands. Around 230,000 people were killed.

▼ The town of Kalutara in Sri Lanka, shown in satellite images before (left) and after (right) being swamped by the deadly 2004 tsunami.

Our atmosphere

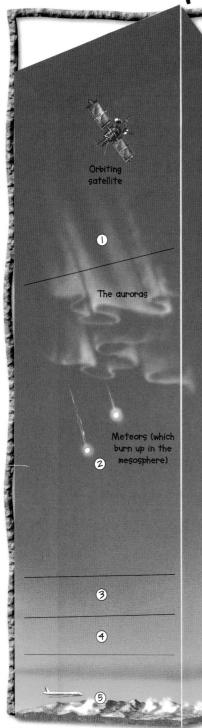

Orbiting
satellite

①

The auroras

Meteors (which
burn up in the
mesosphere)

②

③

④

⑤

157 Our planet is wrapped
in a blanket of air. We call this
blanket the atmosphere. It stretches
hundreds of kilometres above our
heads. The blanket keeps in heat,
especially at night when part of
the planet faces away from the
Sun. During the day, the blanket
becomes a sunscreen instead.
Without an atmosphere, there
would be no weather.

158 Most weather happens in the
troposphere. This is the layer of atmosphere
that stretches from the ground to around
10 kilometres above your head. The higher in
the troposphere you go, the cooler the air.
Because of this, clouds are most likely to form
here. Clouds with flattened tops show just
where the troposphere meets the next layer,
the stratosphere.

KEY
① Exosphere 190 to 960 kilometres
② Thermosphere 80 to 190 kilometres
③ Mesosphere 50 to 80 kilometres
④ Stratosphere 10 to 50 kilometres
⑤ Troposphere 0 to 10 kilometres

◀ The atmosphere stretches right into space. Scientists have
split it into five layers, or spheres, such as the troposphere.

159 Air just cannot keep
still. Tiny particles in air, called
molecules, are always bumping
into each other! The more they
smash into each other, the greater
the air pressure. Generally, there
are more smashes lower in the
troposphere, because the pull of
gravity makes the molecules fall
towards the Earth's surface. The
higher you go, the lower the air
pressure, and the less oxygen there
is in the air.

▶ At high altitudes there is less oxygen. That is
why mountaineers often wear breathing equipment.

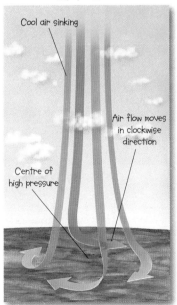

High pressure

Cool air sinking

Air flow moves
in clockwise
direction

Centre of
high pressure

Low pressure

Warm air rising

Air flow moves
in anticlockwise
direction

Centre of
low pressure

160 Warmth makes air
move. When heat from the
Sun warms the molecules in
air, they move faster and
spread out more. This makes
the air lighter, so it rises in
the sky, creating low
pressure. As it gets higher,
the air cools. The molecules
slow down and become
heavier again, so they start
to sink back to Earth.

◀ A high pressure weather system
gives us warmer weather, while low
pressure gives us cooler more
unsettled weather.

Clouds and rain

161 **Rain comes from the sea.** As the Sun heats the surface of the ocean, some seawater turns into water vapour and rises into the air. As it rises, it cools and turns back into water droplets. Lots of water droplets make clouds. The droplets join together to make bigger and bigger drops that eventually fall as rain. Some rain is soaked up by the land, but a lot finds its way back to the sea. This is called the water cycle.

RAIN GAUGE

You will need:
jam jar   waterproof marker pen
ruler   notebook   pen

Put the jar outside. At the same time each day, mark the rainwater level on the jar with your pen. At the end of a week, empty the jar. Measure and record how much rain fell each day and over the whole week.

162 **Some mountains are so tall that their summits (peaks) are hidden by cloud.** Really huge mountains even affect the weather. When moving air hits a mountain slope it is forced upwards. As it travels up, the temperature drops, and clouds form.

◀ Warm, rising air may be forced up the side of a mountain. At a certain level, lower temperatures make the water form clouds.

▼ The water cycle involves all the water on Earth. Water vapour rises from lakes, rivers and the sea to form clouds in the atmosphere.

④ Rain falls, filling rivers

③ Water is given off by forests

② Clouds form

① Water evaporates from the sea

⑤ The rivers run back to the sea, and the cycle starts again

▼ Virga happens when rain reaches a layer of dry air. The rain droplets turn back into water vapour in mid-air, and seem to disappear.

163 **Some rain never reaches the ground.** The raindrops turn back into water vapour because they hit a layer of super-dry air. You can actually see the drops falling like a curtain from the cloud, but the curtain stops in mid-air. This type of weather is called virga.

164 **Clouds gobble up heat and keep the Earth's temperature regular.** From each 2-metre-square patch of land, clouds can remove the equivalent energy created by a 60-Watt lightbulb.

Lightning strikes

165 **Lightning is a giant spark of electricity.** It happens when tiny droplets of water and ice swirl around inside a storm cloud. This makes the cloud develop a strong electrical charge. Eventually, a spark jumps between the base of the cloud and the ground. This allows electricity to flow, releasing the electrical charge. We see the spark as a flash or 'bolt' of lightning.

Positive charge

Negative charge

Negative charge from the cloud meets a positive charge from the ground to create lightning

▲ During a thunderstorm, negative electrical charge builds up at the base of a cloud, while the ground has a positive charge. A lightning spark jumps between them to release the charge.

166 **Thunder and lightning go together.** In fact, thunder is the sound of lightning. When a lightning bolt jumps through the air, it is very hot. It can reach a temperature of 30,000°C. It heats the air around it very quickly. Heat makes air expand (get bigger). It expands so suddenly that it pushes against the air around it, and creates a shock wave. The wave travels through the air and our ears detect it as a loud boom.

167 Long ago, people used to think lightning was a punishment sent by their gods. However, from the 1500s, scientists began learning about electricity and how it worked. Around 1750, US scientist Benjamin Franklin found that lightning was a kind of electricity. He invented the lightning conductor to protect buildings from lightning damage. It is a metal pole that can be fixed to tall buildings. If lightning strikes, the electrical charge runs down the pole and down a metal wire, then flows safely into the ground.

168 It is quite rare for lightning to strike people, and most of those who are struck, survive. However, lightning does kill over 2000 people around the world each year.

▼ Fulgarites occur when lightning strikes sand. The high temperature makes the sand melt. It eventually cools into hollow tubes.

◀ You can clearly see the lightning conductor on the spire of this cathedral in Liverpool, UK.

169 Lightning can make glass. Glass is made by heating up sand. When lightning strikes in a sandy desert or on a sandy beach, this happens naturally. At the place where the lightning hits the ground, it creates a tubelike tunnel of glass in the sand. These natural glass tubes are called fulgurites.

Extreme snow and ice

170 **An ice storm isn't stormy – but it is dangerous.** Cold rain falls onto freezing cold surfaces. The rain freezes solid, forming a thick layer of ice on the ground, trees and other objects. Ice storms cause 'black ice' – invisible ice on roads that causes accidents. Ice-laden trees fall down, breaking power lines and cutting off roads.

◀ Overburdened by the weight of ice from an ice storm, this tree has collapsed across a road.

▲ An avalanche thunders downhill in Silverton, Colorado, USA. This avalanche was started deliberately by dropping explosives, in order to make the mountains safer for visitors.

171 **An avalanche is a massive pile of snow crashing down a mountainside.** Avalanches can happen whenever lots of snow piles up at the top of a slope. They can be deadly if the snow lands on top of mountain walkers or skiers. Sometimes, big avalanches bury whole houses or even whole villages.

172 **A blizzard, or snowstorm, is even more dangerous than an ice storm.** If you get caught outdoors in a blizzard, it's very easy to get lost. Falling snow fills the air, making it impossible to see. Thick snowdrifts build up, making it hard to walk or drive. People have lost their way and died in blizzards, just a short distance from safety.

▲ Ice can form beautiful crystal patterns as it freezes across a window or car windscreen.

173 If you get stuck in a blizzard or avalanche, a hole in the snow can keep you warm. Snow is a great insulator. as heat does not flow through it very well. If you curl up inside a hole dug in the snow, it traps the heat from your body and keeps it close to you. Many people have survived blizzards by making snow holes.

▼ A man uses a reindeer sledge to collect remains of a woolly mammoth discovered buried in ice.

174 We put food in a freezer to keep it fresh — and the same thing happens in nature. Snow and ice can stop dead bodies from rotting away. Woolly mammoths that lived 10,000 years ago have been dug out of the ice in northern Russia, perfectly preserved. In 1991, the body of a 5000-year-old man was found in the ice in mountains in Austria. He was nicknamed Ötzi the Iceman.

Howling hurricanes

▲ Hurricanes can cause widespread devastation and extreme flooding.

175 A hurricane is a huge, swirling mass of stormclouds. Hurricanes form over the ocean, but often travel onto land where they cause floods and destroy whole towns. A typical hurricane is about 500 kilometres wide. In the middle is a small, circular area with no clouds in it, about 70 kilometres wide. This is called the 'eye' of the hurricane.

176 Hurricanes begin in the tropics where the ocean is warm. The ocean surface has to be about 27°C or warmer for a hurricane to start. Warm, wet air rises, forming rainclouds. These begin to swirl in a spiral, caused by the spinning Earth. If the winds reach 118 kilometres an hour, the storm is called a hurricane. Hurricane winds can be as fast as 240 kilometres an hour.

177 The word 'hurricane' is only used to describe storms in the Atlantic Ocean. The scientific name for this type of storm is a tropical cyclone. The same type of storm in the Indian Ocean is known as a cyclone, and in the Pacific Ocean it is called a typhoon.

I DON'T BELIEVE IT!

Surrounding the eye of the hurricane is the eyewall. This is a mass of severe thunderstorms where most of the worst weather occurs.

178 Most hurricanes rage harmlessly over the ocean. If they hit land, less powerful, slow-moving hurricanes can cause more damage than stronger hurricanes, which die out more quickly.

179 Hurricanes and other tropical cyclones can cause terrible disasters. When Hurricane Katrina struck the southern coast of the USA in August 2005, it damaged many cities on the coasts of Mississippi and Louisiana. In New Orleans, huge waves broke through the flood barriers and more than 80 percent of the city was flooded. The hurricane killed over 1800 people and caused damage costing over $80 billion. The Bhola cyclone, which hit Bangladesh in 1970, killed over 300,000 people.

▲ A satellite view from space showing a hurricane swirling across the Gulf of Mexico.

180 Scientists think hurricanes are getting worse. Global warming means that the Earth's temperature is rising, so the seas are getting warmer. This means that more hurricanes are likely. Hurricanes are also becoming bigger and more powerful, as there is more heat energy to fuel them.

▼ These buildings near Lake Pontchartrain, Louisiana, USA, were destroyed by Hurricane Katrina in 2005.

Twisting tornadoes

181 **Tornadoes are also called twisters.** A tornado is an incredibly powerful windstorm that twists around in a swirling 'vortex' shape. It forms a narrow funnel or tube, stretching from the clouds to the ground. Tornadoes often look dark because of all the dirt, dust and broken objects that they pick up as they travel across the land.

182 **You can sometimes tell when a tornado is coming, because the sky turns green.** Tornadoes usually develop from thunderclouds. Scientists are not sure exactly how they form. They think that as warm, damp air rises, drier, colder air is pulled in and begins to swirl around it. This creates a spinning tube of wind that moves along the ground. A tornado can travel at up to 80 kilometres an hour.

183 **Tornadoes contain some of the fastest winds on the planet.** Wind inside a tornado can move at up to 500 kilometres an hour. This powerful wind can cause terrible damage. Tornadoes smash buildings, tear off roofs, make bridges collapse, and suck out doors and windows. They can pick up people, animals and cars, and carry them through the air. In 2006, a tornado in Missouri, USA picked up 19-year-old Matt Suter and carried him nearly 400 metres. He survived with only cuts and bruises.

Cold front

Warm front

◄ Tornadoes often form where a front, or mass, of cold air meets warm air. They spin around each other and form a funnel shape.

TORNADO IN A BOTTLE

You will need:
two plastic drinks bottles the same size
water   sticky tape

1. Fill one of the bottles almost full with water.
2. Position the second bottle upside-down on top of the first, so that their necks join together. Tape them together firmly.
3. Turn both bottles over and swirl them around in a circle as fast as you can.
4. When you hold them still, you should see a tornado shape as the water forms a vortex.

◀ A large, terrifying tornado snakes down to the ground from the base of a big thundercloud.

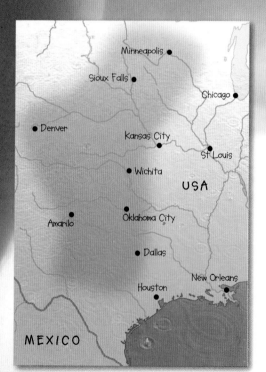

184 Damaging tornadoes happen most often in Tornado Alley. This is an area which stretches across the middle of the USA, between the states of Texas and Illinois. Tornadoes are most common there in the tornado season, from April to August. The Great Tri-State Tornado of 1925 was one of the worst ever. It roared through Missouri, Illionois and Indiana, travelling 350 kilometres. It destroyed 15,000 homes and killed 695 people.

◀ The shaded area on this map shows the part of the USA known as Tornado Alley, where tornadoes are most common.

185 Sometimes, tornadoes occur in deserts, or over the sea. In sandy deserts, small tornadoes pick up sand and carry it along in a whirling tower. They are called sand devils or dust devils. Tornadoes over the sea can suck up water in the same way, and carry it for long distances. They are known as waterspouts.

Flooding the land

186 A flood happens when water overflows and covers what is normally land. Floods can be caused by rivers overflowing their banks after heavy rain. The sea can also flood the land with large waves or tsunamis. Floods can be useful – some rivers flood every year in the rainy season, bringing water and mud that make farmland moist and fertile. However, most floods are bad news.

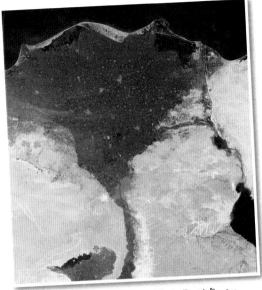

▲ A satellite image of the River Nile in Egypt flowing into the Mediterranean Sea. The green triangular area is the Nile Delta. The Nile used to flood each summer, spreading fertile silt across the land. These floods are now controlled by the Aswan Dam in southern Egypt.

▼ A woman carries a precious pot of clean drinking water through dirty floodwaters during a flood in Bangladesh in 1998.

187 Floods can cause death and destruction. When floodwater flows into houses, it fills them with mud, rubbish and sewage (smelly waste from drains and toilets). It ruins electrical appliances, carpets and furniture. After a flood, homes have to be completely cleaned out and repaired – costing huge amounts of money. Even worse, fast-flowing floodwater can sweep away people, cars and even buildings.

188 **Floods often cause water shortages.** Although there's water everywhere, it's dirty and not safe to drink. The dirty water can fill up water supply pipes and water treatment works. They can't supply clean water, and the taps have to be switched off. During bad floods, the emergency services have to deliver water in bottles or tanks, so that people have enough clean water to drink.

▲ Heavy floods hit many parts of England in the summer of 2007. This aerial photo shows Tewkesbury in Gloucestershire.

189 **More floods are coming.** Because of global warming, the Earth is heating up. In some areas, this means more water will evaporate into the air, causing more clouds and more rain. Global warming also means higher sea levels, so more areas of land are at risk of being flooded.

I DON'T BELIEVE IT!

The Bible tells of a great flood that covered the world in water. Some scientists think flood stories may be based on flooding that happened around 10,000 years ago, as sea levels rose when ice melted after the last Ice Age.

▼ This car was caught in a flash flood (a sudden, unexpected flood) in Texas, USA. Flash floods can wash entire towns away.

Disastrous droughts

190 A drought is a shortage of rainfall that leaves the land dry. Deserts hardly ever get rain, and are dry and dusty all the time. A drought happens when a place gets much less rain than usual. Scientists don't always know why weather patterns change. However, this can be caused by changes in the oceans. Every few years, a change in sea temperatures in the Pacific, called El Niño, affects weather around the world and causes droughts.

▲ During drought conditions, water is precious. Without it people, animals and plants will die.

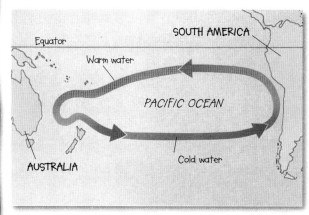

▲ El Niño is a warming of surface ocean waters in the eastern Pacific that can lead to flooding and drought around the world.

191 Droughts are disastrous for people, animals and plants. A shortage of rain means crops can't grow properly, and herds of animals can't get enough drinking water. So people face food and water shortages. Dried-out grass and trees can easily catch fire, and loose dust can blow up into blinding dust storms. Droughts can also cause wars, when people are forced to leave their lands and flock into other areas.

193 Droughts have always happened. They are mentioned in many ancient books, such as the Bible and the writings of the ancient Mesopotamians, who lived in the area around what is now Iraq. However, scientists think that today, global warming is making some droughts worse. As the world gets warmer, weather patterns are changing. Some areas, such as eastern Australia, are now having worse droughts than they used to.

▲ Part of the Murray River in southern Australia, usually flowing with water, lies empty during a drought.

192 The 'Dust Bowl' was a great drought disaster that hit the USA in the 1930s. Several years of drought dried out farm soil in the central states of the USA, such as Oklahoma and Kansas. It blew away in huge dust storms, and farmers could not grow their crops. Hundreds of thousands of people had to leave the area. Many trekked west in search of new lives and jobs.

TRUE OR FALSE?

1. Droughts make forest fires more likely.
2. The Dust Bowl is a volcano in the USA.
3. El Niño is a temperature change in the Indian Ocean.

Answers:
1. True – droughts make forests drier so they burn more easily
2. False – the Dust Bowl was a drought
3. False – El Niño is in the Pacific Ocean

◄ A massive dust storm about to engulf a farm during the Dust Bowl years. Caused by drought conditions, these storms devastated the American prairies.

Global warming

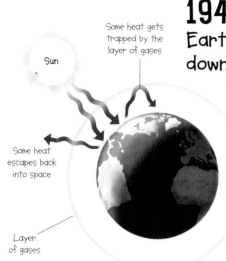

Some heat gets trapped by the layer of gases

Sun

Some heat escapes back into space

Layer of gases

▲ Global warming happens when greenhouse gases collect in the Earth's atmosphere. They let heat from the Sun through, but as it bounces back, it gets trapped close to the Earth, making the planet heat up.

194 **Throughout its history, the Earth has warmed up and cooled down.** Experts think that today's warming is down to humans – and it's happening faster than normal. Carbon dioxide and methane gases are released into the air as pollution. They are known as greenhouse gases and can stop the Sun's heat escaping from the atmosphere.

195 Global warming tells us that the climate is changing. Weather changes every day – we have hot days and cold days – but on average the climate is warming up. Scientists think that average temperatures have risen by one degree Celsius in the last 100 years, and that they will keep rising.

I DON'T BELIEVE IT!

Scientists think that sea levels could rise by one metre by 2100 – maybe even more. Three million years ago when the Earth was hotter, the sea was 200 metres higher than today. We could be heading that way again.

196 Warmer temperatures mean wilder weather. Wind happens when air is heated and gets lighter. It rises up and cold air is sucked in to replace it. Rain occurs when heat makes water in rivers and seas turn into vapour in the air. It rises up and forms rain clouds. Warmer temperatures mean more wind, rain and storms.

KEY

Average area of sea covered by ice from 1980–2000

Predicted area of sea covered by ice for 2080–2100

ARCTIC OCEAN

◄ The ice in the Arctic Ocean is melting so fast that scientists think over half of it could be gone by 2100.

▼ Huge chunks of ice often break off into the sea at Paradise Bay, at the Antarctic.

197 As the Earth heats up, its ice melts. Vast areas of the Earth are covered in ice. It is found around the North and South Poles, and on high mountains. Now, because of global warming, more and more of this ice is melting. It turns into water and flows into the sea. Also, as the water gets warmer, it expands (gets bigger) and the sea takes up more space, making sea levels rise.

► Polar bears depend on large chunks of ice to hunt and rest on. Melting ice in the Arctic is making life much harder for them.

Energy crisis

198 We pump greenhouse gases into the atmosphere because we burn fuels to make energy. Cars, planes and trains run on fuel, and we also burn it in power stations to produce electricity. The main fuels – coal, oil and gas – are called fossil fuels because they formed underground over millions of years.

199 Fossil fuels are running out. Because they take so long to form, we are using up fossil fuels much faster than they can be replaced. Eventually, they will become so rare that it will be too expensive to find them. Experts think this will happen before the end of the 21st century.

Oil platform drilling for oil and gas

Hard rock layer

Gas

Oil

▶ Oil and natural gas formed from the remains of tiny prehistoric sea creatures that collected on the seabed. Layers of rock built up on top and squashed them. Over time, they became underground stores of oil, with pockets of gas above.

Oil and gas move upwards through soft rock layers until reaching a hard rock layer

The layer of dead sea creatures is crushed by rock that forms above, and turns into oil and gas

Tiny sea creatures die and sink to the seabed

QUIZ

Which of these things are used to supply electricity?
A. Burning coal B. Wind
C. The flow of rivers
D. Hamsters on wheels E. Sunshine
F. The energy of earthquakes

Answer:
A, B, C and E. Hamsters could turn tiny turbines, but would make very little electricity. Earthquakes contain vast amounts of energy, but we have not found a way to harness it

200 One thing we can do is find other fuels. Besides fossil fuels, we can burn fuels that come from plants. For example, the rape plant contains oil that can be burned in vehicle engines. However, burning these fuels still releases greenhouse gases.

201 Nuclear power is another kind of energy. By splitting apart atoms – the tiny units that all materials are made of – energy is released, which can be turned into electricity. However, producing this energy creates toxic waste that can make people ill, and may be accidentally released into the air. Safer ways to use nuclear power are being researched.

202 Lots of energy is produced without burning anything. Hydroelectric power stations use the pushing power of flowing rivers to turn turbines. Hydroelectricity is a renewable, or green, energy source – it doesn't use anything up or cause pollution. Scientists are also working on ways to turn the movement of waves and tides into usable energy.

▲ The Grand Coulee Dam in Washington, USA, holds back a river, creating a lake, or reservoir. Water is let through the dam to turn turbines, which create electricity.

203 The wind and the Sun are great renewable sources of energy, too. Wind turbines turn generators, which convert the 'turning movement' into electricity. Solar panels work by collecting sunlight and turning it into an electrical current.

Rotor blade

◀ Solar panels are made of materials that soak up sunlight and turn its energy into a flow of electricity.

▲ Modern wind turbines usually have three blades, which spin around at speed in high winds.

Pollution problems

204 Pollution means dirt, waste and other substances that damage our surroundings. Our farms and factories often release harmful chemicals into rivers and lakes, and cars, lorries and other road vehicles give out poisonous, polluting gases. Litter and rubbish are pollution, too.

▼ A thick layer of smog hangs over the city of Bangkok, the capital of Thailand.

205 Humans make waste – when we go to the toilet. The waste and water from our toilets is called sewage. This usually ends up at sewage works where we process it to make it safe, but in some places sewage flows straight into rivers or the sea. It is smelly and dirty and can contain deadly germs.

206 Pollution can harm our health. Smog is a mixture of smoke from factories and motor vehicles, and fog, and it collects over some cities. It makes it harder to breathe, worsening illnesses such as asthma.

◀ People in Kuala Lumpur, the capital of Malaysia, wear masks to avoid breathing in smog.

◄ People who live near airports have to put up with the sound of low-flying planes flying over their houses.

207 Even noise is a kind of pollution.
Noise from airports disturbs the people who live nearby, and loud noises from ships and submarines can disturb whales. They rely on their own sounds to find their way and send messages, so other noises can confuse them.

208 The more we throw away, the more rubbish piles up.
When we drop rubbish just anywhere, it becomes litter. If we put rubbish in the bin, some of it may get recycled, and the rest gets taken away and dumped in a big hole in the ground, called a landfill site. Either way, there's too much of it!

209 Air pollution can cause acid rain.
The waste gases from power stations and factories mix with water droplets in clouds and form weak acid. This makes soil, rivers and lakes more acidic, which can kill fish and plants. Acid rain can even make rock crumble and dissolve.

▶ At landfill sites, rubbish piles up making huge mountains of waste that have to be flattened down by rollers.

TRUE OR FALSE?

1. Rubbish isn't a problem if you put it in a bin.
2. Acid rain can make your nose fall off.
3. Loud noises in the ocean can make whales get lost.

Answers:
1. False – it still piles up in landfill sites 2. False – the acid is not very strong, but it can dissolve away the stone nose of a statue 3. True – according to some scientists

95

Saving habitats

210 To save wildlife, we need to save habitats. Humans are taking up more and more space and if we don't slow down, there'll be no wild, natural land left. We need to leave plenty of natural areas for wildlife to live in.

▲ These penguins live in Antarctica. Their habitat is ice and freezing water and it could be affected by global warming.

211 One hundred years ago, people went on safari to hunt animals. Today, more tourists go to watch wild animals and plants in their natural habitat – this is called ecotourism and it helps wildlife. Local people can make enough money from tourism, so they don't need to hunt. However, ecotourism can disturb wildlife, so tourists have to take care where they go.

▶ Tourists in a jeep approach a pride of lions in a nature reserve in South Africa.

212 Nature reserves and national parks are safe homes for wildlife. The land is kept wild and unspoiled to preserve natural habitats. There are also guards or wardens to protect the wildlife and watch out for hunters.

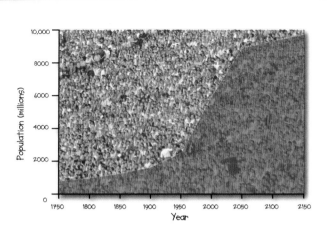

▲ As the human population continues to rise, more and more wild, natural land is being taken over.

214 It can be hard for humans to preserve habitats because we need space too. There are over 7 billion (7,000,000,000) humans on Earth today. Experts think this will rise to at least 9 billion. Some countries have laws to limit the number of children people are allowed to have to try to control the population.

▼ A diver explores a coral reef. The corals are home to many species of fish, crabs and shellfish.

213 You can help to keep habitats safe. In the countryside, don't take stones, shells or flowers. Visit nature reserves – your money helps to run them. Don't buy souvenirs made of coral, or other animals or plants, as this encourages hunting and habitat destruction.

I DON'T BELIEVE IT!

The river Thames in London has just 10 percent of the pollution it had in the 1950s because of pollution prevention, and is home to over 100 species of fish.

SCIENCE

215 Even one hundred books like this could not explain all the reasons why we need science. Toasters, bicycles, mobile phones, computers, cars, light bulbs – all the gadgets and machines we use every day are the results of scientific discoveries. Houses, skyscrapers, bridges and rockets are built using science. Our knowledge of medicines, illnesses and the human body comes from science.

◀ In a big city, science is all around you — everything from sky-scraping buildings to speedy vehicles and useful gadgets is based on science and technology.

216 Many pages in this book mention atoms. They are the smallest bits of a substance. They are so tiny, even a billion atoms would be too small to see. But scientists have carried out experiments to find out what's inside an atom. The answer is — even smaller bits. These are sub-atomic particles, and there are three main kinds.

217 Atoms of the various elements have different numbers of protons and neutrons. An atom of hydrogen has just one proton. An atom of helium, the gas put in party balloons to make them float, has two protons and two neutrons. An atom of the heavy metal called lead has 82 protons and 124 neutrons.

218 At the centre of each at is a blob called the nucleus. It contains two kinds of sub-atomic particles. These are protons and neutrons. Protons are positive, or plu The neutron is neither positive nor negative. Around the centre of each atom are sub-atomic particles called electrons. They whizz round the nucleus. In the same way that a pro in the nucleus is positive or plus, an electron is negative or minus. The number of protons and electrons is usually the same.

I DON'T BELIEVE IT!

One hundred years ago, people thought the electrons were spread out in an atom, like the raisins in a raisin pudding.

▶ The bits inside an atom give each substance its features, from exploding hydrogen to life-giving oxygen.

Hydrogen

Helium

Oxygen

Electron

Proton

Neutron

219 *It is hard to imagine the size of an atom.* A grain of sand, smaller than this o, contains at least 100 billion billion atoms. If you could make the atoms bigger, so that each one becomes as big as a pin head, the grain of sand would be 2 kilometres high!

Electron

Nucleus made from protons and neutrons

Movement of electrons

220 *'Nano' means one–billionth (1/1,000,000,000th), and nanotechnology is science at the smallest level — how atoms join to make molecules.* It is fairly new, but it has already produced many useful products, from stronger materials in jet planes and racing cars, to self-cleaning glass and bouncier tennis balls!

▲ The protons and neutrons in the nucleus of an atom are held together by a powerful force.

▼ Buckyballs are ball–shaped structures made of carbon atoms, used in some types of solar panels and medical research.

◄ This idea for a nano gear–bearing allows the central axle to spin inside the outer collar. It could be used in micromachines.

► Like buckyballs, nanotubes are formed mainly of carbon atoms. They can be combined with plastics in hi–tech equipment such as racing bicycles.

When science is hot!

221 Fire! Flames! Burning! Heat! The science of heat is important in all kinds of ways. Not only do we cook with heat, but we also warm our homes and heat water. Burning happens in all kinds of engines in cars, trucks, planes and rockets. It is also used in factory processes, from making steel to shaping plastics.

▲ A firework burns suddenly as an explosive, producing heat, light and sound. The 'bang' is the sound made by the paper wrapper as it is blown apart.

Heat from the drink is conducted up the metal spoon

222 Heat can move by conduction. A hot object will pass on, or transfer, some of its heat to a cooler one. Dip a metal spoon in a hot drink and the spoon handle soon warms up. Heat is conducted from the drink, through the metal.

223 Heat moves by invisible 'heat rays'. This is called thermal radiation and the rays are infrared waves. Our planet is warmed by the Sun because heat from the Sun radiates through space as infrared waves.

TRUE OR FALSE?

1. Burning happens inside the engine of a plane.
2. A device for measuring temperature is called a calendar.
3. Heat rays are known as infrablue waves.

Answers:
1. True 2. False 3. False

◀ Metal is a good conductor of heat. Put a teaspoon in a hot drink and feel how quickly it heats up.

224 Burning, also called combustion, is a chemical process. Oxygen gas from the air joins to, or combines with, the substance being burned. The chemical change releases lots of heat, and usually light too. If this happens really fast, we call it an explosion.

▲ A burner flame makes glass so hot it becomes soft and bendy, so it can be stretched, shaped and even blown up like a balloon.

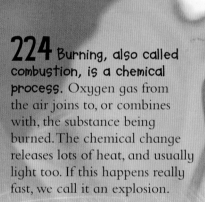

225 Temperature is a measure of how hot or cold something is. It is usually measured in degrees Celsius (°C) or Fahrenheit (°F). Water freezes at 0°C (32°F), and boils at 100°C (212°F). We use thermometers to take our temperatures. Your body temperature is about 37°C (98.6°F).

▶ This thermometer contains alcohol coloured by a red dye. As it warms, the alcohol expands (takes up more space). It moves up the thin tube, showing the temperature on the scale.

226 Heat moves through liquids and gases by convection. Some of the liquid or gas takes in heat, gets lighter, and rises into cooler areas. Then other cooler liquid or gas moves in to do the same and the process repeats. You can see this as 'wavy' hot air rising from a flame.

▶ Hot air shimmering over a candle is a visible sign of the heat being convected away.

Looking at light

227 Almost everything you do depends on light and the science of light, which is called optics. Light is a form of energy that you can see. Light waves are made of electricity and magnetism – and they are tiny. About 2000 of them laid end to end would stretch across this full stop.

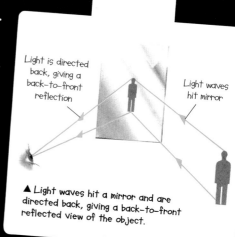

Light is directed back, giving a back–to–front reflection

Light waves hit mirror

▲ Light waves hit a mirror and are directed back, giving a back–to–front reflected view of the object.

▲ A prism of clear glass or clear plastic separates the colours in white light.

228 Like sound, light bounces off surfaces that are very smooth. This is called reflection. A mirror is smooth, hard and flat. When you look at it, you see your reflection.

229 Ordinary light from the Sun or from a light bulb is called white light. But when white light passes through a prism, a triangular block of clear glass, it splits into many colours. These colours are known as the spectrum. Each colour has a different length of wave. A rainbow is made by raindrops, which work like millions of tiny prisms to split up sunlight.

230 Light passes through certain materials, like clear glass and plastic. Materials that let light pass through, to give a clear view, are transparent. Those that do not allow light through, like wood and metal, are opaque.

I DON'T BELIEVE IT!

Light is the fastest thing in the Universe – it travels through space at 300,000 kilometres per second. That's seven times around the world in less than one second!

231 Mirrors and lenses are important parts of many optical (light-using) gadgets. They are found in cameras, binoculars, microscopes, telescopes and lasers. Without them, we would have no close-up photographs of tiny microchips or insects or giant planets – in fact, no photos at all.

▼ A concave lens, which is thin in the middle, makes things look smaller.

Light rays from object

Eye sees light rays coming from this position

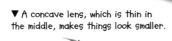

▲ A convex lens, which bulges in the middle, makes things look larger.

232 Light does not usually go straight through glass. It bends slightly where it goes into the glass, then bends back as it comes out. This is called refraction. A lens is a curved piece of glass or plastic that bends light to make things look bigger, smaller or clearer. Spectacle and contact lenses bend light to help people see more clearly.

▲ Glass and water bend, or refract, light waves. This makes a drinking straw look bent where it goes behind the glass and then into the water.

Mysterious magnets

233 Without magnets there would be no electric motors, computers or loudspeakers. Magnetism is an invisible force to do with atoms – tiny particles that make up everything. Atoms are made of even smaller particles, including electrons. Magnetism is linked to the way that these line up and move. Most magnetic substances contain iron. As iron makes up a big part of the metallic substance steel, steel is also magnetic.

▶ For metal recycling, an electromagnet lifts out only iron–containing or ferrous metals, such as steel.

234 A magnet is a lump of iron or steel that has all its electrons and atoms lined up. This means that their magnetic forces all add up. The force surrounds the magnet, in a region called the magnetic field. This is strongest at the two parts of the magnet called the poles.

▲ Maglev (magnetic levitation) trains use pushing or repelling magnetic forces to 'float' above their track.

235 **A magnet has two different poles – north and south.** A north pole repels (pushes away) the north pole of another magnet. Two south poles also repel each other. But a north pole and a south pole attract (pull together). Both magnetic poles attract any substance containing iron, like a nail or a screw.

236 **When electricity flows through a wire, it makes a weak magnetic field around it.** If the wire is wrapped into a coil, the magnetism becomes stronger. This is called an electromagnet. Its magnetic force is the same as an ordinary magnet, but when the electricity goes off, the magnetism does too. Some electromagnets are so strong, they can lift whole cars.

▼ The field around a magnet affects objects that contain iron.

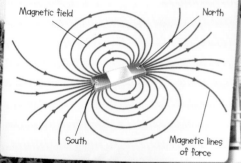

Magnetic field

North

South

Magnetic lines of force

QUIZ

Which of these substances or objects is magnetic?
1. Steel spoon 2. Plastic spoon
3. Pencil 4. Drinks can
5. Food can 6. Screwdriver
7. Cooking foil

Answers:
1.Yes 2.No 3.No
4.No 5.Yes 6.Yes 7.No

Electric sparks!

237 Flick a switch and things happen. The television goes off, the computer comes on, lights shine and music plays. Electricity is our favourite form of energy. We send it along wires and plug hundreds of machines into it.

▼ When an electric current flows, the electrons (small blue balls) all move the same way, jumping from one atom to the next. (The red balls are the centres or nuclei of the atoms.)

238 Electricity depends on electrons. In certain substances, when electrons are 'pushed', they hop from one atom to the next. When billions do this every second, electricity flows. The 'push' is from a battery or a generator. Electricity only flows in a complete loop or circuit. Break the circuit and the flow stops.

Atom

Electron

▼ Solar panels contain many hundreds of fingernail-sized PV (photovoltaic) cells. These convert light energy ('photo') to electrical energy ('voltaic').

▼ A battery has a chemical paste inside its metal casing.

Positive contact

Negative contact on base

239 A battery makes electricity from chemicals. Two different chemicals next to each other, such as an acid and a metal, swap electrons and get the flow going. Electricity's pushing strength is measured in volts. Most batteries are about 1.5, 3, 6 or 9 volts, with 12 volts in cars.

240 Electricity flows easily through some substances, including water and metals. These are electrical conductors. Other substances do not allow electricity to flow. They are insulators. Insulators include wood, plastic, glass, card and ceramics. Metal wires and cables have coverings of plastic, to stop the electricity leaking away.

241 **Electricity from power stations is carried along cables on high pylons, or buried underground.** This is known as the distribution grid. At thousands of volts, this electricity is extremely dangerous. For use in the home, it is changed to 220 volts (in the UK).

▼ Electricity generators are housed in huge casings, some bigger than trucks.

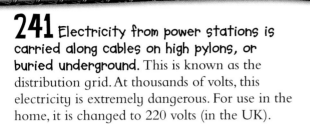

Pylon holds cables off the ground

◄ To check and repair high-voltage cables, the electricity must be turned off well in advance.

MAKE A CIRCUIT
You will need:
lightbulb battery wire
plastic ruler metal spoon
dry card

Join a bulb to a battery with pieces of wire, as shown. Electricity flows round the circuit and lights the bulb. Make a gap in the circuit and put various objects into it, to see if they allow electricity to flow again. Try a plastic ruler, a metal spoon and some dry card.

242 **Mains electricity is made at a power station.** A fuel such as coal or oil is burned to heat water into high-pressure steam. The steam pushes past the blades of a turbine and makes them spin. The turbines turn generators, which have wire coils near powerful magnets, and the spinning motion makes electricity flow in the coils.

How do planes fly?

243 A plane flies by moving through the air. The engines drive the plane forwards with a force called thrust. However, air pushes in the opposite direction and slows the plane down. This is called drag. Weight is the force that tries to pull the plane down. When moving through the air, the wings give an upwards force called lift.

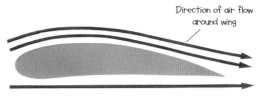

Direction of air flow around wing

▲ As the wing moves forwards, air streams under and over it, lifting it up.

244 Air flowing over the wings gives an upwards lift. The wings are a special shape called an aerofoil. The top curves upwards while the bottom is flatter. As the plane moves forwards, air flowing over the top has further to go and is more spread out than the air beneath. The air beneath pushes the wing harder than the air above it, so the wing lifts, taking the plane with it.

A force called lift pulls the plane up

LIFTING FORCE

Wrap a strip of narrow paper around a pencil. Holding one end of the strip, blow hard over the top of it. Watch the free end of the paper lift upwards. This shows how an aircraft wing lifts as it moves through the air, keeping the heavy aircraft in the air. The faster you blow, the higher the paper lifts.

A force called thrust pulls the plane forwards

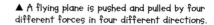

▲ A flying plane is pushed and pulled by four different forces in four different directions.

A force called weight pulls the plane down

Aileron

▶ Flaps on the wings, called ailerons, direct the air flow up or down.

245 The engines give the thrust that drives the plane forwards in the air. As the plane travels faster, the lifting force grows stronger. This force must be equal to the weight of the plane before it can rise into the air and fly. This means that the thrust from the engines must drive the plane quickly to give it enough lift to fly.

246 As the plane moves forwards it pushes against the air. The air pushes back, which slows the plane down and makes it use more fuel. Aircraft builders try to make the drag as minimal as possible by designing the plane to be smooth and streamlined so it cuts cleanly through the air.

247 The weight of a plane is always trying to pull it down. For this reason, planes are built to be as light as possible, using light but strong materials. Even so, a Boeing 747 jumbo jet with all its passengers and luggage can weigh as much as 360 tonnes and still take off.

A force called drag pulls the plane backwards

▼ Jet engines or propellers thrust a plane forwards.

Propeller engine

248 Planes get thrust from jet engines or propellers. Jet engines are more powerful and better for flying high up where the air is thinner. Airliners and fighter planes have jet engines. Propellers are more useful for planes that fly slower and nearer the ground. Most small private planes and some large planes that carry heavy cargo use propeller engines.

Jet engine

Powerful engines

249 **A jet engine thrusts a plane forwards by shooting out a jet of hot gases.** A turbojet engine uses spinning blades called a compressor to suck air into the front of the engine and squeeze it tightly. This air is then mixed with fuel inside the engine, as the fuel requires air to burn. The burning fuel creates hot gases that shoot out of a nozzle at the back of the engine.

BALLOON JET
Blow up a balloon then let it go. Watch the balloon shoot away as the air rushes out. In the same way, a plane shoots forwards when gases rush out of its jet engines.

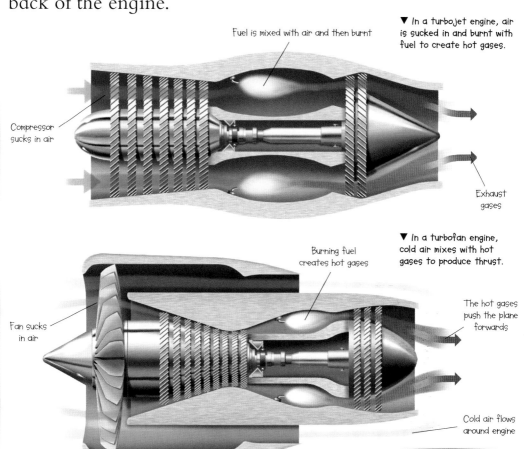

Fuel is mixed with air and then burnt

▼ In a turbojet engine, air is sucked in and burnt with fuel to create hot gases.

Compressor sucks in air

Exhaust gases

Burning fuel creates hot gases

▼ In a turbofan engine, cold air mixes with hot gases to produce thrust.

Fan sucks in air

The hot gases push the plane forwards

Cold air flows around engine

250 A turbofan engine is another type of jet engine used by modern airliners. These are less noisy than turbojet engines and cheaper to run. A large fan at the front sucks in air, but not all of it is squeezed and mixed with fuel. Some of the air flows around the outside of the engine and mixes with the hot gases shooting out of the back.

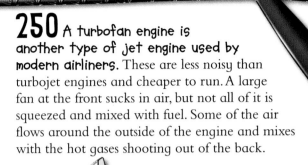

Propeller blade

Hub

▲ When the propellers spin, they pull the plane through the air.

251 Propellers whiz round at high speed, pulling the plane through the air. The propeller has two or more blades sticking out from the centre. Each blade is like a small wing and as it spins, it pushes the air backwards so the plane moves forwards. Small planes have just one propeller at the front, but larger planes may have two or more propellers, each driven by its own engine.

252 Propellers can be driven by two different types of engine. Early planes had engines that worked like the engine in a car. Many small planes still use this type of engine. Turboprop engines are jet engines but the hot gases are used to turn the propeller. This drives the plane instead of a jet of hot gas.

▼ Hot gases from a jet engine turn the propeller in a turboprop engine.

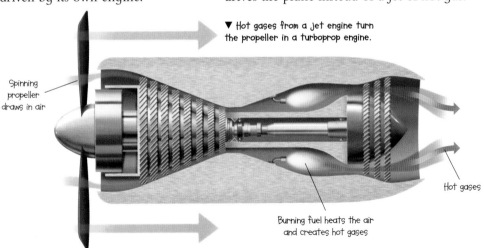

Spinning propeller draws in air

Hot gases

Burning fuel heats the air and creates hot gases

Making sounds and pictures

253 **The air is full of waves we cannot see or hear, unless we have the right machine.** Radio waves are a form of electrical and magnetic energy, just like heat and light waves, microwaves and X-rays. All of these are called electromagnetic waves and they travel at an equal speed – the speed of light.

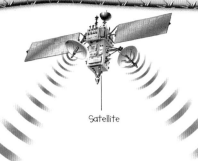

Satellite

Radio waves

255 **Radio waves carry their information by being altered, or modulated, in a certain pattern.** The height of a wave is called its amplitude. If this is altered, it is known as AM (amplitude modulation). Look for AM on the radio display.

254 **Radio waves are used for both radio and television.** They travel vast distances. Long waves curve around the Earth's surface. Short waves bounce between the Earth and the sky.

▼ This range of waves, with different wavelengths, are electrical and magnetic energy. They are called the electromagnetic spectrum.

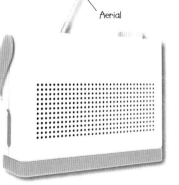

Aerial

▲ A radio set picks up radio waves using its aerial or antenna.

256 **The number of waves per second is called the frequency.** If this is altered, it is known as FM (frequency modulation). FM radio is clearer than AM, and less affected by weather and thunderstorms.

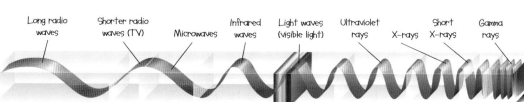

| Long radio waves | Shorter radio waves (TV) | Microwaves | Infrared waves | Light waves (visible light) | Ultraviolet rays | X-rays | Short X-rays | Gamma rays |

257 Radio waves are sent out, or transmitted, from antennae on tall masts or on satellites, to reach a very wide area. A radio receiver converts the pattern of waves to sounds. A television receiver or TV set changes them to pictures and sounds.

I DON'T BELIEVE IT!

You could send and receive radio signals on the Moon, but not in the sea. Radio waves travel easily through space, but only a few metres in water.

▼ A dish-shaped receiver picks up radio waves for TV channels.

258 Digital radio uses incredibly short bursts of radio waves with gaps between them – many thousands each second. Each burst represents the digit (number) 1, and a gap is 0. The order of the 1s and 0s carries information in the form of binary code, as in a computer.

▶ A plasma screen has thousands of tiny boxes, or cells, of three colours – red, green and blue. Electric pulses heat the gas inside for a split second into plasma, which gives out a burst of light. Combinations of these colours gives all the other colours.

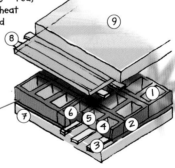

▼ Flat-screen TVs can be LCD or plasma. They use less electricity than cathode-ray TVs and produce a better picture.

KEY
① Glowing 'on' cell
② Dark 'off' cell
③ Rear grid of electrical contacts
④ – ⑥ Coloured phosphors inside cells
⑦ Backing plate
⑧ Front grid of electrical contacts
⑨ Transparent front cover

Compu-science

259 Computers are amazing machines, but they have to be told exactly what to do. So we put in instructions and information, by various means. These include typing on a keyboard, inserting a disc or memory stick, downloading from the Internet, using a joystick or games controller, or linking up a camera, scanner or another computer.

Flat screen monitor

260 Most computers are controlled by instructions from a keyboard and a mouse. The mouse moves a pointer around on the screen and its click buttons select choices from lists called menus.

Silicon 'wafer'

Plastic casing

USB (Universal Serial Bus) sockets

◄ This close up of a slice of silicon 'wafer' shows the tiny parts that receive and send information in a computer.

External monitor (screen) socket

Headphone socket

Wire 'feet' link to other part in the computer

261 Some computers are controlled by talking to them! They pick up the sounds using a microphone. This is speech recognition technology.

262 The 'main brain' of a computer is its Central Processing Unit. It is usually a microchip – millions of electronic parts on a chip of silicon, hardly larger than a fingernail. It receives information and instructions from other microchips, carries out the work, and sends back the results.

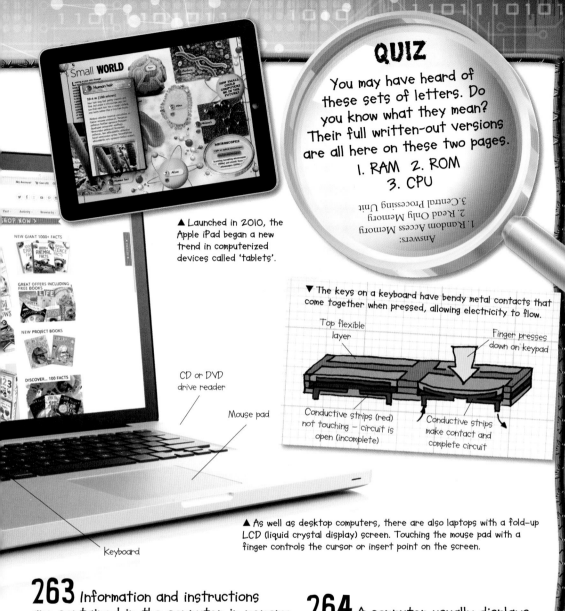

Small **WORLD**

QUIZ

You may have heard of these sets of letters. Do you know what they mean? Their full written-out versions are all here on these two pages.

1. RAM   2. ROM
3. CPU

Answers:
1. Random Access Memory
2. Read Only Memory
3. Central Processing Unit

▲ Launched in 2010, the Apple iPad began a new trend in computerized devices called 'tablets'.

NEW GIANT 1000+ FACTS

GREAT OFFERS INCLUDING FREE BOOKS

NEW PROJECT BOOKS

DISCOVER... 100 FACTS

CD or DVD drive reader

Mouse pad

Keyboard

▼ The keys on a keyboard have bendy metal contacts that come together when pressed, allowing electricity to flow.

Top flexible layer

Finger presses down on keypad

Conductive strips (red) not touching — circuit is open (incomplete)

Conductive strips make contact and complete circuit

▲ As well as desktop computers, there are also laptops with a fold-up LCD (liquid crystal display) screen. Touching the mouse pad with a finger controls the cursor or insert point on the screen.

263 Information and instructions are contained in the computer in memory microchips. There are two kinds. Random Access Memory is like a jotting pad. It keeps changing as the computer carries out its tasks. Read Only Memory is like an instruction book. It usually contains the instructions for how the computer starts up and how all the microchips work together.

264 A computer usually displays its progress on a monitor screen. It feeds information to output devices such as printers, loudspeakers and robot arms. Information can be stored on CDs, DVDs, memory sticks (chips), external HDs (hard drive discs), or uploaded to the Internet.

What's it made of?

265 You wouldn't make a bridge out of straw, or a cup out of bubblewrap! Choosing the right substance for the job is important. All the substances in the world can be divided into several groups. For example, metals such as iron, silver and gold are strong, hard and shiny, and conduct heat and electricity well. They are used to make things that have to be strong and long-lasting.

266 Plastics are made mainly from the substances in petroleum (crude oil). There are so many kinds – some are hard and brittle while others are soft and bendy. They are usually long-lasting, not affected by weather or damp, and they resist heat and electricity.

KEY

① The front wing is a special shape – this produces a force that presses the car down onto the track

② The main body of the car is made from carbon fibre, a light but very strong material

③ The car's axles are made from titanium – a very strong, light metal

④ The engine is made from various alloys, or mixtures of metals, based on aluminium. It produces up to ten times the power of a family car engine

⑤ Each tyre is made of thick, tough rubber to withstand high speeds

⑥ The rear wing is also carbon fibre composite

▼ A racing car has thousands of parts made from hundreds of materials. Each is suited to certain conditions such as stress, temperature and vibrations.

267 Ceramics are materials based on clay or other substances dug from the Earth. They can be shaped and dried, like a clay bowl. Or they can be fired – baked in a hot oven called a kiln. This makes them hard and long-lasting, but brittle and prone to cracks. Ceramics resist heat and electricity very well.

Metal

Fibre

Ceramic

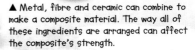

▲ Metal, fibre and ceramic can combine to make a composite material. The way all of these ingredients are arranged can affect the composite's strength.

◀ In 2007, the Interstate 35W bridge collapsed in Minneapolis, USA, killing 13 people. It was due to cracking of small steel connecting plates that were too thin for the weight.

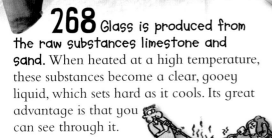

268 Glass is produced from the raw substances limestone and sand. When heated at a high temperature, these substances become a clear, gooey liquid, which sets hard as it cools. Its great advantage is that you can see through it.

269 Composites are mixtures or combinations of different materials. For example, glass strands are coated with plastic to make GRP – glass-reinforced plastic. This composite has the advantages of both materials.

MAKE YOUR OWN COMPOSITE

You will need:
flour   newspaper strips
water   balloon   pin

You can make a composite called pâpier maché from flour, newspaper and water. Tear newspaper into strips. Mix flour and water into a paste. Dip each strip in the paste and place it around a blown-up balloon. Cover the balloon and allow it to dry. Pop the balloon with a pin, and the composite should stay in shape.

270 The world seems to be made of millions of different substances — such as soil, wood, concrete, plastics and air. These are combinations of simpler substances. If you could take them apart, you would see that they are made of pure substances called elements.

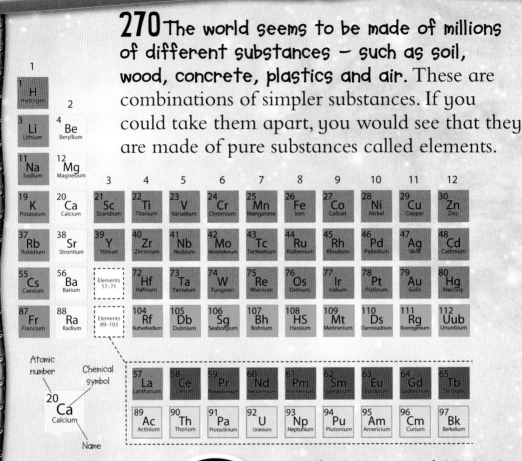

1											
1 H Hydrogen	2										
3 Li Lithium	4 Be Beryllium										
11 Na Sodium	12 Mg Magnesium	3	4	5	6	7	8	9	10	11	12
19 K Potassium	20 Ca Calcium	21 Sc Scandium	22 Ti Titanium	23 V Vanadium	24 Cr Chromium	25 Mn Manganese	26 Fe Iron	27 Co Colbalt	28 Ni Nickel	29 Cu Copper	30 Zn Zinc
37 Rb Rubidium	38 Sr Strontium	39 Y Yttrium	40 Zr Zirconium	41 Nb Niobium	42 Mo Molybdenum	43 Tc Technetium	44 Ru Ruthenium	45 Rh Rhodium	46 Pd Palladium	47 Ag Silver	48 Cd Cadmium
55 Cs Caesium	56 Ba Barium	Elements 57–71	72 Hf Hafnium	73 Ta Tantalum	74 W Tungsten	75 Re Rhenium	76 Os Osmium	77 Ir Iridium	78 Pt Platinum	79 Au Gold	80 Hg Mercury
87 Fr Francium	88 Ra Radium	Elements 89–103	104 Rf Rutherfordium	105 Db Dubnium	106 Sg Seaborgium	107 Bh Bohrium	108 HS Hassium	109 Mt Meitnerium	110 Ds Darmstadtium	111 Rg Roentgenium	112 Uub Ununbium

Atomic number — Chemical symbol

20 Ca Calcium

Name

57 La Lanthanum	58 Ce Cerium	59 Pr Praseodymium	60 Nd Neodymium	61 Pm Promethium	62 Sm Samarium	63 Eu Europium	64 Gd Gadolinium	65 Tb Terbium
89 Ac Actinium	90 Th Thorium	91 Pa Protactinium	92 U Uranium	93 Np Neptunium	94 Pu Plutonium	95 Am Americium	96 Cm Curium	97 Bk Berkelium

▶ Stars are made mainly of burning hydrogen, which is why they are so hot and bright.

▲ The Periodic Table is a chart of all the elements. In each row the atoms get heavier from left to right. Each column (up–down) contains elements with similar chemical features. Every element has a chemical symbol, name, and atomic number, which is the number of particles called protons in its central part, or nucleus.

271 Hydrogen is the simplest element and it is the first in the Periodic Table. This means it has the smallest atoms. It is a very light gas, which floats upwards in air. Hydrogen was used to fill giant airships. But there was a problem – hydrogen catches fire easily and explodes.

272 About 90 elements are found naturally on and in the Earth. In an element, all of its particles, called atoms, are exactly the same as each other. Just as important, they are all different from the atoms of any other element.

Element types

- ■ Alkali metals
- □ Alkaline metals
- ■ Transition metals
- □ Other metals
- ▦ Other non-metals
- ▦ Halogens
- ■ Inert gases
- ■ Lanthanides
- □ Actinides
- ■ Trans-actinides

Note: Elements 113–118 are synthetic elements that have only been created briefly, so their properties cannot be known for certain.

18
2 **He** Helium

13	14	15	16	17	
5 **B** Boron	6 **C** Carbon	7 **N** Nitrogen	8 **O** Oxygen	9 **F** Fluorine	10 **Ne** Neon
13 **Al** Aluminium	14 **Si** Silicon	15 **P** Phosphorus	16 **S** Sulphur	17 **Cl** Chlorine	18 **Ar** Argon
31 **Ga** Gallium	32 **Ge** Germanium	33 **As** Arsenic	34 **Se** Selenium	35 **Br** Bromine	36 **Kr** Krypton
49 **In** Indium	50 **Sn** Tin	51 **Sb** Antimony	52 **Te** Tellurium	53 **I** Iodine	54 **Xe** Xenon
81 **Ti** Thallium	82 **Pb** Lead	83 **Bi** Bismuth	84 **Po** Polonium	85 **At** Astatine	86 **Rn** Radon
113 **Nh** Nihonium	114 **Fl** Flerovium	115 **Mc** Moscovium	116 **Lv** Livermorium	117 **Ts** Tennessine	118 **Og** Oganesson

66 **Dy** Dysprosium	67 **Ho** Holmium	68 **Er** Erbium	69 **Tm** Thulium	70 **Yb** Ytterbium	71 **Lu** Lutetium
98 **Cf** Californium	99 **Es** Einsteinium	100 **Fm** Fermium	101 **Md** Mendelevium	102 **No** Nobelium	103 **Lr** Lawrencium

274 Uranium is a heavy and dangerous element. It gives off harmful rays and tiny particles. This process is called radioactivity and it can cause sickness, burns and diseases such as cancer. Radioactivity is a form of energy and, under careful control, radioactive elements are used as fuel in nuclear power stations.

▶ Aluminium is a strong but light metal that is ideal for forming the body of vehicles such as planes.

273 Carbon is a very important element in living things — including our own bodies. It joins easily with atoms of other elements to make large groups of atoms called molecules. When it is pure, carbon can be two different forms. These are soft, powdery soot, and hard, glittering diamond. The form depends on how the carbon atoms join to each other.

275 Aluminium is an element that is a metal, and it is one of the most useful in modern life. It is light and strong, it does not rust, and it is resistant to corrosion. Saucepans, drinks cans, cooking foil and jet planes are made mainly of aluminium.

Bond (link) Atom

◀ Diamond is a form of the element carbon where the atoms are linked, or bonded, in a very strong box-like pattern.

Baby body

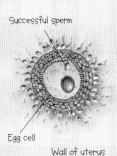

Successful sperm

Egg cell

276 A full-grown human body is made of billions of microscopic parts, called cells. But in the beginning, the body is a single cell, smaller than this full stop. Yet it contains all the instructions, known as genes, for the whole body to grow and develop.

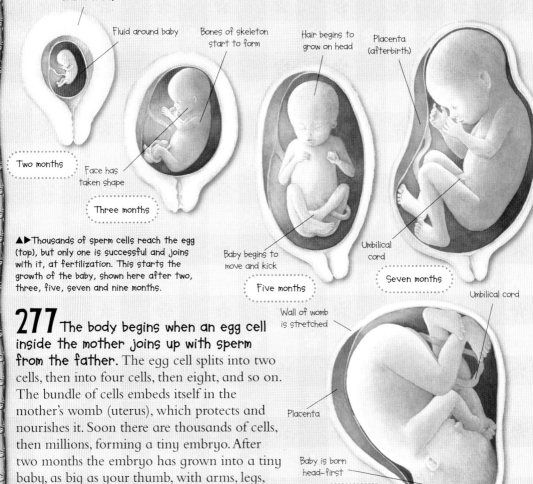

Wall of uterus

Fluid around baby

Bones of skeleton start to form

Hair begins to grow on head

Placenta (afterbirth)

Two months

Face has taken shape

Three months

▲▶Thousands of sperm cells reach the egg (top), but only one is successful and joins with it, at fertilization. This starts the growth of the baby, shown here after two, three, five, seven and nine months.

Baby begins to move and kick

Five months

Umbilical cord

Seven months

Umbilical cord

277 The body begins when an egg cell inside the mother joins up with sperm from the father. The egg cell splits into two cells, then into four cells, then eight, and so on. The bundle of cells embeds itself in the mother's womb (uterus), which protects and nourishes it. Soon there are thousands of cells, then millions, forming a tiny embryo. After two months the embryo has grown into a tiny baby, as big as your thumb, with arms, legs, eyes, ears and a mouth.

Wall of womb is stretched

Placenta

Baby is born head-first

Nine months

Cervix (neck of womb)

278 After nine months in the womb, the baby is ready to be born. Strong muscles in the walls of the womb tighten, or contract. They push the baby through the opening, or neck of the womb, called the cervix, and along the birth canal. The baby enters the outside world.

279 A newborn baby may be frightened and usually starts to cry. Inside the womb it was warm, wet, dark, quiet and cramped. Outside there are lights, noises, voices, fresh air and room to stretch. The crying is also helpful to start the baby breathing, using its own lungs.

280 Being born can take an hour or two – or a whole day or two. It is very tiring for both the baby and its mother. After birth, the baby starts to feel hungry and it feeds on its mother's milk. Finally, mother and baby settle down for a rest and some sleep.

I DON'T BELIEVE IT!

The human body never grows as fast again as it does during the first weeks in the womb. If the body kept growing at that rate, every day for 50 years, it would be bigger than the biggest mountain in the world!

▲ Once the baby is settled it is time for its mother to admire her newborn and rest.

On the body's outside

281 Skin's surface is made of tiny cells that have filled up with a hard, tough substance called keratin, and then died. So when you look at a human body, most of what you see is 'dead'! The cells get rubbed off as you move, have a wash and get dry.

282 Skin rubs off all the time, and grows all the time too. Just under the surface, living cells make more new cells that gradually fill with keratin, die and move up to the surface. It takes about four weeks from a new skin cell being made to when it reaches the surface and is rubbed off. This upper layer of skin is called the epidermis.

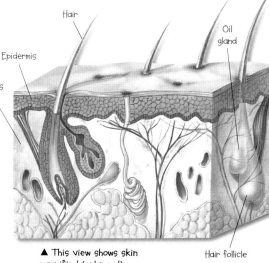

Hair

Oil gland

Epidermis

Dermis

▲ This view shows skin magnified (enlarged) about 50 times.

Hair follicle

▲ Lots of dead skin is removed without you realizing when you dry yourself after a shower.

283 Skin's lower layer, the dermis, is thicker than the epidermis. It is made of tiny, bendy, thread-like fibres of the substance collagen. The dermis also contains small blood vessels, tiny sweat glands, and micro-sensors that detect touch.

284 One of skin's important jobs is to protect the body. It stops the delicate inner parts from being rubbed, knocked or scraped. Skin also prevents body fluids from leaking away and it keeps out dirt and germs.

285 Skin helps to keep the body at the same temperature. If you become too hot, sweat oozes onto your skin and, as it dries, draws heat from the body. Also, the blood vessels in the lower layer of skin widen, to lose more heat through the skin. This is why a hot person looks sweaty and red in the face.

286 Skin gives us our sense of touch. Millions of microscopic sensors in the lower layer of skin, the dermis, are joined by nerves to the brain. These sensors detect different kinds of touch, from a light stroke to heavy pressure, heat or cold, and movement. Pain sensors detect when skin is damaged. Ouch!

Safety helmet protects head and brain

Elbow-pads cushion fall

Gloves save fingers from scrapes and breaks

Knee-pads prevent hard bumps

▲ Skin is tough, but it sometimes needs help to protect the body. Otherwise it, and the body parts beneath, may get damaged.

SENSITIVE SKIN

You will need:
friend   sticky-tack
two used matchsticks   ruler

1. Press some sticky-tack on the end of the ruler. Press two matchsticks into the sticky-tack, standing upright, about 1 centimetre apart.
2. Make your friend look away. Touch the back of their hand with both matchstick ends. Ask your friend: 'Is that one matchstick or two?' Sensitive skin can detect both ends.
3. Try this at several places, such as on the finger, wrist, forearm, neck and cheek.

The bony body

287 **Without bones, the body would be as floppy as a jellyfish!** Bones do many jobs. The long bones in the arms work like levers to reach out the hands. The finger bones grasp and grip. Bones protect softer body parts. The dome-like skull protects the brain. The ribs shield the lungs and heart. Bones also produce blood cells, as explained on the opposite page.

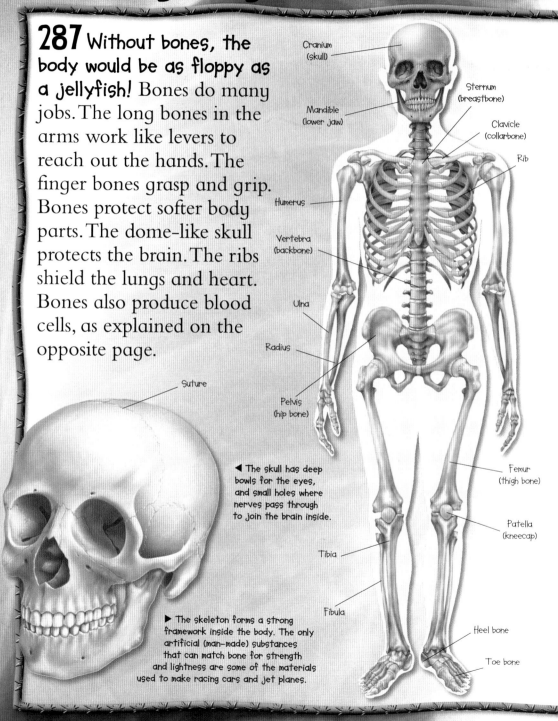

Cranium (skull)

Sternum (breastbone)

Mandible (lower jaw)

Clavicle (collarbone)

Rib

Humerus

Vertebra (backbone)

Ulna

Radius

Pelvis (hip bone)

Suture

◀ The skull has deep bowls for the eyes, and small holes where nerves pass through to join the brain inside.

Femur (thigh bone)

Patella (kneecap)

Tibia

Fibula

Heel bone

Toe bone

▶ The skeleton forms a strong framework inside the body. The only artificial (man-made) substances that can match bone for strength and lightness are some of the materials used to make racing cars and jet planes.

288 All the bones together make up the skeleton. Most people have 206 bones, from head to toe as follows:
- 8 in the upper part of the skull, the cranium or braincase
- 14 in the face
- 6 tiny ear bones, 3 deep in each ear
- 1 in the neck, which is floating and not directly connected to any other bone
- 26 in the spinal column or backbone
- 25 in the chest, being 24 ribs and the breastbone
- 32 in each arm, from shoulder to fingertips (8 in each wrist)
- 31 in each leg, from hip to toetips (7 in each ankle)

289 Bone contains threads of the tough, slightly bendy substance called collagen. It also has hard minerals such as calcium and phosphate. Together, the collagen and minerals make a bone strong and rigid, yet able to bend slightly under stress. Bones have blood vessels for nourishment and nerves to feel pressure and pain. Also, some bones are not solid. They contain a jelly-like substance called marrow. This makes tiny parts for the blood, called red and white blood cells.

Spongy bone

Marrow

Nerves and blood vessels

Compact (hard) bone

'Skin' of bone (periosteum)

End or head of bone

▲ Bone has a hard layer outside, a spongy layer next, and soft marrow in the middle.

NAME THE BONE!

Every bone has a scientific or medical name, and many have ordinary names too. Can you match up these ordinary and scientific names for various bones?

1. Mandible 2. Femur 3. Clavicle
4. Pelvis 5. Patella 6. Sternum

a. Thigh bone b. Breastbone
c. Kneecap d. Hip bone
e. Collarbone f. Lower jaw bone

Answers:
1f 2a 3e 4d 5c 6b

When muscles pull

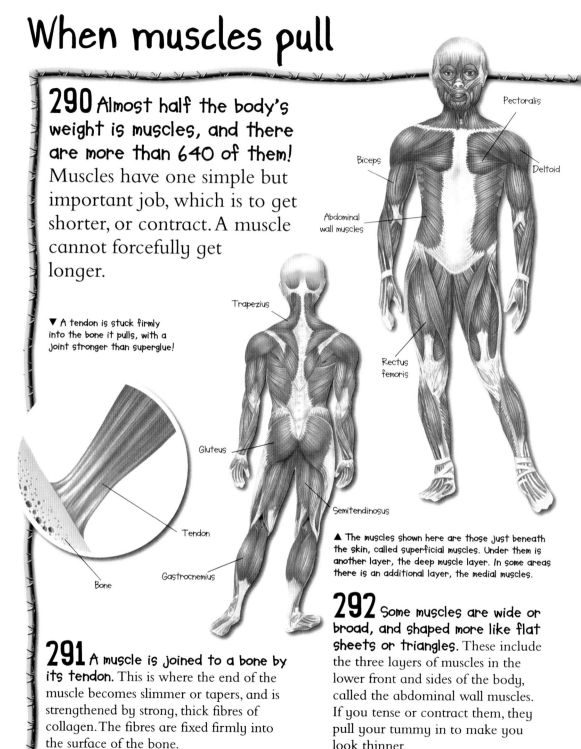

290 Almost half the body's weight is muscles, and there are more than 640 of them! Muscles have one simple but important job, which is to get shorter, or contract. A muscle cannot forcefully get longer.

▼ A tendon is stuck firmly into the bone it pulls, with a joint stronger than superglue!

Bone

Tendon

Trapezius

Gluteus

Semitendinosus

Gastrocnemius

Pectoralis

Biceps

Deltoid

Abdominal wall muscles

Rectus femoris

▲ The muscles shown here are those just beneath the skin, called superficial muscles. Under them is another layer, the deep muscle layer. In some areas there is an additional layer, the medial muscles.

291 A muscle is joined to a bone by its tendon. This is where the end of the muscle becomes slimmer or tapers, and is strengthened by strong, thick fibres of collagen. The fibres are fixed firmly into the surface of the bone.

292 Some muscles are wide or broad, and shaped more like flat sheets or triangles. These include the three layers of muscles in the lower front and sides of the body, called the abdominal wall muscles. If you tense or contract them, they pull your tummy in to make you look thinner.

293 Most muscles are long and slim, and joined to bones at each end. As they contract they pull on the bones and move them. As this happens, the muscle becomes wider, or more bulging in the middle. To move the bone back again, a muscle on the other side of it contracts, while the first muscle relaxes and is pulled longer.

294 Every muscle in the body has a scientific or medical name, which is often quite long and complicated. Some of these names are familiar to people who do exercise and sports. The 'pecs' are the pectoralis major muscles across the chest. The 'biceps' are the biceps brachii muscles in the upper arms, which bulge when you bend your elbow.

► A breakdancer needs endurance, strength and control over their muscles to carry out moves such as this.

295 If you take plenty of exercise or play sport, you do not gain new muscles. But the muscles you have become larger and stronger. This keeps them fit and healthy. Muscles which are not used much may become weak and floppy.

Biceps gets shorter and bends the elbow

To move the forearm back down, the triceps shorten and the biceps gets longer

► Muscles work in two-way pairs, like the biceps and triceps, which bend and straighten the elbow.

Biceps   Triceps

Breathing parts

296 The main parts of the respiratory (breathing) system are the two lungs in the chest. Each one is shaped like a tall cone, with the pointed end at shoulder level.

297 Air comes in and out of the lungs along the windpipe, which branches at its base to form two main air tubes, the bronchi. One goes to each lung. Inside the lung, each bronchus divides again and again, becoming narrower each time. Finally the air tubes, thinner than hairs, end at groups of tiny 'bubbles' called alveoli.

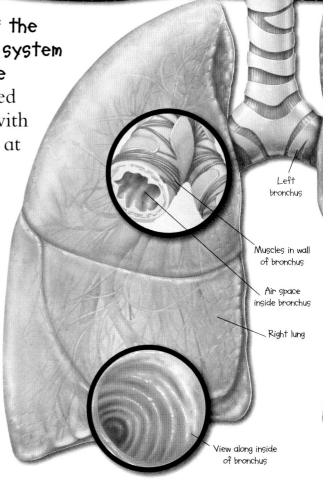

Left bronchus

Muscles in wall of bronchus

Air space inside bronchus

Right lung

View along inside of bronchus

I DON'T BELIEVE IT!

On average, the air breathed in and out through the night by a sleeping person, would fill an average-sized bedroom. This is why some people like to sleep with the door or window open!

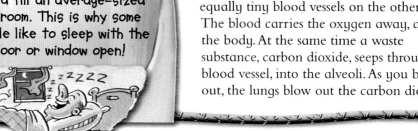

298 There are more than 200 million tiny air bubbles, or alveoli, in each lung. Inside, oxygen from breathed-in air passes through the very thin linings of the alveoli to equally tiny blood vessels on the other side. The blood carries the oxygen away, around the body. At the same time a waste substance, carbon dioxide, seeps through the blood vessel, into the alveoli. As you breathe out, the lungs blow out the carbon dioxide.

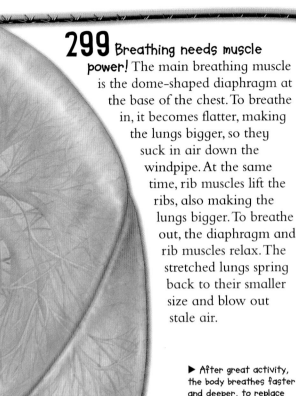

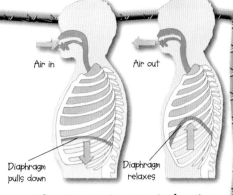

299 **Breathing needs muscle power!** The main breathing muscle is the dome-shaped diaphragm at the base of the chest. To breathe in, it becomes flatter, making the lungs bigger, so they suck in air down the windpipe. At the same time, rib muscles lift the ribs, also making the lungs bigger. To breathe out, the diaphragm and rib muscles relax. The stretched lungs spring back to their smaller size and blow out stale air.

Air in — Air out

Diaphragm pulls down — Diaphragm relaxes

▲ Breathing uses two main sets of muscles, the diaphragm and those between the ribs.

▶ After great activity, the body breathes faster and deeper, to replace the oxygen used by the muscles for energy.

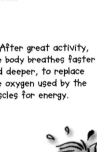

Bronchiole

Blood vessel

Air space in alveoli

Alveoli

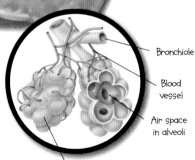

▲ Inside each lung, the main bronchus divides again and again, into thousands of narrower airways called bronchioles.

300 **As you rest or sleep, each breath sends about half a litre of air in and out, 15 to 20 times each minute.** After great activity, such as running a race, you need more oxygen. So you take deeper breaths faster – 3 litres or more of air, 50 times or more each minute.

Bite, chew, gulp

301 The hardest parts of your whole body are the ones that make holes in your food – teeth. They have a covering of whitish or yellowish enamel, which is stronger than most kinds of rocks! Teeth need to last a lifetime of biting, nibbling, gnashing, munching and chewing. They are your own food processors.

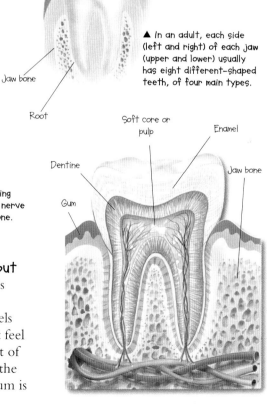

Incisor

Canine

Premolar

Molar

▲ In an adult, each side (left and right) of each jaw (upper and lower) usually has eight different–shaped teeth, of four main types.

302 There are four main shapes of teeth. The front ones are incisors, and each has a straight, sharp edge, like a spade or chisel, to cut through food. Next are canines, which are taller and more pointed, used mainly for tearing and pulling. Behind them are premolars and molars, which are lower and flatter with small bumps, for crushing and grinding.

Jaw bone

Root

Soft core or pulp

Enamel

Dentine

Jaw bone

Gum

▶ At the centre of a tooth is living pulp, with many blood vessels and nerve endings that pass into the jaw bone.

303 A tooth may look almost dead, but it is very much alive. Under the enamel is slightly softer dentine. In the middle of the tooth is the dental pulp. This has blood vessels to nourish the whole tooth, and nerves that feel pressure, heat, cold and pain. The lower part of the tooth, strongly fixed in the jaw bone, is the root. The enamel-covered part above the gum is the crown.

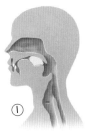

304 Teeth are very strong and tough, but they do need to be cleaned properly and regularly. Germs called bacteria live on old bits of food in the mouth. They make waste products which are acid and eat into the enamel and dentine, causing holes called cavities. Which do you prefer – cleaning your teeth after main meals and before bedtime, or the agony of toothache?

▶ Clean your teeth by brushing in different directions and then flossing between them. They will look better and stay healthier for longer.

▼ The first set of teeth lasts about ten years, while the second set can last ten times longer.

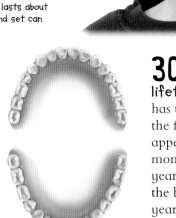

First set
(milk or deciduous teeth)

Second set
(adult or permanent set)

306 Teeth are designed to last a lifetime. Well, not quite, because the body has two sets. There are 20 small teeth in the first or baby set. The first ones usually appear above the gum by about six months of age, the last ones at three years old. As you and your mouth grow, the baby teeth fall out from about seven years old. They are replaced by 32 larger teeth in the adult set.

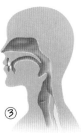

305 After chewing, food is swallowed into the gullet (oesophagus). This pushes the food powerfully down through the chest, past the heart and lungs, into the stomach.

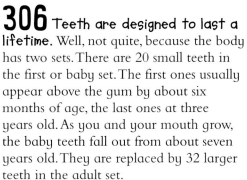

① Tongue pushes food to the back of the throat

② Throat muscles squeeze the food downwards

③ The oesophagus pushes food to the stomach

133

Food's long journey

307 The digestive system is like a tunnel about 9 metres long, through the body. It includes parts of the body that bite food, chew it, swallow it, churn it up and break it down with natural juices and acids, take in its goodness, and then get rid of the leftovers.

308 The stomach is a bag with strong, muscular walls. It stretches as it fills with food and drink, and its lining makes powerful digestive acids and juices called enzymes, to attack the food. The muscles in its walls squirm and squeeze to mix the food and juices.

309 The stomach digests food for a few hours into a thick mush, which oozes into the small intestine. This is only 4 centimetres wide, but more than 5 metres long. It takes nutrients and useful substances through its lining, into the body.

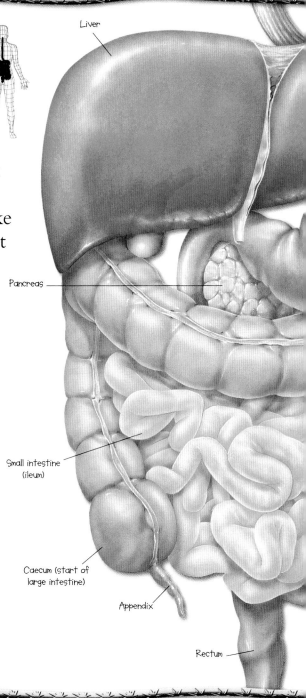

Liver

Pancreas

Small intestine
(ileum)

Caecum (start of
large intestine)

Appendix

Rectum

310 The large intestine follows the small one, and it is certainly wider, at about 6 centimetres, but much shorter, only 1.5 metres. It takes in fluids and a few more nutrients from the food, and then squashes what's left into brown lumps, ready to leave the body.

Stomach

Villus

Vessels inside villus

Large intestine

▶ The lining of the small intestine has thousands of tiny finger-like parts called the villi, which take nutrients from food, into the blood and lymph system.

Vessels in intestine lining

◀ The digestive parts almost fill the lower part of the main body, called the abdomen.

I DON'T BELIEVE IT!

What's in the leftovers?
The brown lumps called bowel motions or faeces are only about one-half undigested or leftover food. Some of the rest is rubbed-off parts of the stomach and intestine lining. The rest is millions of 'friendly' but dead microbes (bacteria) from the intestine. They help to digest our food for us, and in return we give them a warm, food-filled place to live.

311 The liver and pancreas are also parts of the digestive system. The liver sorts out and changes the many nutrients from digestion, and stores some of them. The pancreas makes powerful digestive juices that pass to the small intestine to work on the food there.

Blood in the body

312 The heart beats to pump the blood all around the body and pass its vital oxygen and nutrients to every part. The same blood goes round and round, or circulates, in its network of blood vessels. So the heart, blood vessels and blood are known as the circulatory system.

Carotid artery

◀ Blood vessels divide, or branch, to reach every body part.

Blood vessels in lung

▶ There are three main kinds of blood vessels.

Heart

Iliac artery

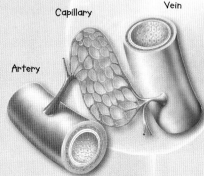

Capillary

Vein

Artery

313 Blood travels from the heart through strong, thick–walled vessels called arteries. These divide again and again, becoming smaller until they form tiny vessels narrower than hairs, called capillaries. Oxygen and nutrients seep from the blood through the thin capillary walls to the body parts around. At the same time, carbon dioxide and waste substances seep from body parts into the blood, to be carried away. Capillaries join again and again to form wide vessels called veins, which take blood back to the heart.

314 In addition to delivering oxygen and nutrients, and carrying away carbon dioxide and wastes, blood has many other vital tasks. It carries body control substances called hormones. It spreads heat evenly around the body from busy, warmer parts such as the heart, liver and muscles. It forms a sticky clot to seal a cut. It carries many substances that attack germs and other tiny invaders.

315 Blood has four main parts.

The largest is billions of tiny, saucer-shaped red cells, which make up almost half of the total volume of blood and carry oxygen. Second is the white cells, which clean the blood, prevent disease and fight germs. The third part is billions of tiny platelets, which help blood to clot. Fourth is watery plasma, in which the other parts float.

Muscle layer

Elastic layer

▼ A blood vessel wall has several layers, and blood itself contains different types of cells.

White cell

Tough outer cover

Inner lining

Plasma

Red cell

▶ Each kidney has about one million tiny filters, called nephrons, in its outer layer, or cortex.

Cortex   Medulla

Blood vessels

Ureter

▼ Blood donation is vital and saves many lives every year.

Platelet

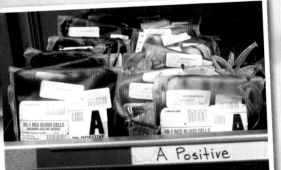

A Positive

316 Blood is cleaned by two kidneys, situated in the middle of your back.

They filter the blood and make a liquid called urine, which contains unwanted and waste substances, plus excess or 'spare' water. The urine trickles from each kidney down a tube, the ureter, into a stretchy bag, the bladder. It's stored here until you can get rid of it – at your convenience.

The beating body

317 **The heart is about as big as its owner's clenched fist.** It is a hollow bag of very strong muscle, called cardiac muscle or myocardium. This muscle never tires. It contracts once every second or more often, all through life. The contraction, or heartbeat, squeezes blood inside the heart out into the arteries. As the heart relaxes it fills again with blood from the veins.

318 **Inside, the heart is not one bag-like pump, but two pumps side by side.** The left pump sends blood all around the body, from head to toe, to deliver its oxygen (systemic circulation). The blood comes back to the right pump and is sent to the lungs, to collect more oxygen (pulmonary circulation). The blood returns to the left pump and starts the whole journey again.

▶ The heart is two pumps side by side, and each pump has two chambers, the upper atrium and the lower ventricle.

Aorta (main artery)

To upper body

From upper body

Pulmonary artery to lung

To lung

From lung

Right atrium

Valve

Right ventricle

From lower body

To lower body

319 Inside the heart are four sets of bendy flaps called valves. These open to let blood flow the right way. If the blood tries to move the wrong way, it pushes the flaps together and the valve closes. Valves make sure the blood flows the correct way, rather than sloshing to and fro, in and out of the heart, with each beat.

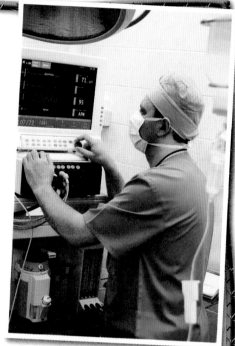

▲ Doctors use ECG machines to monitor the electrical activity of the heart.

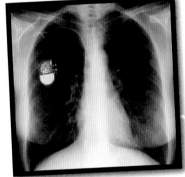

► This X-ray of a chest shows a pacemaker that has been implanted to control an irregular heartbeat.

320 The heart is the body's most active part, and it needs plenty of energy brought by the blood. The blood flows through small vessels, which branch across its surface and down into its thick walls. These are called the coronary vessels.

321 The heart beats at different rates, depending on what the body is doing. When the muscles are active they need more energy and oxygen, brought by the blood. So the heart beats faster, 120 times each minute or more. At rest, the heart slows to 60 to 80 beats per minute.

HOW FAST IS YOUR HEARTBEAT?

You will need:
plastic funnel   tracing paper
plastic tube (like hosepipe)   sticky-tape

You can hear your heart and count its beats with a sound-funnel device called a stethoscope.
1. Stretch the tracing paper over the funnel's wide end and tape in place. Push a short length of tube over the funnel's narrow end.
2. Place the funnel's wide end over your heart, on your chest, just to the left, and put the tube end to your ear. Listen to and count your heartbeat.

Looking and listening

322 The body finds out about the world around it by its senses – and the main sense is eyesight. The eyes detect the brightness, colours and patterns of light rays, and change these into patterns of nerve signals that they send to the brain. More than half of the knowledge, information and memories stored in the brain come into the body through the eyes.

▶ The eye is moved by six tiny muscles, and inside, it is filled with a clear fluid, vitreous humour.

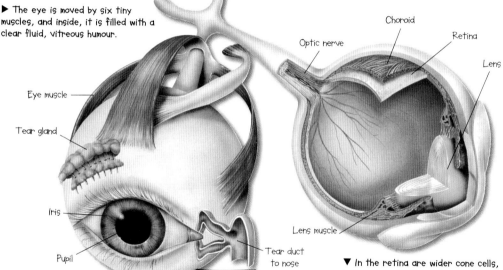

Choroid

Retina

Optic nerve

Lens

Eye muscle

Tear gland

Iris

Pupil

Lens muscle

Tear duct to nose

323 Each eye is a ball about 2.5 centimetres across. At the front is a clear dome, the cornea, which lets light through a small, dark-looking hole just behind it, the pupil. The light then passes through a pea-shaped lens, which bends the rays so they shine a clear picture onto the inside back of the eye, the retina. This has 125 million tiny cells, rods and cones, which detect the light and make nerve signals to send along the optic nerve to the brain.

▼ In the retina are wider cone cells, narrower rod cells, and many nerve cells with long fibres connecting them.

Rod cell

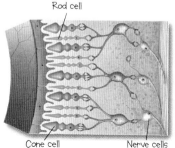

Cone cell

Nerve cells

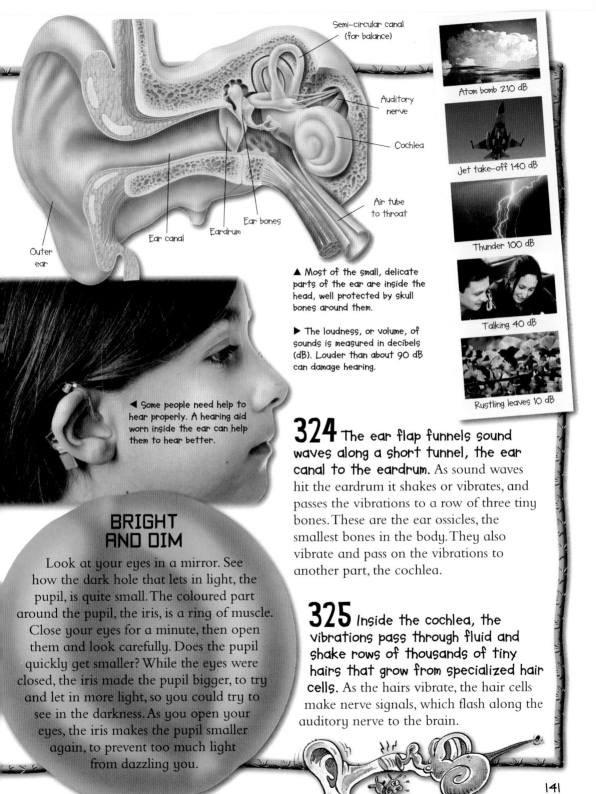

Semi-circular canal (for balance)

Auditory nerve

Cochlea

Air tube to throat

Ear bones

Eardrum

Ear canal

Outer ear

Atom bomb 210 dB

Jet take-off 140 dB

Thunder 100 dB

Talking 40 dB

Rustling leaves 10 dB

▲ Most of the small, delicate parts of the ear are inside the head, well protected by skull bones around them.

▶ The loudness, or volume, of sounds is measured in decibels (dB). Louder than about 90 dB can damage hearing.

◀ Some people need help to hear properly. A hearing aid worn inside the ear can help them to hear better.

BRIGHT AND DIM

Look at your eyes in a mirror. See how the dark hole that lets in light, the pupil, is quite small. The coloured part around the pupil, the iris, is a ring of muscle. Close your eyes for a minute, then open them and look carefully. Does the pupil quickly get smaller? While the eyes were closed, the iris made the pupil bigger, to try and let in more light, so you could try to see in the darkness. As you open your eyes, the iris makes the pupil smaller again, to prevent too much light from dazzling you.

324 The ear flap funnels sound waves along a short tunnel, the ear canal to the eardrum. As sound waves hit the eardrum it shakes or vibrates, and passes the vibrations to a row of three tiny bones. These are the ear ossicles, the smallest bones in the body. They also vibrate and pass on the vibrations to another part, the cochlea.

325 Inside the cochlea, the vibrations pass through fluid and shake rows of thousands of tiny hairs that grow from specialized hair cells. As the hairs vibrate, the hair cells make nerve signals, which flash along the auditory nerve to the brain.

141

Smelling and tasting

▼ The parts that carry out smelling are in the roof of the large chamber inside the nose.

Olfactory cells

Nasal cavity

Mucus lining

326 You cannot see smells, which are tiny particles floating in the air – but your nose can smell them. Your nose can detect more than 10,000 different scents, odours and fragrances. Smell is useful because it warns us if food is bad or rotten, and perhaps dangerous to eat. That's why we sniff a new or strange food item before trying it.

327 Smell particles drift with breathed-in air into the nose and through the nasal chamber behind it. At the top of the chamber are two patches of lining, each about the area of a thumbnail and with 5 million olfactory cells. The particles land on their sticky hairs, and if they fit into landing sites called receptors there, like a key into a lock, then nerve signals flash along the olfactory nerve to the brain.

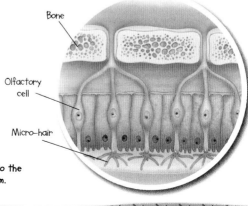

Bone

Olfactory cell

Micro-hair

▶ Olfactory (smell) cells have micro-hairs facing down into the nasal chamber, which detect smell particles landing on them.

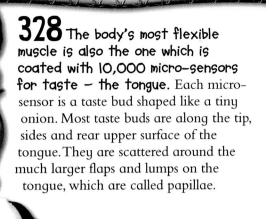

328 The body's most flexible muscle is also the one which is coated with 10,000 micro-sensors for taste – the tongue. Each micro-sensor is a taste bud shaped like a tiny onion. Most taste buds are along the tip, sides and rear upper surface of the tongue. They are scattered around the much larger flaps and lumps on the tongue, which are called papillae.

◀ The tongue is sensitive to flavours, texture and temperature.

329 Taste works in a similar way to smell, but it detects flavour particles in foods and drinks. The particles touch tiny hairs sticking up from hair cells in the taste buds. If the particles fit into receptors there, then the hair cell makes nerve signals, which go along the facial and other nerves to the brain.

SWEET AND SOUR

The tongue detects five basic flavours.
Which of these foods is sweet, salty, savoury (umami), bitter or sour?
1. Coffee 2. Lemon 3. Bacon
4. Ice cream 5. Mushroom

Answers:
1. bitter 2. sour 3. salty
4. sweet 5. savoury

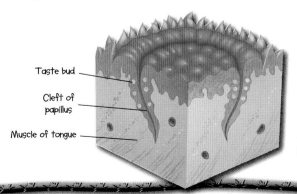

Taste bud

Cleft of papillus

Muscle of tongue

◀ The large pimple-like lumps at the back of the tongue, called papillae, have tiny taste buds in their deep clefts.

The nervous body

330 **The body is not quite a 'bag of nerves', but it does contain thousands of kilometres of these pale, shiny threads.** Nerves carry tiny electrical pulses known as nerve signals or neural messages. They form a vast information-sending network that reaches every part, almost like the body's own Internet.

Brain

Spinal cord

Sciatic nerve

Tibial nerve

331 **Each nerve is a bundle of much thinner parts called nerve fibres.** Like wires in a telephone cable, these carry their own tiny electrical nerve signals. A typical nerve signal has a strength of 0.1 volts (one-fifteenth as strong as a torch battery). The slowest nerve signals travel about half a metre each second, the fastest at more than 100 metres per second.

Axon

▲ Nerves branch from the brain and spinal cord to every body part.

Dendrites

Synapse (junction between nerve cells)

332 **All nerve signals are similar, but there are two main kinds, depending on where they are going.** Sensory nerve signals travel from the sensory parts (eyes, ears, nose, tongue and skin) to the brain. Motor nerve signals travel from the brain out to the muscles, to make the body move about.

▶ The brain and nerves are made of billions of specialized cells, nerve cells or neurons. Each has many tiny branches, dendrites, to collect nerve messages, and a longer, thicker branch, the axon or fibre, to pass on the messages.

333 Hormones are part of the body's inner control system. A hormone is a chemical made by a gland. It travels in the blood and affects other body parts, for example, making them work faster or release more of their product.

334 The main hormonal gland, the pituitary, is also the smallest. Just under the brain, it has close links with the nervous system. It mainly controls other hormonal glands. One is the thyroid in the neck, which affects the body's growth and how fast its chemical processes work. The pancreas controls how the body uses energy by its hormone, insulin. The adrenal glands are involved in the body's balance of water, minerals and salts, and how we react to stress and fear.

▲ Sports such as snowboarding cause us to produce more adrenaline due to excitement and fear.

◄ Female and male bodies have much the same hormone-making glands, except for the reproductive parts – ovaries in the female (left) and testes in the male (right).

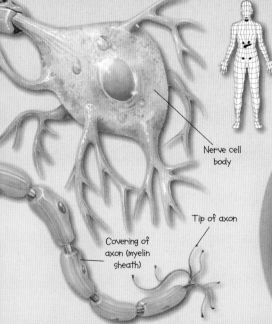

Nerve cell body

Tip of axon

Covering of axon (myelin sheath)

TIME TO REACT!

You will need:
friend   ruler

1. Ask a friend to hold a ruler by the highest measurement so it hangs down. Put your thumb and fingers level with the other end, ready to grab.
2. When your friend lets go grasp it and measure where your thumb is on the ruler. Swap places so your friend has a go.
3. The person who grabs the ruler nearest its lower end has the fastest reactions. To grab the ruler, nerve signals travel from the eye, to the brain, and back to the muscles in the arm and hand.

The brainy body

335 Your brain is as big as your two fists side by side. It's the place where you think, learn, work out problems, remember, feel happy and sad, wonder, worry, have ideas, sleep and dream.

▶ The two wrinkled hemispheres (halves) of the cerebrum, where thinking happens, are the largest brain parts.

336 The brain looks like a wrinkly lump of grey–pink jelly! On average, it weighs about 1.4 kilograms. It doesn't move, but its amazing nerve activity uses up one-fifth of all the energy needed by the body.

▼ Different areas or centres of the brain's outer layer, the cerebral cortex, deal with messages from and to certain parts of the body.

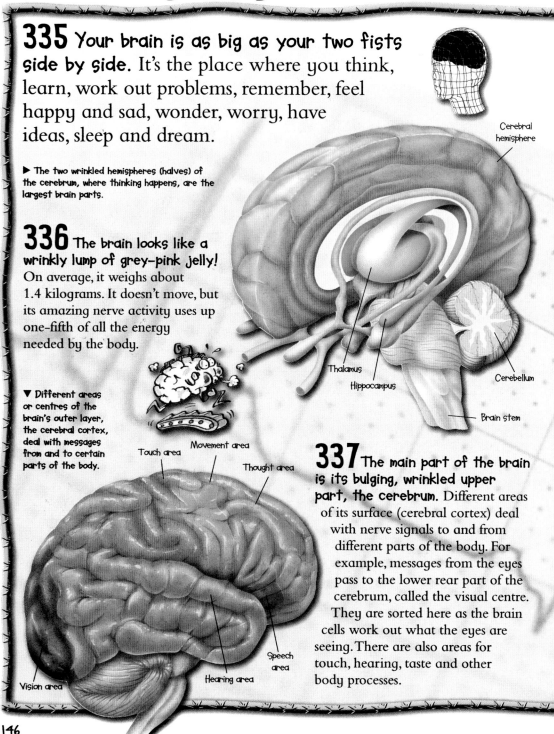

Cerebral hemisphere

Thalamus

Hippocampus

Cerebellum

Brain stem

Touch area

Movement area

Thought area

Speech area

Hearing area

Vision area

337 The main part of the brain is its bulging, wrinkled upper part, the cerebrum. Different areas of its surface (cerebral cortex) deal with nerve signals to and from different parts of the body. For example, messages from the eyes pass to the lower rear part of the cerebrum, called the visual centre. They are sorted here as the brain cells work out what the eyes are seeing. There are also areas for touch, hearing, taste and other body processes.

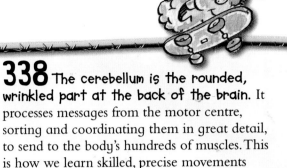

338 The cerebellum is the rounded, wrinkled part at the back of the brain. It processes messages from the motor centre, sorting and coordinating them in great detail, to send to the body's hundreds of muscles. This is how we learn skilled, precise movements such as writing, skateboarding or playing music (or all three), almost without thinking.

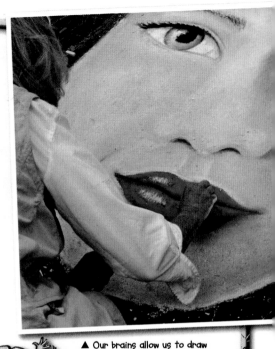

339 The brain stem is the lower part of the brain, where it joins the body's main nerve, the spinal cord. The brain stem controls basic processes vital for life, like breathing, heartbeat, digesting food and removing wastes.

▲ Our brains allow us to draw from memory, expressing emotions.

340 The brain really does have 'brain waves'. Every second it receives, sorts and sends millions of nerve signals. Special pads attached to the head can detect these tiny electrical pulses. They are shown on a screen or paper strip as wavy lines called an EEG, electro-encephalogram.

▼ The brain's 'waves' or EEG recordings change, depending on whether the person is alert and thinking hard, resting, falling asleep or deeply asleep.

I DON'T BELIEVE IT!

The brain never sleeps! EEG waves show that it is almost as busy at night as when we are awake. It still controls heartbeat, breathing and digestion. It also sifts through the day's events and stores memories.

PREHISTORIC LIFE

341 The Earth was once covered by huge sheets of ice.
This happened several times during Earth's history and we
call these frozen times ice ages. However, the ice ages are a
tiny part of prehistory. Before then, the world was warm
and lakes and seas covered the land. Even earlier than this,
there was little rain for thousands of years, and the land
was covered in deserts. Over millions of years weather and
conditions changed. Living things changed too, in order
to survive. This change is called 'evolution'.

Woolly rhinoceros

Cave lion

▼A scene from the last ice age, about 10,000 years ago. Animals grew thick fur coats to protect themselves from the cold. Many animals, such as woolly mammoths, survived on plants such as mosses. Others, such as cave lions, were fierce hunters, needing meat to survive.

Aurochs

Woolly mammoths

Megaloceros

Life begins

342 Life began a very, very long time ago. We know this from the remains of prehistoric life forms that died and were buried. Over millions of years, their remains turned into shapes in rocks, called fossils. The first fossils are over 3000 million years old. They are tiny 'blobs' called bacteria – living things that still survive today.

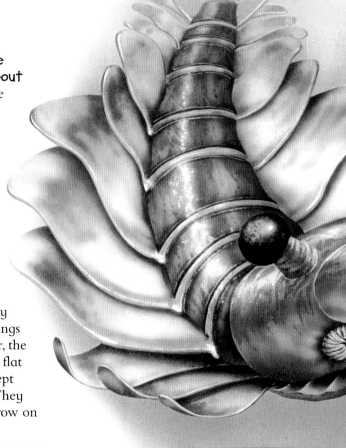

▼ Fossils of *Anomalocaris* have been found in Canada. It had a circular mouth and finlike body parts. Its body was covered by a shell.

343 The first plants were seaweeds, which appeared about 1000 million years ago. Unlike bacteria and blue-green algae, which each had just one living cell, these plants had thousands of cells. Some seaweeds were many metres long. They were called algae – the same name that scientists use today.

344 By about 800 million years ago, some plants were starting to grow on land. They were mixed with other living things called moulds, or fungi. Together, the algae (plants) and fungi formed flat green-and-yellow crusts that crept over rocks and soaked up rain. They were called lichens. These still grow on rocks and trees today.

Jellyfish

Charnia

345 The first animals lived in the sea – and they were as soft as jelly! Over 600 million years ago, some of the first animals were jellyfish, floating in the water. On the seabed lived groups of soft, feathery-looking creatures called *Charnia*. This animal was an early type of coral. Animals need to take in food by eating other living things. *Charnia* caught tiny plants in its 'feathers'.

◀ *Charnia* looked like a prehistoric plant, but it was actually an animal!

346 One of the first hunting animals was *Anomalocaris*. It lived 520 million years ago, swimming through the sea in search of prey. It caught smaller creatures in its pincers, then pushed them into its mouth. *Anomalocaris* was a cousin of crabs and insects. It was one of the biggest hunting animals of its time, even though it was only 60 centimetres long.

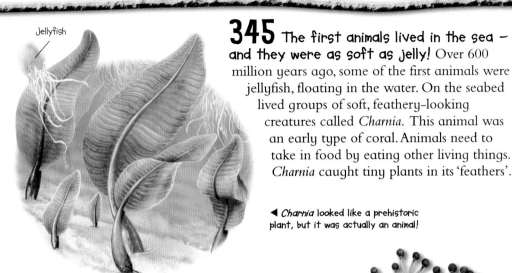

▲ The *Cooksonia* plant had forked stems that carried water. The earliest examples have been found in Ireland.

347 By 400 million years ago, plants on land were growing taller. They had stiff stems that held them upright and carried water to their topmost parts. An early upright plant was *Cooksonia*. It was the tallest living thing on land, yet it was only 5 centimetres high – hardly the size of your thumb!

Very fishy

348 The first fish could not bite — they were suckers! About 500 million years ago, new animals appeared in the sea — the first fish. They had no jaws or teeth and probably sucked in worms and small pieces of food from the mud.

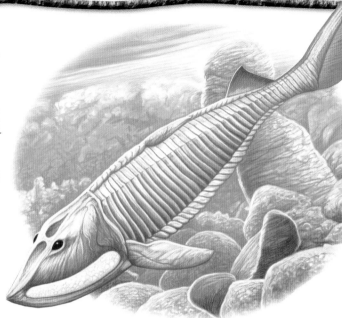

349 **Some early fish wore suits of armour!** They had hard, curved plates of bone all over their bodies for protection. These fish were called placoderms and most were fierce hunters. Some had huge jaws with sharp sheets of bone for slicing up prey.

▲ *Hemicyclaspis* was an early jawless fish. It had eyes on top of its head and probably lived on the seabed. This way it could keep a look out for predators above.

350 **Spiny sharks had spines, but they were not really sharks.** These fish were similar in shape to today's sharks, but they lived in rivers and lakes, not the sea, about 430 million years ago. *Climatius* was a spiny shark that looked fierce, but it was only as big as your finger!

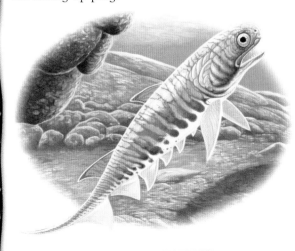

◀ The fins on the back of *Climatius* were supported by needle-sharp spines. These helped to protect it from attacks by squid or other fish.

351 The first really big hunting fish was bigger than today's great white shark! *Dunkleosteus* grew to almost 10 metres long and swam in the oceans 360 million years ago. It sliced up prey, such as other fish, using its massive teeth made of narrow blades of bone, each one as big as this book.

352 Some early fish started to 'walk' out of water. Types of fish called lobefins appeared 390 million years ago. Their side fins each had a 'stump' at the base made of muscle. If the water in their pool dried up, lobefins could use their fins like stubby legs to waddle over land to another pool. *Eusthenopteron* was a lobefin fish about one metre long. Over millions of years, some lobefins evolved into four-legged animals called tetrapods.

VERY FISHY!

You will need:
waxed card (like the kind used to make milk cartons) crayons scissors piece of soap

Place the piece of waxed card face down. Fold the card up at the edges. Draw a fish on the card. Cut a small notch in the rear of the card and wedge the piece of soap in it. Put the 'fish' in a bath of cold water and watch it swim away.

▼ *Eusthenopteron* could clamber about on dry land when moving from one stretch of water to another.

Animals invade the land

353 **The first land animals lived about 450 million years ago.** These early creatures, which came from the sea, were arthropods – creatures with hard outer body casings and jointed legs. They included prehistoric insects, spiders and millipedes. *Arthropleura* was a millipede – it was 2 metres in length!

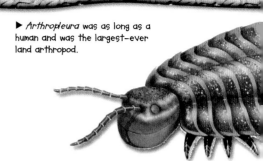

▶ *Arthropleura* was as long as a human and was the largest-ever land arthropod.

354 **Some amphibians were fierce hunters.** *Gerrothorax* was about one metre long and spent most of its time at the bottom of ponds or streams. Its eyes pointed upward, to see fish swimming past, just above. *Gerrothorax* would then jump up to grab the fish in its wide jaws.

355 **The first four-legged animal had eight toes on each front foot!** *Acanthostega* used its toes to grip water plants as it swam. It lived about 380 million years ago and was one metre long. Creatures like it soon began to walk on land, too. They were called tetrapods, which means 'four legs'. They were a big advance in evolution – the first land animals with backbones.

◀ *Acanthostega* probably spent most of its time in water. It had gills for breathing underwater as well as lungs for breathing air.

357 Soon four-legged animals called amphibians were racing across the land. Amphibians were the first backboned animals to move fast out of the water. *Aphaneramma* had long legs and could run quickly. However, prehistoric amphibians, like those of today such as frogs and newts, had to return to the water to lay their eggs.

356 Fins became legs for walking on land, and tails changed, too. As the fins of lobefin fish evolved into legs, their tails became longer and more muscular. *Ichthyostega* had a long tail with a fin along its upper side. This tail design was good for swimming in water, and also helpful when wriggling across a swamp.

358 Some amphibians grew as big as crocodiles! *Eogyrinus* was almost 5 metres long and had strong jaws and teeth, like a crocodile. However, it lived about 300 million years ago, long before any crocodiles appeared. Although *Eogyrinus* could walk on dry land, it spent most of its time in streams and swamps.

◄ *Ichthyostega* had short legs, so it could probably only move slowly on land.

Living with the dinosaurs

359 **Some reptiles were as big and fierce as dinosaurs – but they lived in the sea.** One of these was *Mosasaurus.* It grew up to 10 metres in length and may have weighed 10 tonnes, far bigger than today's great white shark.

360 **One sea reptile had teeth the size of saucers!** The huge, round, flat teeth of *Placodus* were more than 10 centimetres across. It used them to crush shellfish and sea urchins. *Placodus* was 2 metres long and lived at the same time as the first dinosaurs, about 230 million years ago.

I DON'T BELIEVE IT!
Fossils of *Mosasaurus* were found in the same place over 200 years apart! The first was found in a quarry in the Netherlands in 1780. The second was found in the same place in 1998.

▼ *Mosasaurus* was a huge sea reptile. It had razor-sharp teeth and could swim with speed to catch its prey.

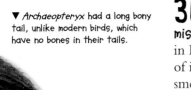

▼ *Archaeopteryx* had a long bony tail, unlike modern birds, which have no bones in their tails.

361 Fossils of the first bird were mistaken for a dinosaur. *Archaeopteryx* lived in Europe about 155 million years ago. Some of its fossils look very similar to the fossils of small dinosaurs. So *Archaeopteryx* was thought to be a dinosaur, until scientists saw the faint shape of its feathers and realized it was a bird.

362 Soon there were many kinds of birds flying above the dinosaurs. *Confuciusornis* was about 60 centimetres long and lived in what is now China, 120 million years ago. It had a backwards-pointing big toe on each foot, which suggests it climbed through the trees. It is also the earliest-known bird to have a true beak.

▲ Fossils of *Confuciusornis* have been found in China. It is named after the famous Chinese wise man, Confucius.

363 Mammals lived at the same time as dinosaurs. These animals have warm blood, and fur or hair, unlike a reptile's scaly skin. *Megazostrodon* was the earliest mammal known to scientists. It lived in southern Africa about 215 million years ago – only 15 million years or so after the dinosaurs began life on Earth. It was just 12 centimetres long, and probably hunted insects.

▼ *Megazostrodon* probably came out at night to hunt for its insect prey. It looked a little like a modern-day shrew.

The dinosaurs arrive!

364 **The earliest dinosaurs stalked the Earth almost 230 million years ago.** They lived in what is now Argentina, in South America. They included *Eoraptor* and *Herrerasaurus*. Slim, fast creatures, they could stand almost upright and run on their two rear legs. Few other animals of the time could run upright like this, on legs that were straight below their bodies. Most other animals had legs that stuck out sideways.

▶ *Herrerasaurus* was about 3 metres long from nose to tail.

The legs were underneath the body, not sticking out to the sides as in other reptiles, such as lizards and crocodiles

365 These early dinosaurs were probably **meat eaters.** They hunted small reptiles such as lizards, insects and worms. They had lightweight bodies and long, strong legs to chase after prey. Their claws were long and sharp for grabbing victims. Their large mouths were filled with pointed teeth to tear up their food.

TWO LEGS GOOD!

You will need:
stiff card   sticky tape
safe scissors   split pins

Cut out a model of *Herrerasaurus*; the head, body, arms and tail are one piece of card. Next, cut out each leg from another piece. Fix the legs on either side of the hip area of the body using a split pin. Adjust the angle of the head, body and tail to stand over the legs. This is how many dinosaurs stood and ran, well balanced over their rear legs and using little effort.

Herrerasaurus had a pointed head and a long, bendy neck, which helped it to look around and sniff for prey

The long tail balanced the head and body over the rear legs

Herrerasaurus could run rapidly on its two rear legs, or walk slowly on all fours

Getting bigger

366 **As the early dinosaurs spread over the land they began to change.** This gradual and natural change in living things has happened since life began on Earth. New kinds of plants and animals appear, do well for a time, and then die out as yet more new kinds appear. The slow and gradual change of living things over time is called evolution.

Plateosaurus

367 **Some kinds of dinosaurs became larger and began to eat plants rather than animals.** *Plateosaurus* was one of the first big plant-eating dinosaurs. It grew up to 8 metres long and lived 220 million years ago in what is now Europe. It could rear up on its back legs and use its long neck to reach food high off the ground.

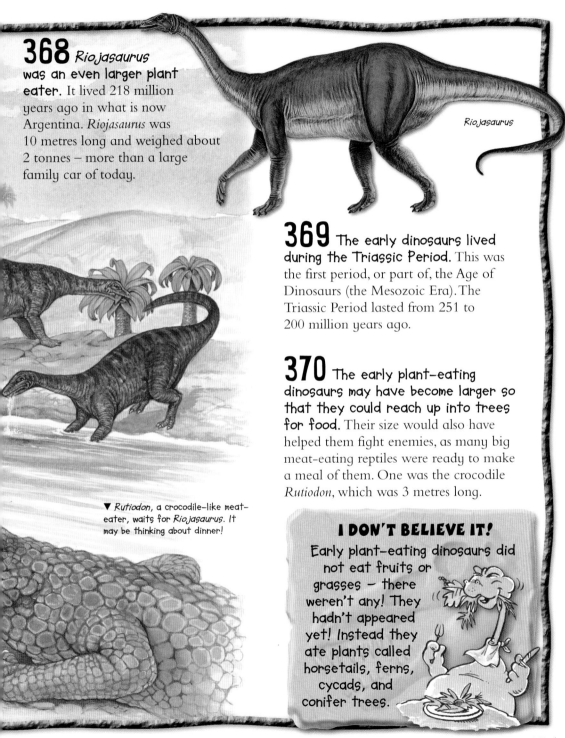

368 *Riojasaurus* was an even larger plant eater. It lived 218 million years ago in what is now Argentina. *Riojasaurus* was 10 metres long and weighed about 2 tonnes – more than a large family car of today.

Riojasaurus

369 The early dinosaurs lived during the Triassic Period. This was the first period, or part of, the Age of Dinosaurs (the Mesozoic Era). The Triassic Period lasted from 251 to 200 million years ago.

370 The early plant-eating dinosaurs may have become larger so that they could reach up into trees for food. Their size would also have helped them fight enemies, as many big meat-eating reptiles were ready to make a meal of them. One was the crocodile *Rutiodon*, which was 3 metres long.

▼ *Rutiodon*, a crocodile-like meat-eater, waits for *Riojasaurus*. It may be thinking about dinner!

I DON'T BELIEVE IT!

Early plant-eating dinosaurs did not eat fruits or grasses – there weren't any! They hadn't appeared yet! Instead they ate plants called horsetails, ferns, cycads, and conifer trees.

Super-size dinosaurs

371 The true giants of the Age of Dinosaurs were the sauropods. These vast dinosaurs all had a small head, long neck, barrel-shaped body, long tapering tail and four pillar-like legs. The biggest sauropods included *Brachiosaurus*, *Mamenchisaurus*, *Barosaurus*, *Diplodocus* and *Argentinosaurus*.

▲ *Argentinosaurus* was up to 40 metres long, and weighed up to 100 tonnes.

372 Sauropod dinosaurs probably lived in groups or herds. We know this from their footprints, which have been preserved as fossils. Each foot left a print as large as a chair seat. Hundreds of footprints together shows that many sauropods walked along in groups.

373 Sauropod dinosaurs may have swallowed pebbles — on purpose! Their peg-like teeth could only rake in plant food, not chew it. Pebbles and stones gulped into the stomach helped to grind and crush the food. These pebbles, smooth and polished by the grinding, have been found with the fossil bones of sauropods.

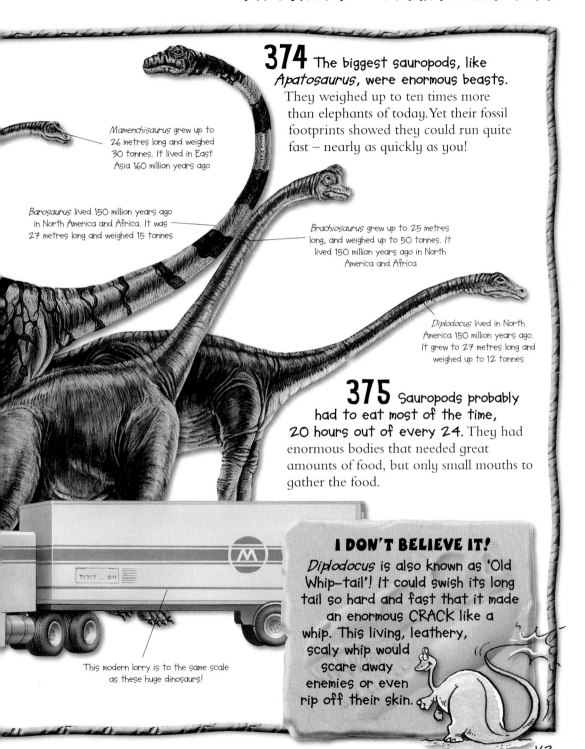

374 The biggest sauropods, like *Apatosaurus*, were enormous beasts. They weighed up to ten times more than elephants of today. Yet their fossil footprints showed they could run quite fast – nearly as quickly as you!

Mamenchisaurus grew up to 26 metres long and weighed 30 tonnes. It lived in East Asia 160 million years ago

Barosaurus lived 150 million years ago in North America and Africa. It was 27 metres long and weighed 15 tonnes

Brachiosaurus grew up to 25 metres long, and weighed up to 50 tonnes. It lived 150 million years ago in North America and Africa

Diplodocus lived in North America 150 million years ago. It grew to 27 metres long and weighed up to 12 tonnes

375 Sauropods probably had to eat most of the time, 20 hours out of every 24. They had enormous bodies that needed great amounts of food, but only small mouths to gather the food.

This modern lorry is to the same scale as these huge dinosaurs!

I DON'T BELIEVE IT!

Diplodocus is also known as 'Old Whip-tail'! It could swish its long tail so hard and fast that it made an enormous CRACK like a whip. This living, leathery, scaly whip would scare away enemies or even rip off their skin.

Claws for killing

376 Nearly all dinosaurs had claws on their fingers and toes. These claws were shaped for different jobs in different dinosaurs. They were made from a tough substance called keratin – the same as your fingernails and toenails.

Hypsilophodon

377 *Hypsilophodon* had strong, sturdy claws. This small plant eater, 2 metres long, probably used them to scrabble and dig in soil for seeds and roots.

378 *Deinonychus* had long, sharp, hooked claws on its hands. This meat eater, about 3 metres long, would grab a victim and tear at its skin and flesh.

379 *Deinonychus* had a huge hooked claw, as big as your hand, on the second toe of each foot. This claw could kick out and flick down like a pointed knife to slash pieces out of the prey.

Deinonychus

380 *Baryonyx* also had a large claw but this was on the thumb of each hand. It may have worked as a fish-hook to snatch fish from water. This is another clue that *Baryonyx* probably ate fish.

◀ These giant arms of the dinosaur *Deinocheirus* were found in Mongolia. Each one was bigger than a human, but nothing else of the skeleton has yet been found.

381 /guanodon had claws on its feet. But these were rounded and blunt and looked more like hooves.

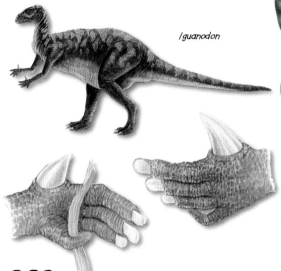

/guanodon

382 /guanodon also had stubby claws on its hands. However its thumb claw was longer and shaped like a spike, perhaps for stabbing enemies.

383 Giant sauropod dinosaurs had almost flat claws. Dinosaurs like *Apatosaurus* looked like they had toenails on their huge feet!

Deadly meat eaters

384 **The biggest meat-eating dinosaurs were the largest predators (hunters) ever to walk the Earth.** Different types came and went during the Age of Dinosaurs. *Allosaurus* was from the middle of this time span. One of the last dinosaurs was also one of the largest predators – *Tyrannosaurus rex*. An earlier hunting dinosaur from South America was even bigger – *Giganotosaurus*.

▼ A group of *Tyrannosaurus rex*.

Giganotosaurus

385 These great predators were well equipped for hunting large prey — including other dinosaurs. They all had massive mouths armed with long sharp teeth in powerful jaws. They had long, strong back legs for fast running, and enormous toe claws for kicking and holding down victims.

386 Meat–eating dinosaurs probably caught their food in various ways. They may have lurked behind rocks or trees and rushed out to surprise a victim. They may have raced as fast as possible after prey that ran away or plodded steadily for a great time to tire out their meal. They might even have scavenged — feasted on the bodies of creatures that were dead or dying.

Albertosaurus was from North America. It was 9 metres long and weighed one tonne

Allosaurus was 11 metres long and weighed 2 tonnes. It came from North America

Carnotaurus from South America was 7.5 metres long and weighed one tonne

The famous Tyrannosaurus rex was over 12 metres long and weighed 5 tonnes. It lived in North America

Spinosaurus came from Africa. It was 14 metres long and weighed 4 tonnes

The biggest carnivore was Giganotosaurus. It was over 13 metres long and weighed over 6 tonnes

Profile of *T rex*

387 Fossil experts can work out what an extinct animal such a *Tyrannosaurus rex* looked like when it was alive. They study the size, shape, length, thickness and other details of its fossil bones, teeth, claws and other parts.

388 The tail of *T rex* was almost half its total length. It had a wide, muscular base and was thick and strong almost to the tip, quite unlike the long, thin, whip-like tails of other dinosaurs such as *Diplodocus*.

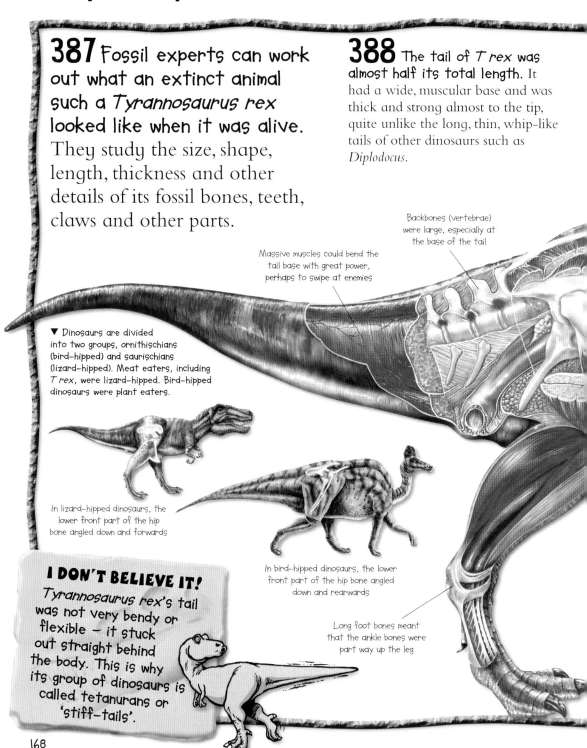

Backbones (vertebrae) were large, especially at the base of the tail

Massive muscles could bend the tail base with great power, perhaps to swipe at enemies

▼ Dinosaurs are divided into two groups, ornithischians (bird-hipped) and saurischians (lizard-hipped). Meat eaters, including *T rex*, were lizard-hipped. Bird-hipped dinosaurs were plant eaters.

In lizard-hipped dinosaurs, the lower front part of the hip bone angled down and forwards

In bird-hipped dinosaurs, the lower front part of the hip bone angled down and rearwards

Long foot bones meant that the ankle bones were part way up the leg

I DON'T BELIEVE IT!

Tyrannosaurus rex's tail was not very bendy or flexible – it stuck out straight behind the body. This is why its group of dinosaurs is called tetanurans or 'stiff-tails'.

389 The fossil bones of *T rex* show that it was a large, heavily built, powerful dinosaur. It had a huge skull, so its head and mouth were massive. There were holes in the skull for the eyes, ears and nasal openings or nostrils. There were also smaller holes in the bones for blood vessels and nerves.

▼ A cutaway *T rex* shows the thick, strong bones of its skeleton, which have been found preserved in many different fossil remains.

Head was long and low with eyebrow ridges and a large snout

Ribs curved around to protect the soft inner organs

Lungs took in air as the dinosaur breathed in and out

390 The main body of *T rex* was strong and sturdy, with a broad chest and a short but powerful neck. As in other reptiles, the upper body contained the heart, and the lungs for breathing. The lower body contained the stomach, guts and other soft parts.

Guts digested high–nutrient meaty meals, so were smaller in comparison to the guts of plant-eating dinosaurs

Front view shows the narrow body

Long, strong toe bones were tipped with big, sharp claws

391 One of the amazing features of *Tyrannosaurus rex* was its tiny arms (front legs), compared to the massive, pillar–like back legs. Almost no other dinosaur had front limbs that were so different in size from its back limbs.

169

Look! Listen! Sniff!

392 Like the reptiles of today, dinosaurs could see, hear and smell the world around them. We know this from fossils. The preserved fossil skulls have spaces for eyes, ears and nostrils.

393 Some dinosaurs, like *Troodon*, had very big eyes. There are large, bowl-shaped hollows in their fossil skulls. Today's animals with big eyes can see well in the dark, like mice, owls and night-time lizards. Perhaps *Troodon* prowled through the forest at night, peering in the gloom, looking for small creatures to eat.

Ear
Eye
Nostril

▶ *Troodon* were small, predatory dinosaurs that may have hunted in groups.

394 There are also spaces on the sides of the head where *Troodon* had its ears. Dinosaur ears were round and flat, like the ears of other reptiles. *Troodon* could hear the tiny noises of little animals moving about in the dark.

◀ *Troodon* was about 2 metres long and lived in North America 70 million years ago. You can see here the large eye sockets.

395 The nostrils of *Troodon* were two holes at the front of its snout. With its delicate sense of smell, *Troodon* could sniff out its prey of insects, worms, little reptiles such as lizards, and small shrew–like mammals.

▲ *Corythosaurus* had a bony plate on its head, instead of a tube like *Parasaurolophus*.

BIGGER EYES, BETTER SIGHT

You will need:

stiff card   elastic   safe scissors

Make a *Troodon* mask from card. Carefully cut out the shape as shown, with two small eye holes, each just one centimetre across. Attach elastic so you can wear the mask and find out how little you can see. Carefully make the eye holes as large as the eyes of the real *Troodon*. Now you can have a much clearer view of the world!

396 Dinosaurs used their eyes, ears and noses not only to find food, but also to detect enemies — and each other. *Parasaurolophus* had a long, hollow, tube–like crest on its head. Perhaps it blew air along this to make a noise like a trumpet, as an elephant does today with its trunk.

▶ *Parasaurolophus* was a 'duck–billed' dinosaur or hadrosaur. It was about 10 metres long and lived 80 million years ago in North America.

397 Dinosaurs like *Parasaurolophus* may have made noises to send messages to other members of their group or herd. Different messages could tell the others about finding food or warn them about enemies.

Dinosaur tanks

398 Some dinosaurs had body defences against predators. These might be large horns and spikes, or thick hard lumps of bonelike armour-plating. Most armoured dinosaurs were plant eaters. They had to defend themselves against big meat-eating dinosaurs such as *Tyrannosaurus rex*.

399 *Triceratops* had three horns, one on its nose and two much longer ones above its eyes. It also had a wide shield-like piece of bone over its neck and shoulders. The horns and neck frill made *Triceratops* look very fearsome. But most of the time it quietly ate plants. If it was attacked, *Triceratops* could charge at the enemy and jab with its horns, like a rhino does today.

▲ *Triceratops* was 9 metres long and weighed over 5 tonnes. It lived 65 million years ago in North America.

400 *Euoplocephalus* was a well-armoured dinosaur. It had bands of thick, leathery skin across its back. Big, hard, pointed lumps of bone were set into this skin like studs on a leather belt. *Euoplocephalus* also had a great lump of bone on its tail. It measured almost one metre across and looked like a massive hammer or club. *Euoplocephalus* could swing it at predators to injure them or break their legs.

DESIGN A DINOSAUR!

Make an imaginary dinosaur! It might have the body armour and tail club of *Euoplocephalus*, or the head horns and neck frill of *Triceratops*. You can draw your dinosaur, or make it out of pieces of card or from modelling clay. You can give it a made-up name, like *Euoplo-ceratops* or *Tri-cephalus*.

How well protected is your dinosaur? How does it compare to some well-armoured creatures of today, such as a tortoise, armadillo or porcupine?

Styracosaurus

Euoplocephalus

Protoceratops

In and over the sea

401 One prehistoric reptile had the bendiest neck ever! The sea reptile *Elasmosaurus* had a neck over 5 metres long – the same as three people lying head-to-toe. Its neck was so bendy that *Elasmosaurus* could twist it around in a circle as it looked for fish and other creatures to eat.

402 The first big flying animals were not birds, but pterosaurs. They lived at the same time as the dinosaurs, and died out at the same time too, about 65 million years ago. *Pteranodon* was one of the later pterosaurs and lived about 70 million years ago. It swooped over the sea to scoop up fish.

▼ *Pteranodon* scoops up prey while long-necked *Elasmosaurus* snaps its jaws in search of food.

Pteranodon

403 **The largest flying animal of all time was as big as a plane!** With wings measuring up to 14 metres from tip to tip, the pterosaur *Quetzalcoatlus* was twice as big as any flying bird. It may have lived like a vulture, soaring high in the sky, and then landing to peck at a dead body of a dinosaur.

404 **Some fossils of sea creatures are found thousands of kilometres from the sea.** Around 100 to 70 million years ago, much of what is now North America was flooded. The shallow waters teemed with all kinds of fish, reptiles and other creatures. Today their fossils are found on dry land.

Elasmosaurus

Rise of mammals

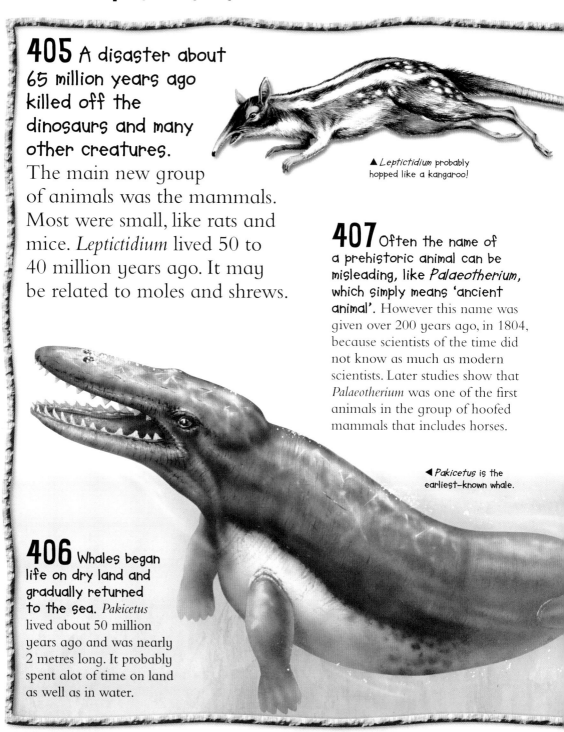

405 A disaster about 65 million years ago killed off the dinosaurs and many other creatures. The main new group of animals was the mammals. Most were small, like rats and mice. *Leptictidium* lived 50 to 40 million years ago. It may be related to moles and shrews.

▲ *Leptictidium* probably hopped like a kangaroo!

407 Often the name of a prehistoric animal can be misleading, like *Palaeotherium*, which simply means 'ancient animal'. However this name was given over 200 years ago, in 1804, because scientists of the time did not know as much as modern scientists. Later studies show that *Palaeotherium* was one of the first animals in the group of hoofed mammals that includes horses.

◄ *Pakicetus* is the earliest-known whale.

406 Whales began life on dry land and gradually returned to the sea. *Pakicetus* lived about 50 million years ago and was nearly 2 metres long. It probably spent alot of time on land as well as in water.

▼ A mother *Uintatherium* and her baby. This strange-looking creature was the largest land animal of its time. Its head was covered in horns and it had small tusks.

408 Around 40 million years ago, the largest animal walking the Earth was *Uintatherium*. This plant eater was over 3 metres long and nearly 2 metres tall at the shoulder – about the same size as a cow. Its fossils were found near the Uinta River in Colorado, USA. *Uintatherium* is thought to be a cousin of horses and elephants.

409 An animal's looks can be misleading. *Patriofelis* means 'father of the cats'. It lived 45 million years ago and was named because scientists thought it looked like an early cat. Later they realized it was really a member of an extinct group of hunting animals called creodonts.

QUIZ

1. What does the name *Patriofelis* mean?
2. How long was *Pakicetus*?
3. In what year were *Palaeotherium* fossils found?
4. How tall was *Uintatherium*?
5. When did dinosaurs die out and mammals start to take over?

Answers:
1. 'Father of the cats'
2. About 2 metres 3. 1804
4. Almost 2 metres tall at the shoulder
5. 65 million years ago

As the world cooled down

410 Before the world started to cool 30 million years ago, palm trees grew almost everywhere – but they became rare. These trees had thrived in warm, wet conditions. But as Earth cooled, other plants took over, such as magnolias, pines, oaks and birch. These changes meant that animals changed too.

411 *Pyrotherium* means 'fire beast', but not because this plant eater could walk through fire. Its fossils were found in layers of ash from an ancient volcano in Argentina, South America. The volcano probably erupted, and its fumes and ash suffocated and burned all the animals nearby. *Pyrotherium* was about as big as a cow and looked like a combination of a pig and a short-tusked elephant.

412 Many prehistoric animals have exciting names – *Brontotherium* means 'thunder beast'. Where the fossils of *Brontotherium* were found in North America, local people thought they were bones of the gods. They thought that these gods rode chariots across the sky and started thunderstorms, which led to the animal's name.

413 *Andrewsarchus* was a real big-head! At one metre long, it had the biggest head of any hunting mammal on land, and its strong jaws were filled with sharp, pointed teeth. Its whole body was bigger than a tiger of today. *Andrewsarchus* probably lived like a hyena, crunching up bones and gristle from dead animals. Yet it belonged to a mammal group that was mostly plant eaters. It lived 30 million years ago in what is now the deserts of Mongolia, Asia.

▲ *Andrewsarchus* was the biggest meat-eating land animal ever to have lived.

▲ The horns on *Arsinoitherium*'s head were hollow and may have been used to make mating calls.

QUIZ

1. What does *Brontotherium* mean?
2. What does *Pyrotherium* mean?
3. How long was the head of *Andrewsarchus*?
4. Where did *Arsinoitherium* live?

Answers:
1. 'Thunder beast' 2. 'Fire beast' 3. One metre 4. Northern Africa

414 Some animals had horns as tall as people! *Arsinoitherium*'s two massive horns looked like powerful weapons – but they were light, fragile and made of very thin bone. This plant eater lived in northern Africa about 35 million years ago. It was almost as big as an elephant and may have been an ancient cousin of the elephant group.

Amazing ancient elephants

415 The first elephant had tiny tusks and almost no trunk. *Moeritherium* lived in northern Africa about 36 million years ago. It stood just 60 centimetres tall and may have weighed around 20 kilograms – about the size of a large pet dog.

I DON'T BELIEVE IT!

The tusks of *Anancus* were over 4 metres long – almost as long as the animal itself.

▶ Woolly mammoths had coats of shaggy hair. This hair kept their warm inner fur dry and waterproof in the freezing conditions of the ice age.

416 Some elephants were very hairy. The woolly mammoth was covered in thick, long dense hair to keep out the cold of the ice age. It was larger than a modern elephant and was probably hunted by early people. The last woolly mammoths may have died out less than 10,000 years ago.

417 One elephant had tusks like shovels. *Platybelodon* lived about nine million years ago in Europe, Asia and Africa. Its lower tusks were shaped like broad, flat shovels. Perhaps it used them to scoop up water plants to eat.

418 Some elephants had four tusks. *Tetralophodon* lived about eight million years ago and stood 3 metres tall. Its fossils have been found in Europe, Asia, Africa and America, so it was a very widespread and successful animal.

419 The biggest elephant was the Columbian mammoth. It stood 4 metres tall and may have weighed over 10 tonnes – twice as much as most elephants today. It lived on the grasslands of southern North America.

▼ The Columbian mammoth had tusks that twisted into curved, spiral shapes.

420 Elephants were more varied and common long ago, than they are today. *Anancus* roamed Europe and Asia two million years ago. Like modern elephants, it used its trunk to pull leaves from branches and its tusks to dig up roots. However most kinds of prehistoric elephants died out. Only two kinds survive today, in Africa and Asia.

Our prehistoric relations

421 Monkeys, apes and humans first appeared over 50 million years ago – the first kinds looked like squirrels. This group is called the primates. *Plesiadapis* was one of the first primates. It lived 55 million years ago in Europe and North America.

◀ *Plesiadapis* had claws on its fingers and toes, unlike monkeys and apes, which had nails.

422 Early apes walked on all fours. About 20 million years ago, *Dryopithecus* lived in Europe and Asia. It used its arms and legs to climb trees. When it came down to the ground, it walked on all fours. It was 60 centimetres long and ate fruit and leaves.

I DON'T BELIEVE IT

The first fossils of the giant ape *Gigantopithecus* to be studied by scientists came from a second-hand shop in Hong Kong, over 70 years ago.

▶ The early ape *Dryopithecus* walked flat on its feet, unlike other apes, which walked on their knuckles.

▼ The need to see longer distances on grasslands may have caused the first apes to walk on two legs.

423 Some kinds of apes may have walked on their two back legs, like us. About 4.5 million years ago *Ardipithecus* lived in Africa. Only a few of its fossils have been found. However, experts think it may have walked upright on its back legs. It could have made the first steps in the change, or evolution, from apes to humans.

424 One prehistoric ape was a real giant – over 3 metres tall! Its name, *Gigantopithecus*, means 'giant ape'. It was much larger than today's biggest ape, the gorilla, which grows to 2 metres tall. *Gigantopithecus* probably ate roots and seeds, and may have hunted small animals such as birds, rats and lizards.

▶ The enormous *Gigantopithecus* could probably stand on its hind legs to reach food.

425 Scientists work out which animals are our closest cousins partly from fossils – and also from chemicals. The chemical called DNA contains genes, which are instructions for how living things grow and work. The living animals with DNA most similar to ours are the great apes, chimpanzees and gorillas, both from Africa. So our ancient cousins were probably apes like them. The orang-utan, from Southeast Asia, is less similar.

What are fossils?

426 Fossils are the preserved remains of once-living things, such as bones, teeth and claws. Usually the remains were buried in sediments – layers of tiny particles such as sand, silt or mud. Very slowly, the layers and the remains inside them turned into solid rock.

427 In general it takes at least 10,000 years, but usually millions, for fossils to form. So the remains of living things that are a few hundred or thousand years old, such as the bandage-wrapped mummies of pharaohs in ancient Egypt, are not true fossils.

▲ A seed cone fossil of the extinct plant *Williamsonia*.

428 Many kinds of once-living things have formed fossils. They include all kinds of animals from enormous whales and dinosaurs to tiny flies and beetles. There are fossils of plants, too, from small mosses and flowers to immense trees. Even microscopic bacteria have been preserved.

◄ Teeth are very hard and so make excellent fossils – especially those from *Tyrannosaurus rex*!

▶ It is unusual for thin, delicate bones, such as those of the bat *Icaronycteris*, to fossilize.

429 In most cases, fossils formed from the hard parts of living things that did not rot away soon after death. As well as bones, teeth and claws these include shells, scales and the bark, roots, cones and seeds of plants.

430 Much more rarely, soft parts have been preserved as fossils, such as flower petals and worm bodies. Where this has happened, it gives a fascinating glimpse into how these ancient life-forms looked and lived.

▼ The tube worms' soft bodies soon decayed but their hard, coiled tubes were preserved in the seabed mud.

QUIZ

Which of these are true fossils?

A. A bird called the dodo, which died out over 300 years ago

B. Two thousand-year-old pots and vases from ancient Rome

C. The first shellfish that appeared in the sea over 500 million years ago

Answer:
C is a true fossil.
The others are much too recent

How fossils form

▼ All living things die. Those living in water, such as this ichthyosaur, are more likely to leave fossils than those on land.

431 **When a living thing dies, its flesh and other soft parts start to rot.** Sometimes they are eaten by scavenging creatures such as worms and insects. The harder parts, such as teeth and bones, rot more slowly and last longer.

432 Fossil formation usually begins like this, and very often in water. Sediments tend to settle on dead animals and plants in ponds, lakes, rivers and seas. This is the main reason why most fossils are of plants and animals that lived in water or somehow got washed into water.

① After death, the ichthyosaur sinks to the seabed. Worms, crabs and other scavengers eat its soft body parts.

START SOME FOSSILS

You will need:

small stones   glass mixing jug
sand   water

Imagine the stones are 'bones' of an ancient creature. They get washed into a river – put them in the jug and half-fill with water. Then the 'bones' are covered by sediment – sprinkle in the sand.

433 Over time, more sediment layers settle on top of the remains. As they are covered deeper, further rotting or scavenging is less likely.

② Sediments cover the hard body parts, such as bones and teeth, which gradually turn into solid rock.

434 Water trickles into the sediments and once-living remains. The water contains dissolved substances such as minerals and salts. Gradually, these replace the once-living parts and turn them and the sediments into solid rock. This is called permineralization.

435 Most living things rot away soon after death, so the chances of anything becoming a fossil are slim. Also, sedimentary rock layers change over time, becoming heated and bent, which can destroy fossils in them. The chances of anyone finding a fossil are even tinier. This is why the record of fossils in rocks represents only a tiny proportion of prehistoric life.

③ Millions of years later the upper rock layers wear away and the fossil remains are exposed.

Fossils and time

436 Fossils are studied by many kinds of scientist. Palaeontologists are general experts on fossils and prehistoric life. Palaeozoologists specialize in prehistoric creatures, and palaeobotanists in prehistoric plants. Geologists study rocks, soil and other substances that make up the Earth. All of these sciences allow us to work out the immense prehistory of the Earth.

437 Earth's existence is divided into enormous lengths of time called eons, which are split into eras, then periods, epochs and finally, stages. Each of these time divisions is marked by changes in the rocks formed at the time – and if the rocks are sedimentary, by the fossils they contain. The whole time span, from the formation of the Earth 4600 million years ago to today, is known as the geological time scale.

▼ Starting with the Cambrian Period (far right), this timeline shows 11 major time periods in Earth's history. It gives examples of some of the fossil animals and plants that have been found for each period. 'MYA' stands for 'millions of years ago'.

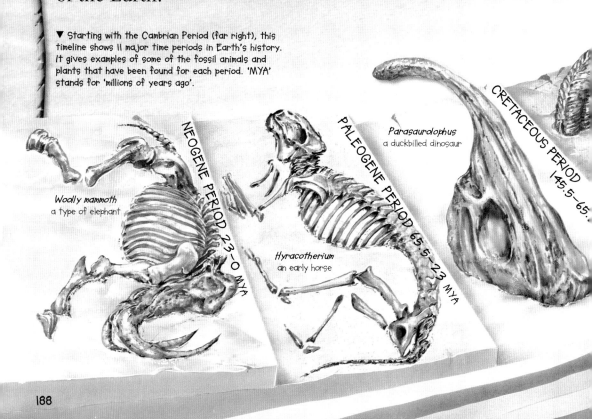

NEOGENE PERIOD 23–0 MYA

Woolly mammoth
a type of elephant

PALEOGENE PERIOD 65.5–23 MYA

Hyracotherium
an early horse

Parasaurolophus
a duckbilled dinosaur

CRETACEOUS PERIOD 145.5–65.

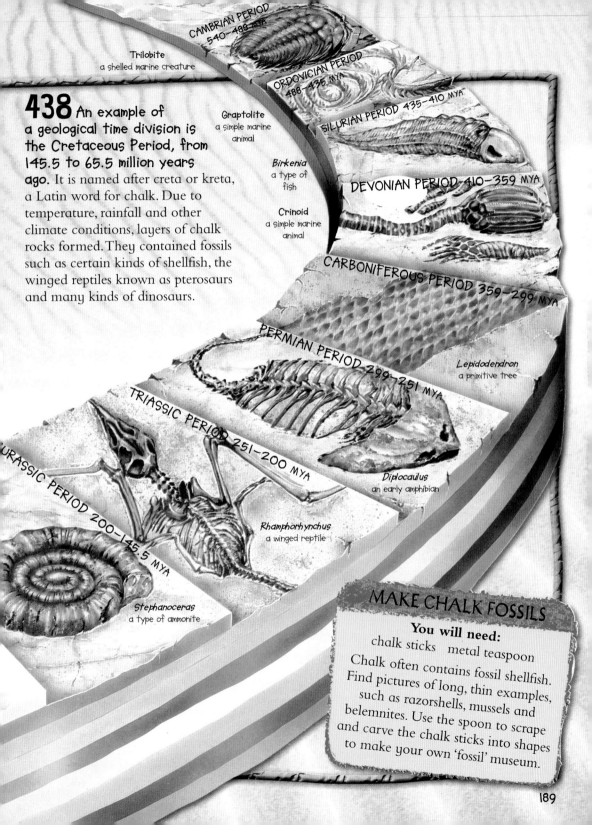

CAMBRIAN PERIOD
540–488 MYA

Trilobite
a shelled marine creature

ORDOVICIAN PERIOD
488–435 MYA

Graptolite
a simple marine
animal

SILURIAN PERIOD 435–410 MYA

Birkenia
a type of
fish

DEVONIAN PERIOD 410–359 MYA

Crinoid
a simple marine
animal

CARBONIFEROUS PERIOD 359–299 MYA

PERMIAN PERIOD 299–251 MYA

Lepidodendron
a primitive tree

TRIASSIC PERIOD 251–200 MYA

JURASSIC PERIOD 200–145.5 MYA

Diplocaulus
an early amphibian

Rhamphorhynchus
a winged reptile

Stephanoceras
a type of ammonite

438 An example of a geological time division is the Cretaceous Period, from 145.5 to 65.5 million years ago. It is named after creta or kreta, a Latin word for chalk. Due to temperature, rainfall and other climate conditions, layers of chalk rocks formed. They contained fossils such as certain kinds of shellfish, the winged reptiles known as pterosaurs and many kinds of dinosaurs.

MAKE CHALK FOSSILS

You will need:
chalk sticks   metal teaspoon
Chalk often contains fossil shellfish.
Find pictures of long, thin examples,
such as razorshells, mussels and
belemnites. Use the spoon to scrape
and carve the chalk sticks into shapes
to make your own 'fossil' museum.

439 Our planet is full of animals. They live almost everywhere, from the tops of mountains to the darkest depths of oceans. The greatest variety of animals live in places such as rainforests or coral reefs, where there is plenty of food and shelter.

▼ African animals gather round a waterhole in the dry season. The great grasslands of Africa are one of the last places where huge herds of grazing animals still survive.

440 Animals come in all shapes and sizes. Some, such as elephants, are giants, while others, such as fleas, are almost too small to see. There are at least five million different kinds of animals alive today. Scientists discover new kinds every day.

441 For at least 650 million years, animals have been living on our planet. Sponges are among the oldest known animals. They live in oceans today, but remains of sponges that lived 650 million years ago have been found preserved in Australia.

What is an animal?

442 Animals are living things that need to eat food, such as plants or other animals. This gives them the energy they need to survive. Animals use their senses to detect food and react to their surroundings.

▶ Animals can be divided into groups according to their features. Each group has certain characteristics in common.

443 An animal's body is usually made of many cells, which are grouped into tissues. Tissues may be joined together to form organs, such as the brain, heart or lungs.

Animal families

Invertebrates are usually small creatures, such as crabs and insects. Some have a hard shell, others are soft.

Fish live in the waters of oceans, rivers and lakes. They breathe in oxygen from the water through flaps called gills.

Amphibians, such as frogs, live partly in water and partly on land. Most lay eggs in water.

Reptiles, such as snakes and lizards, usually live on land in warm places. Most baby reptiles hatch out of eggs.

Birds have wings instead of arms, and most can fly. All birds lay eggs that have a hard shell.

Mammals, such as bears, dolphins and humans, are covered in fur or hair. They breathe air, even if they live in water.

444 Well over 90 percent of all animals are invertebrates. These animals do not have an internal backbone to support their bodies. They rely on the support of their body fluids or a hard outer casing, called an exoskeleton.

◀ The organs inside a chimpanzee are very similar to those inside a human being.

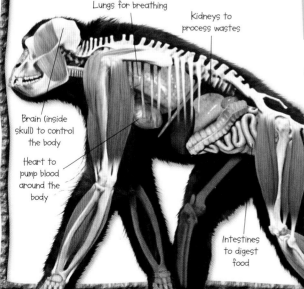

Lungs for breathing

Kidneys to process wastes

Brain (inside skull) to control the body

Heart to pump blood around the body

Intestines to digest food

445 Animals with a backbone are called vertebrates. Their backbone forms part of an internal skeleton, which is usually made of bone. However, sharks and rays have a skeleton made of rubbery cartilage. A skeleton supports the body, helps it to move and protects the internal organs.

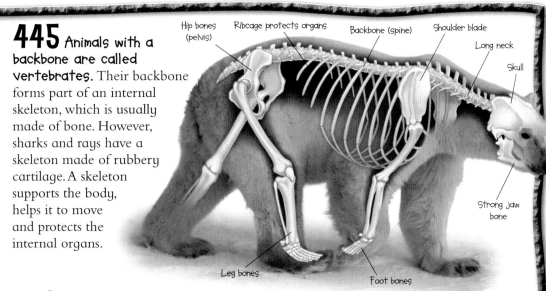

Hip bones (pelvis)

Ribcage protects organs

Backbone (spine)

Shoulder blade

Long neck

Skull

Strong jaw bone

Leg bones

Foot bones

446 Vertebrates have different coverings on the outsides of their bodies. Fish and reptiles have scales made from hard skin or bone. Frogs usually have smooth skin. Birds are the only animals with feathers, and mammals are the only animals with fur or hair.

▲ A polar bear has a short, strong backbone and powerful leg and hip bones. Its skull is long and slim to help it swim.

▶ Foals will feed from their mothers for several months, or up to one year in the wild.

447 Humans are mammals. Mammals are the most intelligent of all animals. Female mammals feed their young on milk, which they produce themselves. There are about 5500 different kinds of mammals and up to one-quarter of them are bats!

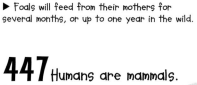

Super senses

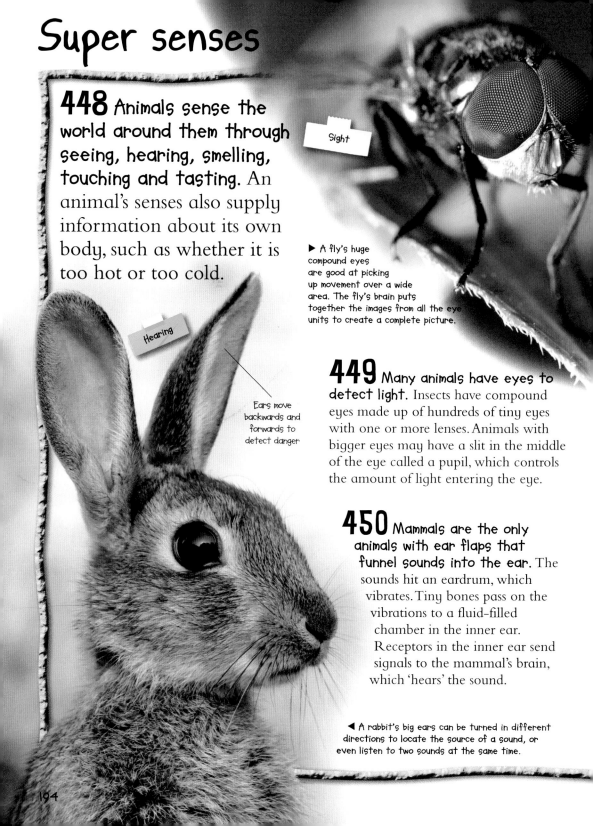

448 Animals sense the world around them through seeing, hearing, smelling, touching and tasting. An animal's senses also supply information about its own body, such as whether it is too hot or too cold.

Sight

▶ A fly's huge compound eyes are good at picking up movement over a wide area. The fly's brain puts together the images from all the eye units to create a complete picture.

Hearing

Ears move backwards and forwards to detect danger

449 Many animals have eyes to detect light. Insects have compound eyes made up of hundreds of tiny eyes with one or more lenses. Animals with bigger eyes may have a slit in the middle of the eye called a pupil, which controls the amount of light entering the eye.

450 Mammals are the only animals with ear flaps that funnel sounds into the ear. The sounds hit an eardrum, which vibrates. Tiny bones pass on the vibrations to a fluid-filled chamber in the inner ear. Receptors in the inner ear send signals to the mammal's brain, which 'hears' the sound.

◀ A rabbit's big ears can be turned in different directions to locate the source of a sound, or even listen to two sounds at the same time.

451 **An animal's senses of taste and smell often work together.** A snake flicks its forked tongue in and out of its mouth to smell and taste the air. Most vertebrates taste with their tongues, but adult insects often taste with their feet!

Smell and taste

▶ Snakes have special smell detectors on the roofs of their mouths, so they use their tongues to pick up smells in the air.

452 Many animals, such as insects and crabs, have two long, thin feelers called **antennae on their heads.** The antennae help to detect and identify smells, air currents and textures. Male moths often have feathery antennae to pick up the scent given off by female moths.

453 **A sense of touch provides information about an animal's immediate surroundings and the position of its body.** Most animals have touch receptors all over their bodies. Some receptors are linked to structures such as whiskers.

Whiskers

▼ The star-nosed mole is named after the sensitive tentacles around its nose, which help it to find prey in dark, underground tunnels. Its nose is six times more sensitive to touch than the human hand.

Touch

195

Predators and prey

454 An animal that hunts and eats other animals is called a predator. Its victim is known as its prey. Predators have to find, catch and kill their prey. They need strength, keen senses, quick reactions and lethal weapons.

455 After dark, many predators rely on their excellent sense of hearing to find prey. Some bats hunt insects at night by producing high-pitched squeaks. They listen for the echoes that bounce back from their prey.

▼ Bats have large ears to pick up the sound echoes bouncing back from their prey.

Sounds made by bat

Echoes from prey

456 Some predators hide and wait for their prey to come to them. They may build traps, such as the webs of spiders, or lure their prey within close reach. The alligator snapping turtle has a false 'worm' on its tongue to make fish swim right into its open jaws.

'Worm'

◀ The alligator snapping turtle wriggles the 'worm' on its tongue to make it look alive. It stabs larger prey with the hooked tips of its strong jaws.

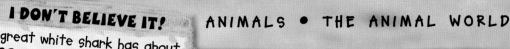

◀ ▶ A cheetah can only run at top speed for a few hundred metres before it gets too hot and exhausted, and has to stop. If this warthog keeps running, it might get away.

457 Active predators need a set of weapons for attacking and killing their prey without being injured themselves. These weapons range from pointed teeth and powerful jaws, to curved claws, sharp bills and poisonous stings or fangs.

◀ Ospreys use their strong, needle-sharp claws, called talons, to snatch fish from the water. Spines under their toes help them to hold their slippery prey.

458 Many spiders are agile, fast-moving hunters that stalk their prey. Jumping spiders prowl around, using their eight eyes to spot a meal. They pounce on their prey and kill it with a bite from their poisonous fangs. Some predators save energy by sneaking up on their prey, then attacking suddenly at the last minute. Many are well camouflaged so they can creep close to their prey.

▶ Chameleons creep very slowly along branches, but they shoot out their long, sticky tongues at lightning speed to catch insects.

Survival skills

459 The world is a dangerous place for animals, and they have different ways of staying alive. Many move fast to escape an attack. Others are protected by armour-plating, thick shells, horns, tusks or spines.

460 Animals may have colours, patterns or shapes that help them to blend in with their surroundings. Some disguise themselves by looking like twigs, thorns or leaves. This is called camouflage.

▼ A poison arrow frog makes poison in its skin. Just a few drops of this poison are strong enough to kill an animal as big as a horse.

▲ A rattlesnake shakes the 'rattle' on its tail to warn predators to keep away.

461 Brightly coloured animals are often poisonous. Their colours are a warning message, which means "I am dangerous, don't eat me!" Predators learn to leave these animals alone. Harmless animals may copy these warning colours to protect themselves. This is known as mimicry.

Bony plates
covered by
horny keratin

462 Slow-moving animals often rely on body armour for protection. Tortoises and turtles can pull their soft body parts inside their shells. Armadillos, pangolins and pill millipedes roll up into a ball to protect their soft undersides.

① Armadillo curls into a ball if it senses danger

▲ A three-banded armadillo has body armour on its back, but not underneath. When it rolls up into a tight ball, its body armour protects its soft underparts.

Underside of body is soft and hairy

② Armadillo starts to uncurl when it is safe again

Flexible skin between bands of armour

463 Predators prefer to eat living prey, so some animals survive an attack by pretending to be dead. Snakes such as the grass snake are good at playing dead. They roll onto their backs, open their mouths and keep still. The snake starts to move again when the predator goes away.

③ Armadillo is protected by body armour even when walking

464 Some animals can break off parts of their bodies to escape from predators. Lizards may break off a tail tip, which wriggles about on the ground. This distracts an attacker, giving the lizard time to escape.

▲ The bright blue tail of this skink, a type of lizard, breaks at special fracture points between the bones inside the tail.

Living in groups

465 Many animals, including some insects, fish, birds and mammals, live in groups with others of their kind. They are called social animals and may have female or male leaders.

466 Other animals, such as bears, tigers and orang-utans, live on their own. They do not have to share their food and are able to have young if they find a mate. In a group of social animals, such as wolves, only one pair of animals may have babies.

467 Some animals live in groups just for the breeding season. Penguins and seals form large breeding colonies with hundreds, or even thousands, of members. They warn each other of nearby predators and parents may leave their young in 'nurseries' when they go to find food.

▼ Cape fur seals gather on shorelines in colonies of up to 270,000 individuals to breed and look after their pups.

▲ Flamingos live in colonies that may contain thousands of birds. This helps them to avoid predators and find food.

▲ Male lions (far right) are bigger than females. Their thick manes of hair make them look even bigger and more frightening to their enemies.

468 Lions are one of the few social cats. They live in groups called prides, which consist of several related lionesses, their cubs, and one or more adult males. The males protect the pride from predators and rival lions, while the females do most of the hunting.

469 The young of most insects have to fend for themselves. However, ants and termites, some types of bees and a few wasps live in giant family groups. One or more females lay eggs, while other members of the group care for the young and defend the nest.

▶ Honeybees form a tightly-packed ball of bees, called a swarm, when they leave their nest to start a new colony.

Mammals

Placental mammals

470 There are nearly 5500 different types of mammal. Most mammals have babies that grow inside the mother's body. While a baby mammal grows, a special organ called a placenta supplies it with food and oxygen from the mother's body. These mammals are called placental mammals.

Placenta

Birth canal

▲ A baby elephant in the womb receives nourishment through the placenta.

471 Not all mammals' young develop inside the mother's body. Two smaller groups of mammals do things differently. Monotremes, such as platypuses and echidnas (spiny anteaters), lay eggs. The platypus lays her eggs in a burrow, but the echidna keeps her single egg in a special pouch in her belly until it is ready to hatch.

▶ The echidna keeps her egg in a pouch until it hatches after about ten days.

Monotremes

472 Mammal mothers feed their babies on milk from their own bodies. The baby sucks this milk from teats on special mammary glands, also called udders or breasts, on the mother's body. The milk contains all the food the young animal needs to help it grow.

473 Marsupials give birth to tiny young that finish developing in a pouch. A baby kangaroo is only 2 centimetres long when it is born. Tiny, blind and hairless, it makes its own way to the safety of its mother's pouch. Once there, it latches onto a teat in the pouch and begins to feed.

A joey starts life as a tiny undeveloped baby

Marsupials

▲ A baby kangaroo is called a joey. It stays in the pouch for about six months while it grows.

▼ This reindeer uses its eyes, its ears and especially its nose to sense the world.

474 Most mammals have good senses of sight, smell and hearing. Their senses help them watch out for enemies, find food and keep in touch with each other. For many mammals, smell is their most important sense. Plant-eaters such as rabbits and deer sniff the air to pick up scents of danger, especially those of predators.

I DON'T BELIEVE IT!
Lemmings are very fast breeders. Females can become pregnant at only 14 days old, and they can produce litters of as many as 12 young every month.

Midnight marsupials

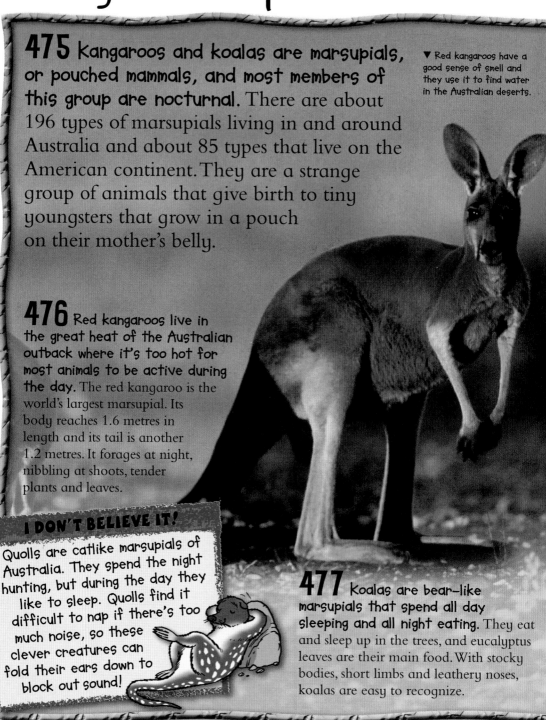

475 Kangaroos and koalas are marsupials, or pouched mammals, and most members of this group are nocturnal. There are about 196 types of marsupials living in and around Australia and about 85 types that live on the American continent. They are a strange group of animals that give birth to tiny youngsters that grow in a pouch on their mother's belly.

▼ Red kangaroos have a good sense of smell and they use it to find water in the Australian deserts.

476 Red kangaroos live in the great heat of the Australian outback where it's too hot for most animals to be active during the day. The red kangaroo is the world's largest marsupial. Its body reaches 1.6 metres in length and its tail is another 1.2 metres. It forages at night, nibbling at shoots, tender plants and leaves.

I DON'T BELIEVE IT!

Quolls are catlike marsupials of Australia. They spend the night hunting, but during the day they like to sleep. Quolls find it difficult to nap if there's too much noise, so these clever creatures can fold their ears down to block out sound!

477 Koalas are bear-like marsupials that spend all day sleeping and all night eating. They eat and sleep up in the trees, and eucalyptus leaves are their main food. With stocky bodies, short limbs and leathery noses, koalas are easy to recognize.

478 Virginia opossums forage at night and survive on all sorts of food, including grubs, fruit, eggs and scraps they scavenge from bins. They live in North and Central America and shelter in piles of vegetation or under buildings. Opossums have an unusual skill – if they are scared they drop down and act dead, with their eyes and mouths open. They do this for up to six hours at a time – long enough for a predator to get bored and wander off!

▲ Tasmanian devils gorge on their meal, and other devils may soon come to join in, drawn by the smell of fresh meat.

▼ A female Virginia opossum has up to 18 young in her litter, but she only has teats to feed 13 of them. She protects her young until they are old enough to fend for themselves.

479 In Australia's southern island of Tasmania, a terrible screeching and barking may be heard in the night – a Tasmanian devil. These marsupials are known for their noisy, aggressive behaviour and if they are alarmed, devils screech and bark. They can smell dead animals from far away and have such powerful jaws they can grind and chew bones and gristle.

Beautiful bats

480 A flutter of wings and the glimpse of a swooping body in the night sky are often the only clues you'll get that a bat is nearby. Bats are the nocturnal masters of the sky. They are small, furry mammals that are so well adapted to life on the wing that they can pass by almost unnoticed by humans and animals alike.

▲ During the day, bats hang upside down and rest — this is called roosting.

481 Except for the polar regions, bats can be found all over the world. They roost in caves, trees, under logs and in buildings. There are nearly 1000 different types, or species, of bat — the smallest have wingspans of 15 centimetres, and the biggest have wingspans of 1.5 metres or more!

482 Bats are the only mammals that have wings. Their wings have developed from forelimbs and have a thin membrane of skin that stretches over long, bony digits, or fingers. Bats can change direction easily in flight, which helps them chase and catch insects.

I DON'T BELIEVE IT!

Bats can live for a surprisingly long time — often for 10 to 25 years. Some wild bats have been known to live to the ripe old age of 30! This is partly because bats are able to avoid being eaten as few animals can catch them when they dash and dart between trees.

483 Although bats have good eyesight, they depend more on their senses of smell and hearing to find their prey at night. Most types of bat have a special sense called echolocation. They produce very high-pitched sounds – too high for most people to hear – that bounce off objects in front of them. When the sound comes back to a bat's ears, like an echo, they can tell by the way it has changed, how far away the object is and its size.

484 There are two main groups of bat – plant-eating bats and hunting bats. Both groups are mainly nocturnal. However, it is the hunters that use echolocation to find their prey. Most plant eaters don't echolocate and tend to be bigger than hunting bats. Some plant-eating bats, such as the Rodrigues fruit bat, are active in the day. The word 'diurnal' (die-ur-nal) is used to describe creatures that are active during the day.

◀ The word 'sonic' means making sounds, and the high-pitched noises of bats can be described as 'ultrasonic' – too high for us to hear.

485 Oilbirds are unique – they are the world's only fruit-eating nocturnal birds, and they echolocate like bats. Oilbirds live in South America and they spend their days in total darkness, sleeping in pitch-black caves. They wake after sunset and travel up to 75 kilometres in search of food.

Echoes bouncing back off the moth

Sound waves from the bat

◀ Bats make high-pitched sounds, called clicks, using their mouths or noses. The sound hits an insect and bounces back to the bat's ears. The reflected sound gives the bat information about the location and size of the insect.

Insect eaters

486 Since many insects, grubs and worms are active night, so are the mammals that hunt them. Aardvarks are unusual ant-eating animals of Africa that snuffle and snort in the darkness. Their name means 'earth-pig' in Afrikaans, one of many languages spoken in South Africa, and they do look quite like long-nosed pigs with their big, fleshy snouts.

◀ Hedgehogs sleep during the day. At night, they come out to search for insects and worms to eat.

488 If they are scared, hedgehogs roll themselves into a tight ball with only their sharp spines showing. They may be able to defend themselves against foxes, but hedgehogs are no match for a car – thousands of these European mammals are killed on roads every year.

▶ Aardvarks live alone and come out at sunset to forage for food. These long-snouted animals can eat up to 50,000 insects in one night!

487 At night, aardvarks search for termites and ants using their good sense of smell as their eyesight is poor. They rip open nests and lick up the insects with their long tongues. Aardvarks also have large front claws, which they use for digging their burrows where they sleep during the day. They can close their ears and nostrils to stop dirt from getting in them as they dig.

489 Few people ever see pangolins as they are shy and secretive nocturnal creatures. Pangolins are armoured animals that live in Africa and Asia. Their bodies are covered in thick, overlapping scales, which are formed from layers of hardened skin. Pangolins don't have teeth, but lick up ants and termites with their long, sticky tongues.

I DON'T BELIEVE IT!

Armadillos are nocturnal, armour-plated relatives of anteaters. Their eyesight is so poor, they have been known to walk straight into the legs of people standing in their way! Armadillos eat almost anything they can find and have been known to dig into graves and munch on dead bodies!

▲ Pangolins have short legs and bodies measuring up to one metre in length. They can climb trees or dig burrows underground using their long, sharp claws.

490 Shrews are active by night as well as day, since they must eat every few hours to survive. They are mouse-like, furry creatures with long snouts and are some of the smallest mammals in the world. They rely mostly on their sense of smell to find food, but some of them use echolocation – a way of locating objects using sound that is used by bats and oilbirds.

◄ A tiny shrew prepares to devour an earthworm, which looks like a giant in comparison.

Chisellers and chewers

491 Some of the world's commonest mammals are nocturnal rodents such as mice, rats, voles and lemmings. This group of animals can exist in almost any habitat all over the world, except the Antarctic. They have big eyes to see in the dark, furry bodies, and teeth that are perfect for gnawing and chewing. Most also have good hearing, and long whiskers to feel their way in the dark.

492 Rats are active in the day, but more so at night. They are experts in survival – able to live almost anywhere. One of the reasons for their success is that they can eat nearly anything. Rats hunt for food but they are just as likely to scavenge rubbish from bins at night or find morsels in the sewers. These unpopular animals have been known to start eating the flesh of living things and spread deadly diseases.

▼ At night, rats roam around towns scavenging any food and scraps they can find.

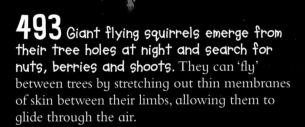

493 Giant flying squirrels emerge from their tree holes at night and search for nuts, berries and shoots. They can 'fly' between trees by stretching out thin membranes of skin between their limbs, allowing them to glide through the air.

494 American beavers are large rodents, often measuring more than one metre in length from nose to tail-tip. They spend the day resting in a lodge, which is a nest made from mud and sticks with underwater entrances. Beavers leave their nests as the sun begins to set and they remain busy through much of the night, feeding on plants. They find their way around using their long whiskers to guide them.

▼ Beavers chisel at trees and branches, cutting them up for use in the dams they build on rivers and streams. These dams create wetlands where many types of animal and plant thrive.

QUIZ

Mammals have hair or fur, and feed their young with milk. Which one of these animals is not a mammal?

Wolf Bat Squirrel
Alligator Dolphin

Answer:
Alligators are reptiles, not mammals

495 Edible dormice are small, nocturnal rodents that live in woods, or make their nests near or under buildings. During the late summer and autumn they fatten themselves up with seeds, fruit and nuts to prepare for hibernation – a long winter sleep. The ancient Romans kept edible dormice and overfed them until they were so fat they could hardly move. They were cooked until crisp and crunchy and served at dinners and parties!

What is a primate?

496 Primates such as monkeys and apes are covered in fur or hair and the young feed on their mothers' milk. They have big brains and can work out solutions to difficult problems. Primates have been known to learn new skills and teach them to their young.

497 Primates are mammals. This means that they have back bones and warm-blooded bodies. They are divided into three groups – prosimians such as bushbabies, monkeys such as baboons, and apes such as gorillas.

▶ A gorilla's bones are strong but lightweight. They support the muscles, hold the body upright and allow movement.

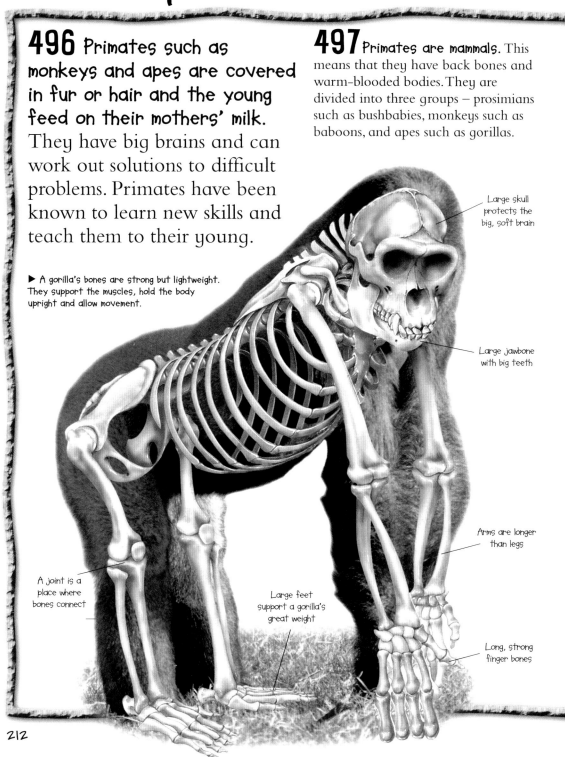

Large skull protects the big, soft brain

Large jawbone with big teeth

Arms are longer than legs

Long, strong finger bones

A joint is a place where bones connect

Large feet support a gorilla's great weight

498 Unlike many other animals, primates have large eyes at the front of their head. This allows them to focus clearly on objects in front of them. Since most primates live in trees and leap between branches, this is a very useful feature. Unlike most other creatures, primates can see in colour.

▼ Primates' hands and feet can grab, hold, pinch and probe. Most primates can grip objects and tools precisely in their hands.

Tarsier hand

Tarsier foot

Spider monkey hand

Spider monkey foot

Chimpanzee hand   Chimpanzee foot

500 Primates have hands that are very similar to ours. Instead of paws and claws, they have fingers and flat fingernails. They can bring their forefingers and thumbs together in a delicate pinching movement.

499 Primates prefer to live in groups. They often live with their families, or large groups of related families. Primates communicate with one another in many ways – using sound, scent, touch and movement. Young primates usually stay with their families for years while they learn how to survive.

▶ In many primate groups, such as the baboons shown here, adults help the mother by finding food and helping to look after the baby. Males will also gather food and play with the young.

Whales and dolphins

501 The mammal group of cetaceans is made up of about 80 kinds of whale, dolphin and porpoise. The whale group is then divided into two main types – baleen whales and toothed whales.

▼ The sperm whale is the biggest of the toothed whales. It only seems to have teeth in its lower jaw because those in its upper jaw can barely be seen.

503 Toothed whales catch prey with their sharp teeth. This subgroup includes sperm whales, beaked whales and pilot whales. One example is the beluga, or white whale. It is one of the noisiest whales, making clicks, squeaks and trills.

502 Baleen whales are the largest members of the cetacean group. They are often called great whales. The sei whale, for example, is about 16 metres long. Baleen whales catch food with long strips in their mouths called baleen, or whalebone.

◄ The beluga lives in the cold waters of the Arctic and can grow up to 5 metres in length.

▼ The finless porpoise, with its blunt 'beak' and bulging forehead, is one of the smallest cetaceans at about 1.5 metres in length.

505 Another group is made up of beaked whales. These are medium-sized whales with long, beak-shaped mouths. There are about 20 kinds, but some are very rare and hardly ever seen. The shepherd's beaked whale, which is about 7 metres in length, has been seen fewer than 20 times.

504 There are six species of porpoise. They are usually quite small, at 2 metres or less in length. They have blunter, more rounded heads than dolphins. The finless porpoise, as its name suggests, has a smooth back with no fin.

Grey patch from eye to the flipper

Back is a dusky blue–black colour

▶ The dusky dolphin is very inquisitive and likes to swim and leap near boats, perhaps in the hope of being fed.

White underside

506 There are more than 35 kinds of dolphin. Most of them are 2 to 3 metres in length. They are fast swimmers and can often be seen leaping above the waves. The dusky dolphin is one of the highest leapers, twisting and somersaulting before it splashes back into the sea.

Polar seals

507 **Many kinds of seal live in the Arctic region.** These include ringed seals, bearded seals, harp seals, spotted seals, ribbon seals and hooded seals. Most feed on fish, squid and small shrimp-like creatures called krill, which are also eaten by whales.

◄ Seals make breathing holes by bashing their noses, teeth and flippers against the thin ice.

508 **Seals have very thick fur to keep out the cold water.** Like their main enemy, the polar bear, they also have a layer of fatty blubber under the skin to keep them warm. They swim well but have to come up to breathe every few minutes. Sometimes they use breathing holes they make in the ice.

509 **In spring, mother seals come onto the ice to give birth.** Their babies, or pups, have very thick, fluffy fur to keep them warm. Each mother seal usually has only one pup. She feeds it on very rich milk, and it grows very quickly.

▼ In the snow, the pup lies perfectly still. Its thick, white fur keeps it warm and hides it in its snowy surroundings. The pup's fur is yellow at birth, but it soon turns white. The pup then grows a new, darker fur coat.

510 Mother seals have to return to the water to feed, leaving their pups alone on the ice. At this time pups are in danger from polar bears, wolves and other predators. Within a couple of weeks the young seal is big enough to look after itself.

511 The walrus is a huge seal with two long upper teeth, called tusks. A big walrus can grow to 3 metres in length and weigh 1.5 tonnes! Walruses often use their flippers and tusks to haul themselves out of the water onto rocky shores, to sunbathe during the brief summer.

▶ Walruses show off their tusks at breeding time to impress a mate. Tusks are used in feeding, to lever shellfish off the seabed.

Dogs and wolves

512 Wolves, coyotes and African hunting dogs belong to the dog family. Most live and hunt in groups, or packs. By working together, a pack can attack and kill large prey, such as deer and bison.

◀ When a wolf feels threatened, the fur on its back, called its hackles, stands on end. This makes it look bigger and fiercer.

513 Wolves have excellent senses of sight, hearing and smell to help them to find their prey. These strong, agile creatures have been known to travel a distance of 100 kilometres in just one night in search of food.

514 Coyotes are wild dogs that live in North America. They normally hunt in pairs or on their own, although they may join together as a group to chase large prey, such as deer.

515 Like wild cats, coyotes hunt by keeping still and watching an animal nearby. They wait for the right moment, then creep towards their prey and pounce, landing on top of the startled victim. Coyotes are swift runners and often chase jackrabbits across rocks and up hills.

BE A WOLF!

1. One person is Mr Wolf and stands with their back to the other players.
2. The players stand 10 paces away and shout, "What's the time, Mr Wolf?".
3. If Mr Wolf shouts, "It's 10 o'clock", the players take 10 steps towards Mr Wolf.
4. Watch out because when Mr Wolf shouts "Dinnertime", he chases the other players and whoever he catches is out of the game!

▼ When African hunting dogs pursue their prey, such as the wildebeest, the chase may go on for several kilometres, but the dogs rarely give up. They wait until their prey tires, then leap in for the kill.

516 African wild dogs are deadly pack hunters. They work as a team to chase and torment their prey. The whole pack shares the meal, tearing at the meat with their sharp teeth.

What is a bear?

517 There are eight types, or species, of bear including polar bears, grizzly bears and giant pandas. All have large, heavy bodies, big heads and short, powerful legs.

518 Most bears are brown in colour. Polar bears have white, or yellow-white coats, which help them blend into their snowy Arctic habitat. Pandas have striking black-and-white markings. Bears have thick fur, which helps to keep them warm – and makes them look even bigger than they actually are.

519 When they show their teeth and growl, bears are a scary sight. They belong to a group of meat-eating creatures called carnivores. The large, sharp teeth at the front of their mouths are called canines, and they use them for stabbing and tearing at meat. These teeth may measure between 5 and 8 centimetres in length.

520 A close look at a bear reveals that its eyes are actually quite small compared to the size of its head. Bears have good eyesight, but their sense of smell is much stronger. They can even smell food hidden in a glove compartment, inside a locked car!

◀ An angry bear may roar, opening its powerful jaw to reveal massive teeth.

▶ A bear's paws and claws are fearsome weapons, but they are most often used for digging up food such as roots. The Malayan sun bear's long, curved claws make it an excellent climber.

I DON'T BELIEVE IT!

Bears may look like they rely on strength rather than speed to survive, but don't be fooled. Brown bears can run at nearly 50 kilometres an hour — much faster than most humans.

521 Bears use their teeth to defend themselves in fights and to hunt other animals.

They have powerful paws to swipe at their attackers, and one blow can knock another animal to the ground. Their claws are long, knife-like, and reach up to 15 centimetres in length.

▼ A bear's skeleton helps to support its weight. The large skull protects the brain and the ribcage protects the internal organs.

Pelvis

Ribcage

Spine

Shoulder

Skull

221

Big cats

522 **All members of the cat family are mammals.** They are all strong but swift and most can climb trees easily. Their faces are rounded and their muzzles short. Cats are predators, which means that they hunt other animals and their teeth are suitable for catching, killing and eating their prey. All cats have excellent eyesight.

▲ The Siberian tiger is covered with thick fur that keeps it warm during the winter months.

523 **The tiger is not only the biggest cat it is also one of the largest carnivores, or meat eaters, living on land.** Of all tigers, Siberian tigers are the biggest. They may weigh as much as 350 kilograms and can measure 3 metres in length.

MAKE A MONSTER CAT!

You will need:
2 cups plain flour   1 cup salt
1 cup water   varnish or paint
bowl   spoon

1. Put the flour into a bowl. Add the salt and water.
2. Mix to form a smooth dough and mould into a cat shape.
3. Put your models onto a greased baking tray. Bake at gas mark 1 or 120°C for one to three hours. Once cool, paint or varnish your model.

▲ A jaguar's spots look like rosettes and often have a dark smudge in the centre.

526 The nimble cheetah does not need to be big to be successful. It has developed into one of the world's greatest predators, proving that skill and speed can make up for a lack of bulky muscles.

527 Sabre-toothed cats became extinct about 10,000 years ago. *Smilodon* was the most famous sabre-toothed cat. It was the size of a large lion and its canine teeth were a massive 25 centimetres long!

524 Jaguars are the biggest cats in the Americas. They measure up to 2.7 metres in length and can weigh an impressive 158 kilograms, which makes them the third largest big cat.

525 Lions hunt in groups called prides. This means that they can catch much larger animals than other big cats that hunt alone. By living and hunting together all the lions in the group eat regularly. Male lions usually eat first, even though the females do most of the hunting.

▲ *Smilodon* probably stabbed thick-skinned animals with its huge teeth.

Enormous elephants

528 There are three main types of elephant — two African and one Asian. African elephants are larger and they can measure up to 5 metres in length. Both males and females have tusks, which are long teeth that grow out of the mouth on either side of the trunk. They only live in Africa, but they are found in many types of habitat.

▶ African savannah elephants have huge ears and long, curved tusks.

529 There are two types of African elephant — forest and savannah. Forest elephants have darker skin than those that live on the savannah. They also have yellow-brown tusks that point downwards rather than curve upwards, and their trunks can be quite hairy. Forest elephants live in areas where there is a lot of thick vegetation.

▲ Asian elephants usually have smaller tusks than their African cousins, and much smaller ears.

530 Asian elephants are found in India and other parts of Southeast Asia. Males can weigh over 5 tonnes and measure more than 3 metres from the toe to the shoulder. Female Asian elephants do not always have visible tusks and are smaller than the males. The teeth of Asian elephants are very like those of mammoths, and it is thought that these two animals are closely related.

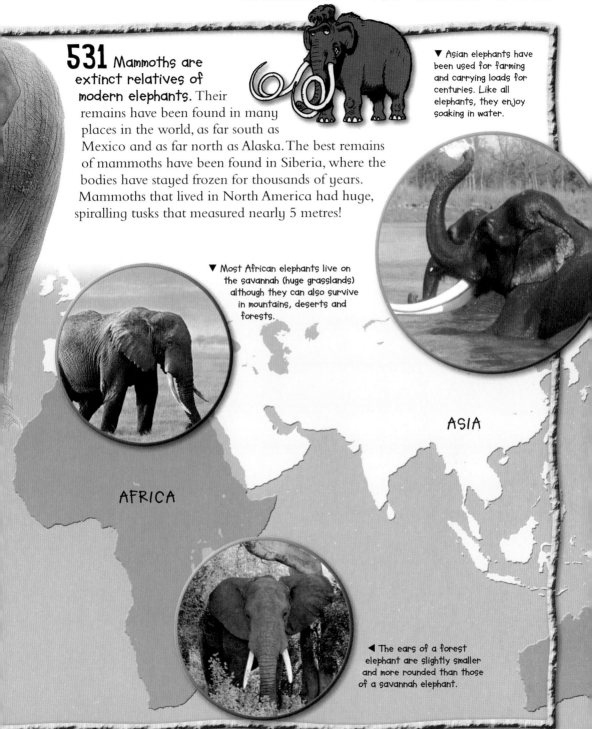

531 Mammoths are extinct relatives of modern elephants. Their remains have been found in many places in the world, as far south as Mexico and as far north as Alaska. The best remains of mammoths have been found in Siberia, where the bodies have stayed frozen for thousands of years. Mammoths that lived in North America had huge, spiralling tusks that measured nearly 5 metres!

▼ Asian elephants have been used for farming and carrying loads for centuries. Like all elephants, they enjoy soaking in water.

▼ Most African elephants live on the savannah (huge grasslands) although they can also survive in mountains, deserts and forests.

ASIA

AFRICA

◄ The ears of a forest elephant are slightly smaller and more rounded than those of a savannah elephant.

Horses, zebras and asses

532 Horses, ponies, zebras and asses all belong to the same animal family – the equids. All members of this family have a single toe on each foot, and are called 'odd-toed' animals (unlike cows and deer, which have two toes on each foot). Like other animals with fur, horses are mammals and they give birth to live young, which they feed with milk.

▲ Zebras are easily recognized by their stripy coats. These wild equids live in Africa.

533 Ponies are smaller than horses. Although horses and ponies are the same type of animal, they are different sizes. Horses are measured in 'hands', not centimetres, and a pony is a horse that is less than 14.2 hands (or 148 centimetres) tall. Ponies also have wider bodies and shorter legs than horses.

534 Equids live all over the world. Wild equids, such as zebras, live on grasslands where they can graze all day on plants. Horses that live and work with humans can be found almost everywhere across the world, and these are known as domestic horses.

535 Equids have manes of long hair on their heads and necks, and thick, tufted tails. Their long legs, deep chests and powerful muscles allow them to run a long way at great speed without getting tired.

▶ A horse's height is measured from its feet to the top of its shoulders, which are known as 'withers'.

MEASURE IN HANDS

Normally we use centimetres and metres as units of measurement, but you can use anything you like – even your hands.

Measure the height of a table using your hands. Then ask an adult to measure it as well. Did you get the same measurement? If not, why not?

536 Wild horses live in large groups called herds. All horses, wild or domestic (tame), are very loyal to one another and can form close bonds with other animals, including humans. Since it is natural for horses to have company, domestic horses should always be kept together, or with other animals such as sheep and cows.

537 Horses are intelligent animals. They can communicate with each other by whinnying or braying, but, like many other animals, horses also sniff and smell one another to communicate. They also enjoy nuzzling and grooming each other's fur.

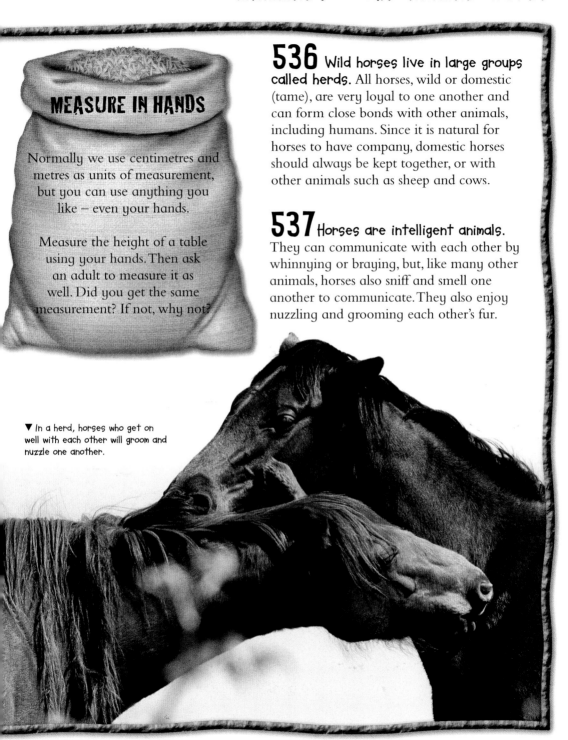

▼ In a herd, horses who get on well with each other will groom and nuzzle one another.

Mighty monsters

538 Not all deadly creatures kill for food. Many of them only attack when they are frightened. Some plant-eating animals fight to protect their young, or when they feel scared.

539 Hippos may appear calm when they are wallowing at the edge of a waterhole, but they kill more people in Africa than any other large animal. These huge creatures fiercely protect their own stretch of water, and females are extremely aggressive when they have calves and feel threatened.

540 African buffaloes can be very aggressive towards other animals and humans. If they become scared, they move quickly and attack with their huge horns. Groups of buffaloes surround a calf or ill member of the herd to protect it. They face outwards to prevent predators getting too close.

541 If an elephant starts flapping its ears and trumpeting, it is giving a warning sign to stay away. However, when an elephant folds its ears back, curls its trunk under its mouth and begins to run – then it really means business. Elephants will attack to keep other animals or humans away from the infants in their herd, and males will fight one another for a mate.

542 With huge bodies and massive horns, rhinos look like fearsome predators. They are actually related to horses and eat a diet of leaves, grass and fruit. Rhinos can become aggressive, however, when they are scared. They have poor eyesight, which may be why they can easily feel confused or threatened, and attack without warning.

◄ Male hippos fight one another using their massive teeth as weapons. Severe injuries can occur, leading to the death of at least one of the hippos.

I DON'T BELIEVE IT!

Adult male elephants are called bulls, and they can become killers. A single stab from an elephant's tusk is enough to cause a fatal wound, and one elephant is strong enough to flip a car over onto its side!

The bird world

543 There are over 9000 different types, or species, of bird. These have been organized by scientists into 29 groups called orders, which contain many different species. The largest is the Passeriformes order.

▼ This chaffinch is in the Passeriformes order. More than half of all bird species belong to this order.

Wings

Crown

Bill, or beak

Throat

Passeriformes order:
Includes robins, sparrows and wrens

Breast

Tail

Toes

Two legs

Common swift

Apodiformes order:
Swifts and hummingbirds

Keel-billed toucan

Piciformes order:
Toucans and woodpeckers

Blue-and-yellow macaw

Psittaciformes order:
Parrots, cockatoos and lorikeets

Pied avocet

Charadriiformes order:
Waders, gulls and auks

▲ The shape of a bird's beak can be used to decide which order a bird belongs to. These pictures show examples from the largest orders.

544 All birds have wings. These are the bird's front limbs and they come in many different shapes. Birds that soar in the sky for hours, such as eagles, have long, broad wings. Small, fast-flying birds such as swifts have slim, pointed wings.

▶ Feathers have different shapes, sizes and textures, suited to the jobs they do.

Tail feather

Flight feather

Contour (body) feather

Down feather

545 Birds are the only creatures that have feathers. They are made of keratin – the same material as our hair and nails. Feathers keep a bird warm, and its wing and tail feathers help it to fly. Some birds have colourful feathers to help attract mates or blend in with their surroundings – camouflage.

546 All birds have a beak, or bill, for eating. The beak is made of bone and is covered with a hard material called horn. Birds have different kinds of beak for different types of food. Insect-eating birds tend to have thin, sharp beaks for picking up their tiny prey. The parrot's strong beak is ideal for cracking nuts. Hunting birds, such as goshawks, have powerful hooked beaks for tearing flesh.

547 Birds lay eggs. It would be impossible for birds to carry their developing young inside their bodies like mammals do – they would be too heavy to fly.

▼ The egg protects the growing chick and provides it with food. While the young develop, the parent birds, such as this common eider, keep the eggs safe and warm. This is called incubation.

231

Fast movers

548 The fastest flying bird is the peregrine falcon. It hunts other birds in the air and makes spectacular high-speed dives to catch its prey. During a hunting dive, a peregrine may reach speeds of 200 kilometres an hour. In normal level flight, it flies at about 100 kilometres an hour. Peregrine falcons live almost everywhere in the world.

Wings are bent for a high-speed dive

▶ When a peregrine falcon spots its prey, it enters into an incredibly fast, powerful dive, called a stoop.

Long slender beak reaches inside a flower to drink nectar

▶ The hummingbird's fast-beating wings make a low buzzing or humming sound that gives these birds their name.

549 A hummingbird's wings beat 50 or more times a second as it hovers in the air. The tiny horned sungem hummingbird beats its wings at an amazing 90 beats per second. When hovering, the hummingbird holds its body upright and beats its wings backwards and forwards.

Large, fan-shaped tail

550 Ducks and geese are also fast fliers. Many of them can fly at speeds of more than 65 kilometres an hour. The red-breasted merganser and the common eider duck can fly at up to 100 kilometres an hour.

▲ The male common eider has a distinctive patch of green feathers on the back of its neck.

551 The swift spends nearly all its life in the air and rarely comes to land. After leaving its nest, a young swift can fly up to 500,000 kilometres, and may not come to land again for two years. The common swift has been recorded flying at 112 kilometres an hour.

Swifts have long, slim wings that are perfect for their life in the air

▲ The swift can eat, drink, catch prey and mate on the wing.

552 The greater roadrunner is a fast mover on land. It runs at speeds of up to 27 kilometres an hour as it hunts for insects, lizards and birds' eggs to eat. It can fly but seems to prefer running or walking.

FEED THE BIRDS!

You will need:
225g of fat (suet, lard or dripping)
500g of seeds, nuts, biscuit crumbs, cake and other scraps   a piece of string

Ask an adult for help. Melt the fat, and mix it with the seeds and scraps. Pour it into an old yogurt pot and leave it to cool and harden. Remove the 'cake' and make a hole through it. Push the string through the hole and knot one end. Hang it from a tree, and watch as birds flock to eat it.

River birds

553 Kingfishers live close to rivers, where they hunt for fish. At breeding time, a pair of birds tunnels into the riverbank, using their strong beaks. They prepare a nesting chamber at the end of the long tunnel. Here the female can safely lay up to eight eggs. Both parents look after the eggs, and feed the chicks when they hatch.

▶ A kingfisher plunges into the water, grabbing a fish in its dagger-like beak.

▼ Ospreys are also known as 'fish hawks'. As they dive into the water, they keep the prey in their sights.

554 The osprey is a bird of prey that feeds mainly on fish. This bird is found almost all over the world near rivers and lakes. It watches for prey from the air then plunges into the water with its feet held out in front. Special spikes on the soles of its feet help it hold onto its slippery catch.

555 The pelican collects fish in the big pouch that hangs beneath its long beak. When the pelican pushes its beak into the water the pouch stretches and fills with water, scooping up fish. When the pelican lifts its head up, the water drains out of the pouch leaving the food behind.

▲ A pelican's massive pouch works like a fishing net to trap prey.

556 The heron catches fish and other creatures such as insects and frogs. This long-legged bird stands on the shore or in shallow water and grabs its prey with a swift thrust of its sharp beak.

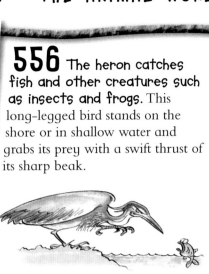

557 A small bird called the dipper is well-adapted to river life. It usually lives around fast-flowing streams and can swim and dive well. It can even walk along the bottom of a stream, snapping up prey such as insects and other small creatures. There are five different types of dipper and they live in North and South America, Asia and Europe.

▶ An African jacana feeds from water lettuce on the head of a hippopotamus.

558 The jacana can walk on water! It has amazingly long toes that spread the bird's weight over a large area. This allows it to walk on floating lily pads as it hunts for food such as insects. Jacanas can also swim and dive. There are eight different types of jacana, also called lilytrotters.

Desert dwellers

559 **The elf owl makes its nest in a hole in a desert cactus.** This prickly, uncomfortable home helps to keep the owl's eggs safe from predators that do not want to struggle through the cactus' spines.

▶ The elf owl is one of the smallest owls in the world and is only about 14 centimetres long. It lives in desert areas in the southwest USA.

I DON'T BELIEVE IT!

The lammergeier vulture drops bones onto rocks to smash them. It then eats the soft marrow and even splinters of bone. Acids in the bird's stomach can digest the bone.

560 **Desert birds may have to travel long distances to find water.** This is not always possible for chicks. To solve this problem, the male sandgrouse has feathers on his tummy that act like sponges to hold water. He soaks his feathers, and then flies back to his young, which gulp down the water that he's brought.

◀ The sandgrouse lives throughout Asia, often in semi-desert areas.

◀ A cactus wren rarely needs to drink water. It can get most of what it needs from its food.

561 Many desert birds have very light, sandy-brown feathers to blend with their surroundings. The cream-coloured courser lives in deserts in Africa and Asia. It searches for prey on the ground, as when it flies, the black-and-white pattern on the underside of its wings makes it easier for predators to spot.

562 The lappet-faced vulture scavenges for its food. It glides over the deserts of Africa and the Middle East, searching for dead animals. The vulture attacks a carcass with its strong hooked bill. Its head and neck are bare so it does not have to clean its feathers after feeding from a messy carcass.

563 The cactus wren eats cactus fruits and berries. This little bird hops among the spines of cactus plants in search of juicy morsels. It also catches insects, small lizards and frogs. Cactus wrens live in the southwestern USA.

▼ The lappet-faced vulture is the largest vulture in Africa. It is strong enough to fight off other birds and even mammals such as jackals, and its large beak can rip through skin and muscle.

What is a penguin?

564 **Like all birds, penguins are covered in feathers and lay eggs.** Most birds have bodies that help them fly, but penguins' bodies are perfectly suited to swimming. There are 17 types of penguin, all quite similar in appearance.

565 **Penguins have stout, upright bodies covered in black-and-white feathers.** Their black backs and white bellies help to camouflage the birds as they swim. When seen from below penguins appear white, blending into the light sky, but when seen from above they blend into the dark sea water.

▶ Birds, like this Chinstrap penguin, are vertebrates – just like reptiles, amphibians and mammals. This means that they have bony skeletons that support their bodies.

Skull

Bill (beak)

Spine

The bones in a penguin's flipper are similar to those in other birds' wings, and a human's arm

Ribcage

Hip bone

Penguins have sharp-clawed toes on their feet

I DON'T BELIEVE IT!

No one knows for sure where penguins got their strange name from, but it may come from the Latin word for 'fat', which is 'pinguis'.

◀ Penguins evolved (gradually changed over millions of years) from flying birds into flightless birds, so their flippers look quite similar to wings.

568 All birds have wings, but not all of them can fly. Wings are limbs, just like arms and legs, but they are mostly used for flying. The wings of penguins are too small and stumpy to be used for flight, but they have evolved for moving through water.

Flipper of a Magellanic penguin

Wing of a herring gull

▼ The long–extinct Waimanu had bird–like wings, rather than flippers, but probably could not fly.

566 The largest penguin that ever lived was almost as tall as a human. Scientists know this from studying fossil bones of penguins that lived millions of years ago. These bones give us clues about how prehistoric penguins looked and behaved. Waimanu, for example, was a small penguin-like bird that lived around 60 million years ago.

567 Male and female penguins usually look alike. It is very difficult to tell them apart, but the males are often taller and slightly heavier. Most penguins build nests or dig burrows where they lay their eggs, and both parents help to take care of the eggs and chicks.

239

Ravenous raptors

569 **Eagles, hawks, kites and ospreys are fearsome predators called birds of prey.** Equipped with incredible eyesight, powerful legs, and sharp claws and bills, they hunt during the day, soaring high in the sky as they look for food.

570 **Birds of prey are also known as raptors, which comes from the Latin word 'rapere', meaning 'to seize'.** Once they have captured their prey, such as a mouse, bird or frog, a raptor usually takes it to its nest to start pulling off fur and feathers. Bones are also thrown away, and the ground near a raptor's nest may be strewn with animal remains.

▶ Like most birds of prey, golden eagles have razor-sharp, hooked bills. They use them to tear the body of their prey apart.

▶ Eagle owls are large, powerful birds. They hunt and capture large animals, including other owls and birds of prey.

571 **Birds do not have teeth.** They have bills, or beaks, instead. Tearing large pieces of meat is a difficult job using just a bill. Birds of prey use their curved claws, called talons, to hold or rip their food apart, or they just swallow it whole.

572 **Little more than the flap of a wing can be heard as an owl swoops down to grab an unsuspecting mouse.** Owls hunt at night. They can even see small movements on the ground, thanks to their large eyes and sharp eyesight. When they hunt in total darkness, they rely on their excellent sense of hearing to find food.

QUIZ

The names of raptors have been jumbled up. Can you work out what they are?

1. GELEA
2. ITKE
3. CFALNO
4. LOW
5. PRYESO
6. KAWH

Answers:
1. Eagle 2. Kite 3. Falcon
4. Owl 5. Osprey 6. Hawk

573 **Peregrine falcons are the fastest hunters in the world and hunt on the wing.** This means that they catch their prey while in flight. They chase their prey to tire it out, before lashing out with their sharp talons.

▼ Bald eagles are one of the largest raptors in the world with a wingspan of over 2 metres.

574 **Bald eagles can soar at great heights when hunting.** They can climb to 3000 metres high and reach 160 kilometres an hour as they dive down to capture fish, turtles, ducks and snakes.

Night hunter

575 Owls are nocturnal birds of prey with superb vision and excellent hearing. Their eyes are large and face forwards, which helps them to judge distance. Their hearing is so good, they can locate their prey in total darkness just by listening!

576 The heart-shaped face of a barn owl works like a pair of ears! It helps to direct sound towards the sides of the owl's head, where the ears are situated at different heights. This helps them to pinpoint exactly where a sound is coming from. As they hover in the sky, barn owls can hear the tiny, high-pitched sounds made by small animals hidden in the vegetation below. Barn owls are able to fly almost silently towards their prey.

I DON'T BELIEVE IT!

Barn owls have white undersides, which may not appear to be the best camouflage for a nocturnal animal. This actually helps them to disappear against the sky when seen from below, allowing them to stalk and attack their prey more easily.

577 Barn owls are the most widespread land birds in the world and live on every continent, except Antarctica. They spend the day roosting (resting) in barns, buildings or trees and at night they come out to hunt. They catch rodents, such as rats, voles and mice.

▲ Barn owls have special adaptations that help them to hunt in the dark. Their soft feathers deaden the noise of flapping wings as they descend towards their unsuspecting prey.

578 Barn owls can see twice as well as humans by day and many times better at night. If an owl and a human were looking at the same image at night, the owl would see the image much more brightly. It would also be able to detect the smallest movement, which would be invisible to the human eye.

579 If they feel threatened or scared, owls slap their beaks together loudly making a clapping noise – this can sometimes be heard after dark. Barn owls shriek and hiss, but tawny owls are much more vocal. Their range of different calls can often be heard in the forests of Europe and Asia where they live. Male tawny owls make a loud 'hu-hooo' sound, which carries far in the still darkness. Females make a 'ke-wick' sound in reply. These noisy birds also make soft warbles and ear-piercing screeches!

Cold-blooded creatures

580 **Reptiles and amphibians are cold-blooded animals.** There are four groups of reptiles – snakes and lizards, the crocodile family, tortoises and turtles, and the tuatara. Amphibians are split into frogs and toads, newts and salamanders, and caecilians.

▼ Crocodiles are the largest reptiles in the world. Their eyes and nostrils are placed high on their heads so that they can stay mostly under water while approaching their prey.

581 **Reptiles do a lot of sunbathing!** They do this, called basking, to get themselves warm with the heat from the sun so that they can move about. When it gets cold, at night or during a cold season, they might sleep or hibernate, which means that they go into a very deep sleep.

582 **Most reptiles have dry, scaly, waterproof skin.** This stops their bodies from drying out. The scales are made of keratin and may form very thick, tough plates. Human nails are also made of the same sort of material.

583 The average amphibian has skin that is moist, fairly smooth and soft. Oxygen can pass easily through their skin, which is important because most adult amphibians breathe through their skin as well as with their lungs. Reptiles breathe only through their lungs.

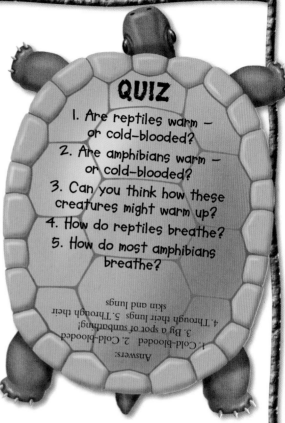

QUIZ

1. Are reptiles warm – or cold-blooded?
2. Are amphibians warm – or cold-blooded?
3. Can you think how these creatures might warm up?
4. How do reptiles breathe?
5. How do most amphibians breathe?

Answers:
1. Cold-blooded 2. Cold-blooded 3. By a spot of sunbathing! 4. Through their lungs 5. Through their skin and lungs

584 Amphibians' skin is kept moist by special glands just under the surface. These glands produce a sticky substance called mucus. Many amphibians also keep their skin moist by making sure that they are never far away from water.

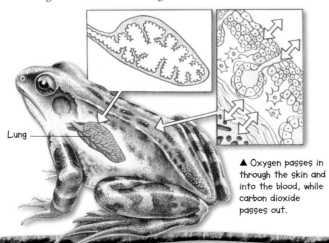

Lung

▲ Oxygen passes in through the skin and into the blood, while carbon dioxide passes out.

585 Some amphibians have no lungs. Humans breathe with their lungs to get oxygen from the air and breathe out carbon dioxide. Although most amphibians breathe through their skin and lungs, lungless salamanders breathe only through their skin and the lining of the mouth.

In the water

586 Amphibians are well known for their links with water, but some types of reptile are also aquatic (live in the water). Different types of amphibian and reptile have developed all kinds of ways of tackling watery lifestyles.

▼ Marine iguanas dive into chilly seawater to graze on seaweed. They can dive up to 9 metres at a time, but then have to bask to warm up again.

I DON'T BELIEVE IT!

Floating sea snakes can be surrounded by fish that gather at the snake's tail to avoid being eaten. When the snake fancies a snack, it swims backwards, fooling the fish into thinking its head is its tail!

587 Newts and salamanders swim rather like fish. They make an 'S' shape as they move. Many have flat tails that help to propel them through the water.

Eastern newt

▲▼ Newts are good swimmers and spend most of their lives in water.

Rough-skinned newt

▼ Green turtles took to the sea about 150 million years ago.

588 Toads and frogs propel themselves by kicking back with their hind legs. They use their front legs as a brake for landing when they dive into the water. Large, webbed feet act like flippers, helping them to push through the water.

① Frog draws its legs up

③ The main kick back with toes spread propels the frog forward through the water

② Then pushes its feet out to the side

④ Frog closes its toes and draws its legs in and up for the next kick

589 A swimming snake may seem unlikely, but most snakes are experts in the water. Sea snakes can stay submerged for five hours and move rapidly through the water. European grass snakes are also good swimmers. They have to be because they eat animals that live around water.

▼ Sea snakes return to land to lay eggs.

Yellow-bellied sea snake

590 Sea turtles have light, flat shells so they can move along more easily under water. Some have managed speeds of 29 kilometres an hour. Their flipper-like front legs 'fly' through the water. Their back legs form mini-rudders for steering.

Banded sea snake

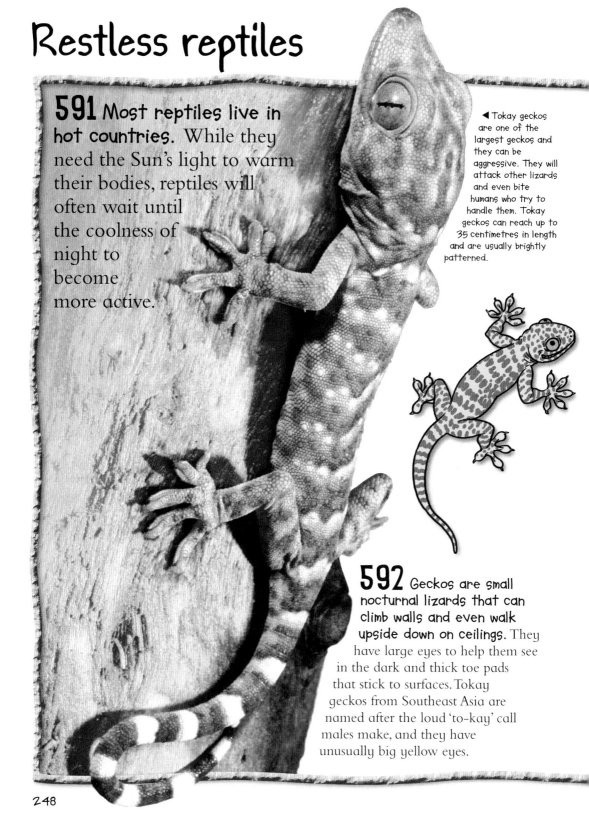

Restless reptiles

591 **Most reptiles live in hot countries.** While they need the Sun's light to warm their bodies, reptiles will often wait until the coolness of night to become more active.

◄ Tokay geckos are one of the largest geckos and they can be aggressive. They will attack other lizards and even bite humans who try to handle them. Tokay geckos can reach up to 35 centimetres in length and are usually brightly patterned.

592 Geckos are small nocturnal lizards that can climb walls and even walk upside down on ceilings. They have large eyes to help them see in the dark and thick toe pads that stick to surfaces. Tokay geckos from Southeast Asia are named after the loud 'to-kay' call males make, and they have unusually big yellow eyes.

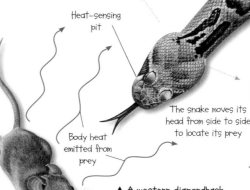

593 Nocturnal snakes are superb hunters because their senses are so well adapted to detecting prey in the dark. Some snakes have an extra skill – they can feel the heat from another animal's body. Snakes, such as the western diamond rattlesnake, do this using special heat-detecting pits between their eyes and nostrils. Using this extra sense, the snake can find its prey in the dark and strike with deadly accuracy.

Heat-sensing pit

The snake moves its head from side to side to locate its prey

Body heat emitted from prey

▲ A western diamondback rattlesnake uses its heat-detecting pits to work out the distance and direction of its prey.

594 Some reptiles are huge and fearsome night-time hunters. Black caimans, which are members of the crocodile family, can reach 6 metres in length. They live in South America in freshwater rivers and lakes and at night they come to shallow water or land to hunt. Their dark skin colour means they can creep up on prey, such as deer or large rodents, unnoticed.

▼ Black caimans are nocturnal hunters. They wait for prey to come to the water's edge to drink then pounce with speed. Adult caimans are big enough to drag deer and tapirs into the water.

QUIZ

Can you work out the names of these amphibians and reptiles by rearranging the letters?
DOAT WENT CEGKO GROF RUTTLE KNASE DROCCOLIE

Answers:
toad newt gecko frog turtle snake crocodile

595 Common kraits are one of the deadliest snakes of Pakistan, India and Sri Lanka, and they are nocturnal. They prey on other snakes and rodents, sometimes straying into buildings to find them. Once they have found their prey, kraits lunge their fangs into it, injecting a lethal venom.

Scary snakes

▶ Venomous snakes, such as the rattlesnake, inject venom using their large fangs. Snakes use their venom to paralyze (stop all movement) or kill their prey.

Venom runs down the groove on the outside of the fangs and is then injected into the victim's body

597 Cobras kill more than 10,000 people in India every year. As a warning sign, cobras spread their neck ribs, or hoods, to make them look more fearsome. Then they quickly lunge forwards and sink their fangs into their prey.

596 With unblinking eyes, sharp fangs and flickering tongues, snakes look like menacing killers. Despite their fearsome reputation, snakes only attack people when they feel threatened.

598 The taipan is one of Australia's most venomous snakes. When this snake attacks, it injects large amounts of venom that can kill a person in less than an hour.

599 Carpet vipers are small snakes found throughout many parts of Africa and Asia. They are responsible for hundreds, maybe thousands, of human deaths every year. Carpet viper venom affects the nervous system and the blood, causing the victim to bleed to death.

I DON'T BELIEVE IT!

Snakes can open their jaws so wide that they can swallow their prey whole. Large snakes, such as constrictors, can even swallow antelopes or pigs!

◀ Primitive snakes have a heavy skull with a short lower jaw and few teeth.

Short jaw that cannot open very wide

◀ Rear-fanged snakes have fangs in the roof of their mouths.

Fangs are towards the rear of the mouth, below the eye

◀ Some snakes have fangs at the front of their mouths.

The fangs are hollow, and positioned at the front of the mouth

600 Gaboon vipers have the longest fangs of any snake, reaching 5 centimetres in length. They produce large amounts of venom, which they inject deeply into the flesh with dagger-like teeth. Although slow and calm by nature, Gaboon vipers attack with great speed and a single bite can kill a human in less than two hours.

▶ Snakes kill their prey with a lethal bite. Then they swallow the victim, such as a rodent, whole.

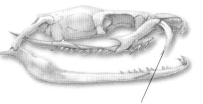

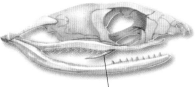

Dragons and monsters

▼ Komodo dragons use their powerful jaws to tear the flesh of their victim, and then eat everything, including bones and fur.

601 Komodo dragons are not really dragons, but lizards. They can reach 3 metres in length and up to 100 kilograms in weight, making them the largest lizards in the world. They hunt their prey using their sensitive sense of smell.

602 Once the Komodo has caught its prey, it sinks its sharp teeth into the victim's flesh. With a mouth full of poisonous bacteria, one bite is enough to kill an animal with an infection, even if it escapes the Komodo's clutches.

QUIZ

1. What colour is the Gila monster?
2. Why does the fire salamander have bold patterns on its skin?
3. How does the Komodo dragon hunt its prey?

Answers:
1. Black, pink and yellow 2. To warn predators that it is poisonous 3. Using its sensitive sense of smell

603 There are only two truly poisonous lizards – the Gila monster and the Mexican beaded lizard. Gila monsters live in North America and they have bands of black, pink and yellow on their scaly skin to warn predators to stay away.

▶ Gila monsters use their sense of smell to hunt small animals and find reptile eggs. They can kill their prey with a single bite.

▼ Fire salamanders are amphibians, like frogs. They hunt insects and earthworms, mainly at night.

604 Fire salamanders look like a cross between a lizard and a frog. They have bold patterns on their skin to warn predators that they are poisonous. The poison, or toxin, is on their skin and tastes foul. They squirt the toxin at predators, irritating or even killing them.

253

Ambush and attack

605 Lurking beneath the surface of the water, a deadly hunter waits, ready to pounce. Lying absolutely still, only its eyes and nostrils are visible. With one swift movement, the victim is dragged underwater. This killer is the crocodile, a relative of the dinosaurs.

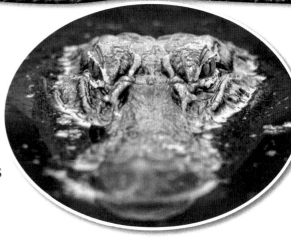

▲ Crocodiles and alligators are well-suited to their aquatic lifestyle. They spend much of their day in water, keeping cool and hidden from view.

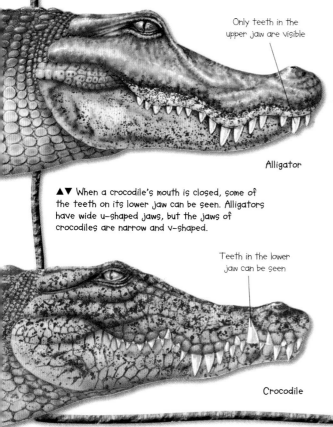

Only teeth in the upper jaw are visible

Alligator

▲▼ When a crocodile's mouth is closed, some of the teeth on its lower jaw can be seen. Alligators have wide u-shaped jaws, but the jaws of crocodiles are narrow and v-shaped.

Teeth in the lower jaw can be seen

Crocodile

606 When a crocodile has its prey in sight, it moves at lightning speed. The prey has little chance to escape as the crocodile pulls it underwater. Gripping the victim in its mighty jaws, the crocodile twists and turns in a 'deathspin' until its victim has drowned.

607 The largest crocodiles in the world live in estuaries, where rivers meet the oceans. They are called estuarine crocodiles and can reach a staggering 7 metres in length. These giant predators are often known as man-eating crocodiles, although they are most likely to catch turtles, snakes, monkeys, cows and pigs.

608 Alligators are very strong reptiles with wide jaws and thick, scaly skin on their backs. They live in marshes, ponds and rivers, often close to where people live. Like all crocodiles and alligators, the American alligator will catch and eat anything. They have even been known to attack humans.

I DON'T BELIEVE IT!

Crocodiles and alligators store their uneaten food underwater for several weeks. The remains rot, making it easier for the reptiles to swallow. Yum!

▼ Crocodiles and alligators have huge jaws, full of teeth. As well as being used for grabbing and holding prey, they use their teeth to slice pieces from the body of the victim.

Cooler customers

609 Many amphibians are common in cooler, damper parts of the world. Amphibians like wet places. Most mate and lay their eggs in water.

▶ Frogs can hide from strong sunlight by resting in trees or under plants.

610 As spring arrives, amphibians come out of hiding. The warmer weather sees many amphibians returning to the pond or stream where they were born. This may mean a very long journey through towns or over busy roads.

◀ Wildlife watchers help common toads cross the road to reach their breeding ponds in safety.

▲ When it is time to hibernate, a frog must find a safe, damp place to stay.

611 When the weather turns especially cold, amphibians often hide away. They simply hibernate in the mud at the bottom of ponds or under stones and logs. This means that they go to sleep in the autumn and don't wake up until spring.

Gills

▶ This is a mudpuppy — a type of salamander. It spends its whole life underwater and breathes using its frilly gills.

▲ Pygmy marbled newts avoid getting too hot by hiding under rotting wood or by resting in mud during the day.

612 Journeys to breeding grounds may be up to 5 kilometres — a long way for an animal only a few centimetres in length. This is like a person walking 90 kilometres away without a map! The animals find their way by scent, landmarks, the Earth's magnetic field and the Sun's position.

Water babies

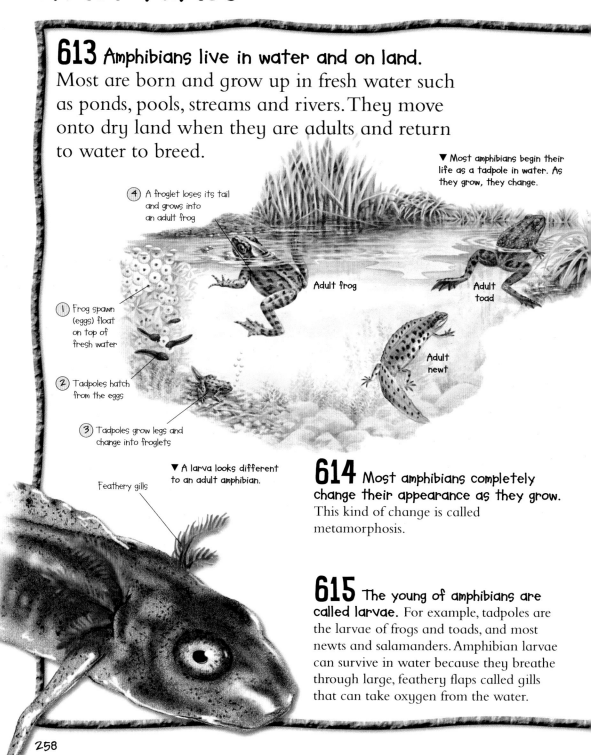

613 Amphibians live in water and on land.
Most are born and grow up in fresh water such
as ponds, pools, streams and rivers. They move
onto dry land when they are adults and return
to water to breed.

▼ Most amphibians begin their
life as a tadpole in water. As
they grow, they change.

④ A froglet loses its tail
and grows into
an adult frog

Adult frog

Adult
toad

① Frog spawn
(eggs) float
on top of
fresh water

Adult
newt

② Tadpoles hatch
from the eggs

③ Tadpoles grow legs and
change into froglets

▼ A larva looks different
to an adult amphibian.

Feathery gills

614 Most amphibians completely
change their appearance as they grow.
This kind of change is called
metamorphosis.

615 The young of amphibians are
called larvae. For example, tadpoles are
the larvae of frogs and toads, and most
newts and salamanders. Amphibian larvae
can survive in water because they breathe
through large, feathery flaps called gills
that can take oxygen from the water.

▲ An axolotl is a strange creature that remains a tadpole all its life.

616 **The axolotl is an amphibian that has never grown up.** This type of water-living salamander has never developed beyond the larval stage. It does, however, develop far enough to be able to breed.

▼ Toads can lay hundreds – even thousands – of eggs at a time.

617 **The majority of amphibians lay soft eggs.** These may be in a jelly-like string or clump of tiny eggs called spawn, as with frogs and toads. Newts lay their eggs singly.

618 **A few amphibians give birth to live young instead of laying eggs.** The eggs of the fire salamander, for example, stay inside their mother, where the young hatch out and develop. The female then gives birth to young that are like miniature adults.

Fearsome frogs

619 At first glance, few frogs appear fearsome. They may not have teeth or claws, but frogs and toads produce a deadly substance in their moist skin. This substance may taste foul or even be poisonous. The most poisonous frogs live in the forests of Central and South America. They are called poison-dart frogs.

620 One of the deadliest frogs is the golden poison-dart frog. It lives in rainforests in western Colombia, and its skin produces a very powerful poison – one of the deadliest known substances. A single touch is enough to cause almost instant death.

▼ The strawberry poison-dart frog is also known as the 'blue jeans' frog because of its blue legs.

621 Many poison-dart frogs are becoming rare in the wild. This is because the rainforests where they live are being cut down. Some poison-dart frogs can be kept in captivity, where they gradually become less poisonous. When they are raised in captivity, these frogs are not poisonous at all.

◀ The male green poison-dart frog carries tadpoles on his back. He takes them to a safe place in water where they will grow into adults.

I DON'T BELIEVE IT!

Poison-dart frogs are brightly coloured or boldly patterned. Their jewel-like appearance warns predators to stay away. This means that these frogs can hunt for bugs during the day, without fear of being eaten.

622 People who live in the rainforests of Central and South America use the poison from frogs to catch food. A hunter wipes the tip of a dart on the poisonous frog's back, then carefully puts it in a blowpipe. One puff sends the lethal dart into the body of an unsuspecting monkey or bird.

▼ Poison is wiped off the back of the golden poison-dart frog with a dart. One frog produces enough poison for more than 50 darts.

623 Looking after eggs is the job of male green poison-dart frogs. The female lays her eggs amongst the leaf litter on the forest floor. The male guards them until they hatch into tadpoles, then carries them to water, where they will grow into frogs.

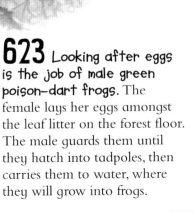

Sharks

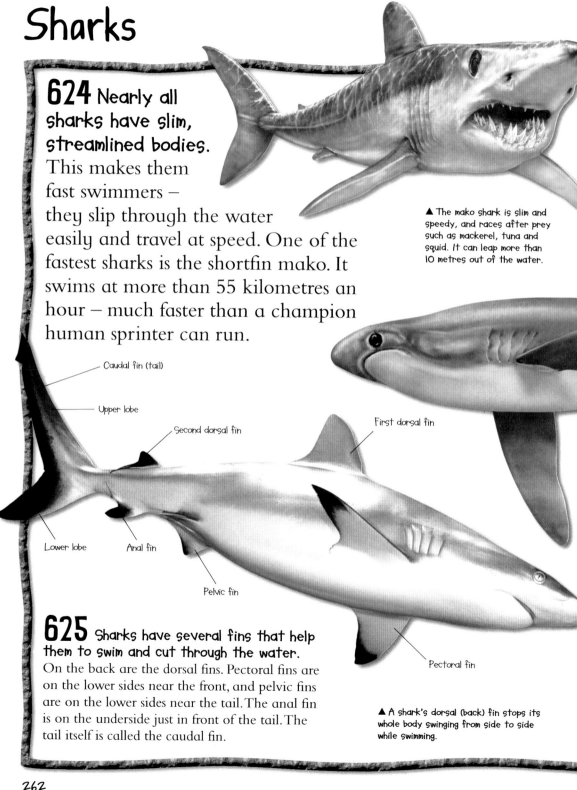

624 Nearly all sharks have slim, streamlined bodies. This makes them fast swimmers – they slip through the water easily and travel at speed. One of the fastest sharks is the shortfin mako. It swims at more than 55 kilometres an hour – much faster than a champion human sprinter can run.

▲ The mako shark is slim and speedy, and races after prey such as mackerel, tuna and squid. It can leap more than 10 metres out of the water.

Caudal fin (tail)

Upper lobe

Second dorsal fin

First dorsal fin

Lower lobe

Anal fin

Pelvic fin

Pectoral fin

625 Sharks have several fins that help them to swim and cut through the water. On the back are the dorsal fins. Pectoral fins are on the lower sides near the front, and pelvic fins are on the lower sides near the tail. The anal fin is on the underside just in front of the tail. The tail itself is called the caudal fin.

▲ A shark's dorsal (back) fin stops its whole body swinging from side to side while swimming.

626 Some sharks have tails longer than their bodies. The common thresher shark is 6 metres long – and half of this is its tail. The thresher uses it to attack smaller fish, so it can eat them.

▼ The thresher shark thrashes its tail from side to side to stun small fish before swallowing them.

627 Shark tails have other uses, too. Some sharks smack the water's surface with their tails to frighten their prey. Others swish away sand or mud on the seabed to reveal any hidden creatures.

BREATHING UNDERWATER

1. Most sharks have five pairs of gills
2. Fine blood vessels allow oxygen to pass from the water to the blood
3. Heart pumps blood around the body

▶ A shark's gill chambers are in its neck region. Most have five gill slits on either side.

628 Like other fish, sharks breathe underwater using their gills. These are under the slits on either side of the head, and are filled with blood. Water flows in through the shark's mouth, over the gills and out through the slits. The gills take in oxygen from the water because sharks need oxygen to survive.

629 Most sharks swim all of the time so that water flows over their gills and they can breathe. However some can lie still and make the water flow over their gills by 'pumping' the muscles of their mouth and neck.

Insects everywhere!

630 The housefly is one of the most common, widespread and annoying insects. There are many other members of the fly group, such as bluebottles, horseflies, craneflies and fruitflies. They all have two wings. Most other kinds of insects have four wings.

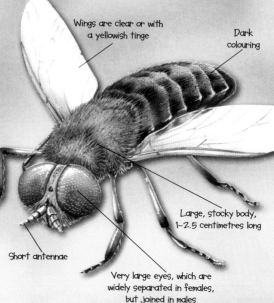

▼ Insects, such as this horsefly, do not have a bony skeleton like we do. Their bodies are covered by horny plates, called an exoskeleton.

Wings are clear or with a yellowish tinge

Dark colouring

Large, stocky body, 1–2.5 centimetres long

Short antennae

Very large eyes, which are widely separated in females, but joined in males

631 The ladybird is a noticeable insect with its bright red or yellow body, and black spots. It is a member of the beetle group – the biggest insect group of all. There are more than half a million kinds, from massive Goliath beetles to tiny flea beetles.

▶ Bright colours warn other animals that ladybirds taste horrible.

632 The cabbage white butterfly is not usually welcome in the garden. Its young, known as caterpillars, eat the leaves of plants. There are thousands of kinds of butterflies, and even more kinds of their night-time cousins, the moths.

▼ When the earwig is threatened, it raises its tail to try to make itself look bigger.

633 The earwig is a familiar insect outside – and sometimes inside. Despite their name, earwigs do not crawl into ears or hide in wigs, but they do like dark, damp corners. Earwigs form one of the smaller insect groups, with fewer than 2000 different kinds.

634 Ants are fine in the garden or wood, but are pests in the house. Ants, bees and wasps make up a large insect group with some 130,000 different kinds. Most can sting, although many are too small to hurt people. However, some types, such as bulldog ants, have a painful bite.

▶ Ants use their antennae and sense of touch as a means of communication. These ants are forming a 'living bridge' so their fellow workers can cross a gap to reach food.

635 The scorpionfly has a nasty-looking sting on a long curved tail. It flies or crawls around bushes and weeds during summer. Only the male scorpionfly has the red tail. It looks like the sting of a scorpion, but is harmless.

SPOT THE INSECTS!

Have you seen any insects so far today? Maybe a fly whizzing around the house or a butterfly flitting among the flowers? On a warm summer's day you will probably spot lots of different insects. On a cold winter's day there are fewer insects about – most are hiding away or have not hatched out of their eggs.

How insects grow

636 Nearly all insects begin life inside an egg. The female insect usually lays her eggs in an out-of-the-way place, such as under a stone, leaf or bark, or in the soil.

▼ The scarlet lily beetle lays her eggs directly onto the lily leaves, which the grubs will eat when they hatch.

637 Usually a female insect mates with a male insect before she can lay her eggs. The female and male come together to check they are both the same kind of insect and are healthy. This is known as courtship. Butterflies often flit through the air together in a 'courtship dance'.

638 When some types of insects hatch, they do not look like their parents. A young beetle, butterfly or fly is soft-bodied, wriggly and worm-like. This young stage is called a larva. A beetle larva is called a grub, a butterfly larva is a caterpillar and a fly larva is a maggot.

◄ Large caterpillars always eat into the centre of the leaf from the edge. Caterpillars grasp the leaf with their legs, while their specially developed front jaws chew their food.

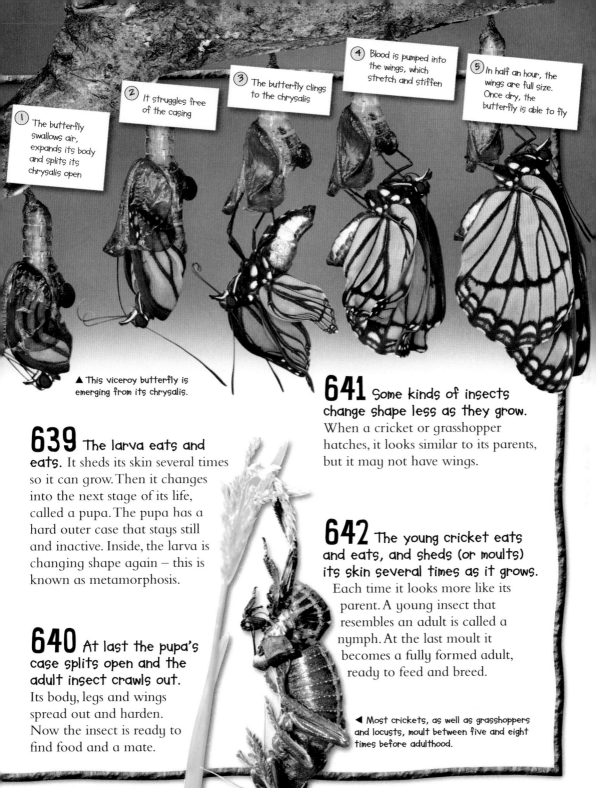

① The butterfly swallows air, expands its body and splits its chrysalis open

② It struggles free of the casing

③ The butterfly clings to the chrysalis

④ Blood is pumped into the wings, which stretch and stiffen

⑤ In half an hour, the wings are full size. Once dry, the butterfly is able to fly

▲ This viceroy butterfly is emerging from its chrysalis.

639 The larva eats and eats. It sheds its skin several times so it can grow. Then it changes into the next stage of its life, called a pupa. The pupa has a hard outer case that stays still and inactive. Inside, the larva is changing shape again – this is known as metamorphosis.

640 At last the pupa's case splits open and the adult insect crawls out. Its body, legs and wings spread out and harden. Now the insect is ready to find food and a mate.

641 Some kinds of insects change shape less as they grow. When a cricket or grasshopper hatches, it looks similar to its parents, but it may not have wings.

642 The young cricket eats and eats, and sheds (or moults) its skin several times as it grows. Each time it looks more like its parent. A young insect that resembles an adult is called a nymph. At the last moult it becomes a fully formed adult, ready to feed and breed.

◀ Most crickets, as well as grasshoppers and locusts, moult between five and eight times before adulthood.

Air aces

643 An insect's wings are attached to the middle part of its body, the thorax. This is like a box with strong walls, called a clickbox. Muscles pull to make the walls click in and out, which in turn makes the wings flick up and down. A large butterfly flaps its wings once or twice each second. Some tiny flies flap almost 1000 times each second.

644 Most kinds of insects have two pairs of wings and use them to fly from place to place. One of the strongest fliers is the Apollo butterfly of Europe and Asia. It flies high over hills and mountains, then rests on a rock or flower in the sunshine.

645 The smallest fliers include gnats, midges and mosquitoes. These are true flies, with one pair of wings. Some are almost too tiny for us to see. Certain types bite animals and people, sucking their blood as food.

◄ Apollo butterflies flit between plants, searching for sweet nectar to drink.

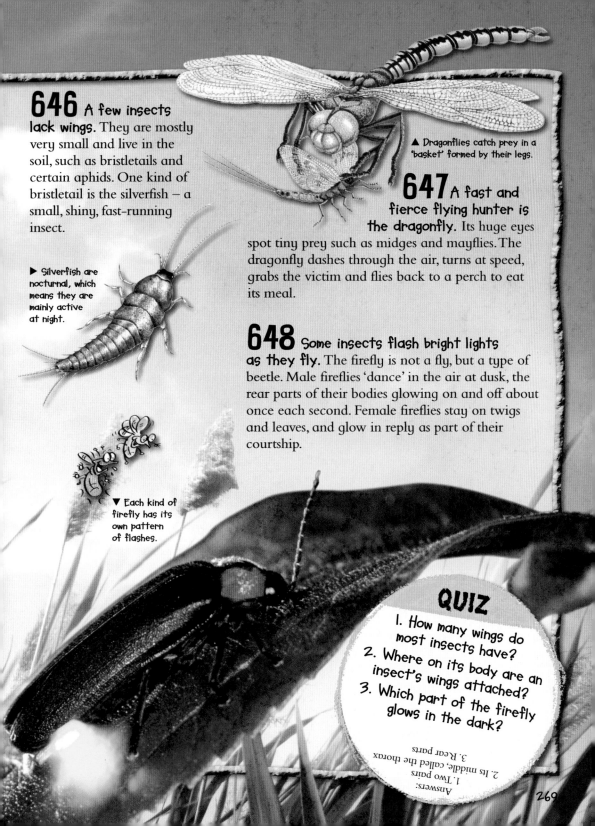

646 A few insects **lack wings.** They are mostly very small and live in the soil, such as bristletails and certain aphids. One kind of bristletail is the silverfish – a small, shiny, fast-running insect.

▲ Dragonflies catch prey in a 'basket' formed by their legs.

▶ Silverfish are nocturnal, which means they are mainly active at night.

647 A fast and fierce flying hunter is **the dragonfly.** Its huge eyes spot tiny prey such as midges and mayflies. The dragonfly dashes through the air, turns at speed, grabs the victim and flies back to a perch to eat its meal.

648 Some insects flash bright lights **as they fly.** The firefly is not a fly, but a type of beetle. Male fireflies 'dance' in the air at dusk, the rear parts of their bodies glowing on and off about once each second. Female fireflies stay on twigs and leaves, and glow in reply as part of their courtship.

▼ Each kind of firefly has its own pattern of flashes.

QUIZ

1. How many wings do most insects have?
2. Where on its body are an insect's wings attached?
3. Which part of the firefly glows in the dark?

Answers:
1. Two pairs
2. Its middle, called the thorax
3. Rear parts

Super sprinters

► Cockroaches are expert
scavengers, able to live
on tiny scraps of our food.
Some kinds spread germs
in their droppings.

649 Some insects rarely fly or
leap. They prefer to run and run…
all day, and sometimes all night
too. Among the champion insect
runners are cockroaches. There are
about 4500 different kinds and they
are tough and adaptable. Some live
in soil or caves, but most scurry
speedily across the ground and dart
into narrow crevices, under logs,
stones, cupboards – even beds!

650 One of the busiest insect walkers is the devil's coach-horse, which resembles an earwig. It belongs to the group known as rove beetles, which walk huge distances to find food.

▼ The devil's coach-horse has powerful mouthparts to tear apart small caterpillars, grubs and worms.

651 Some insects can run along smooth slippery surfaces, such as walls, windows or wet rocks. Others can run along the beds of ponds and rivers. The stonefly nymph has big, strong, wide-splayed legs that grip even smooth stones in rushing streams.

◀ The stonefly nymph, the larva of the stonefly, scuttles over wet rocks and riverbeds searching for food.

652 The green tiger beetle is an active hunter. It races over open ground, chasing smaller creatures such as ants, woodlice, worms and little spiders. It has huge jaws for its size and rips apart any victim.

I DON'T BELIEVE IT!

Green tiger beetles are about 12–15 millimetres long but can run at about 60–70 centimetres per second. That is like a human sprinter running 100 metres in one second!

Watery wonders

653 Many kinds of insects live underwater in ponds, streams, rivers and lakes. Some walk along the bottom, others swim strongly using their legs as oars to row through the water. The great diving beetle hunts small water creatures, such as tadpoles and baby fish. It can give a person a painful bite in self-defence.

▶ Pondskaters row on water with their rear four legs.

654 Some insects even walk on water. The pondskater has a slim, light body with long, wide-splayed legs. It glides across the water surface 'skin' or film, known as surface tension. The pondskater is a member of the bug group of insects and eats tiny animals, which fall into the pond.

▶ The great diving beetle breathes air, which it collects and stores under the hard wing-cases on its back.

Large pincer-like mouthparts

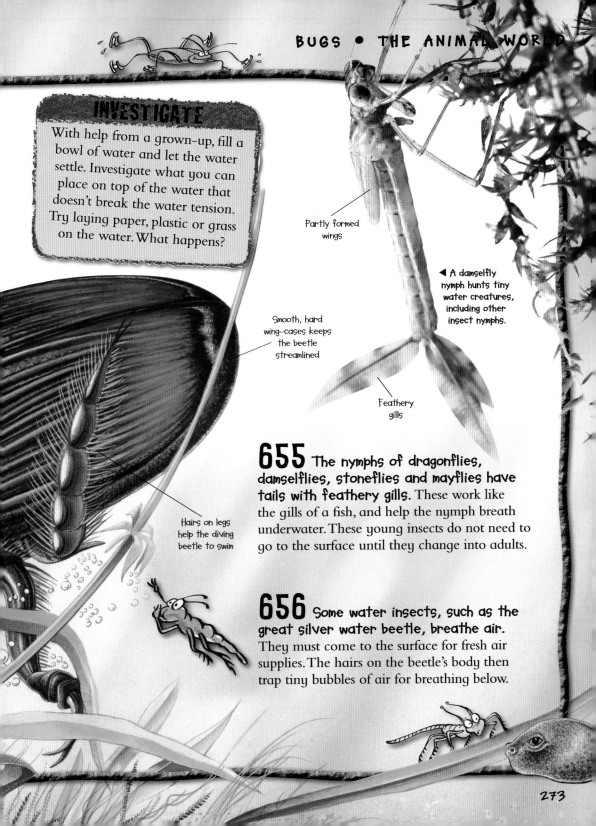

With help from a grown-up, fill a bowl of water and let the water settle. Investigate what you can place on top of the water that doesn't break the water tension. Try laying paper, plastic or grass on the water. What happens?

Partly formed wings

◄ A damselfly nymph hunts tiny water creatures, including other insect nymphs.

Smooth, hard wing-cases keeps the beetle streamlined

Feathery gills

Hairs on legs help the diving beetle to swim

655 The nymphs of dragonflies, damselflies, stoneflies and mayflies have tails with feathery gills. These work like the gills of a fish, and help the nymph breath underwater. These young insects do not need to go to the surface until they change into adults.

656 Some water insects, such as the great silver water beetle, breathe air. They must come to the surface for fresh air supplies. The hairs on the beetle's body then trap tiny bubbles of air for breathing below.

657 Soil teems with millions of creatures – and many are insects. Some are larvae or grubs, others are fully-grown insects, such as burrowing beetles, ants, termites and earwigs. These soil insects are a vital source of food for all kinds of larger animals, from spiders and shrews to moles and birds.

658 The larva of the click beetle is shiny orange, up to 25 millimetres long and called a **wireworm**. It stays undergound, feeding on plant parts, for up to five years. Then it changes into an adult and leaves the soil. Wireworms can be serious pests of crops such as barley, oats, wheat, potatoes and beet.

▶ Many insects pose a threat to farmers' crops. Farmers can use pesticides – chemicals to kill the insects – but many people think that this harms other plants and animals.

659 The larva of the cranefly ('daddy long-legs') is called a leatherjacket because of its tough, leathery skin. Leatherjackets eat the roots of grasses, including cereal crops, such as wheat. They hatch from their eggs in late summer and feed in the soil. They change into pupae and then adults the following summer.

INSECT LARVAE

1. African fruit beetle larva
2. Black cutworm caterpillar
3. Cicada grub
4. Click beetle larva
5. Cockchafer grub
6. Leatherjacket
7. Japanese beetle larva

ADULT INSECTS

1. African fruit beetle
2. Black cutworm moth
3. Cicada
4. Click beetle
5. Cockchafer
6. Cranefly
7. Japanese beetle

660 The larva of the cicada may live underground for more than ten years. Different types of cicadas stay in the soil for different periods of time. The American periodic cicada is probably the record holder, taking 17 years to change into a pupa and then an adult. Adults make loud chirping or buzzing sounds.

▶ Adult cicadas suck the sap of bushes and trees.

Veggie bugs

▲ Most shield bugs feed on plant sap using their sucking mouth parts.

661 About nine out of ten kinds of insects eat some kind of plant food. Many feed on soft, rich, nutritious substances. These include the sap in stems and leaves, the mineral-rich liquid in roots, the nectar in flowers and the soft flesh of squashy fruits and berries.

662 Solid wood may not seem very tasty, but many kinds of insects eat it. They usually consume the wood when they are larvae or grubs, making tunnels as they eat their way through trees, logs and timber structures, such as bridges, fences, houses and furniture.

▶ Woodworms are various kinds of wood-eating beetle larvae. Some stay in the wood for three years or more.

663 Animal droppings are delicious to many kinds of insects. Various types of beetles lay their eggs in warm, steamy piles of droppings. When the larvae hatch out, they eat the dung.

▲ Dung beetles mould soft dung into a ball shape. They roll the ball into a hole, which they have dug to lay their eggs in. The ball then covers their eggs.

◄ A lacebug jabs its sharp mouthparts into a plant to suck up the rich, syrupy sap inside.

664 Insects are not fussy eaters! They feed on old bits of damp and crumbling wood, dying trees, brown and decaying leaves and smelly, rotting fruit. This is nature's way of recycling goodness and nutrients in old plant parts, and returning them to the soil so new trees and other plants can grow.

▲ Fruitworms are insect larvae that may be moth caterpillars or beetle grubs, as shown here.

Clever colonies

665 Some insects live together in huge groups called colonies, which are like insect cities. There are four main types of insects that form colonies. One is the termites. The other three are all in the same insect subgroup and are bees, wasps and ants.

▶ An ants' nest is packed with tunnels and chambers.

666 Different kinds of ants make nests from whatever material is available. Ants might use mud, small sticks and twigs, tiny bits of stone and gravel, or chewed-up pieces of leaves and flowers.

Winged males and females leave to start their own nests

667 Leafcutter ants grow their own food. They harvest leaves to use in the nest to grow fungi, which they eat.

668 In most insect colonies, only one or two members lay eggs. These are the queens and they are usually much bigger than the other ants. A queen can lay over 100 eggs each day.

Nursery chamber with ant larvae

The queen lays eggs in a separate chamber

▼ This wasp is making new cells for larvae.

669 A wasps' nest will have about 5000 wasps in it, but these are small builders in the insect world! A termite colony may have more than 5,000,000 inhabitants! Wood ants form nests of up to 300,000. Honeybees number around 50,000, while bumblebees live in colonies of only 10 or 20.

I DON'T BELIEVE IT!

Ants look after aphids and milk them like cows! They stroke the aphids to obtain a sugary liquid called honeydew, which the ants sip to get energy.

Worker ants care for the eggs and larvae

670 Inside an ants' nest are many kinds of workers, each with different jobs to do. Foragers tunnel into the soil and collect food, such as bits of plants and animals. Guards at the entrances to the nest bite any animals that try to come in. Nursery workers look after the eggs, larvae and pupae, while courtiers feed and clean the queen.

Camouflage

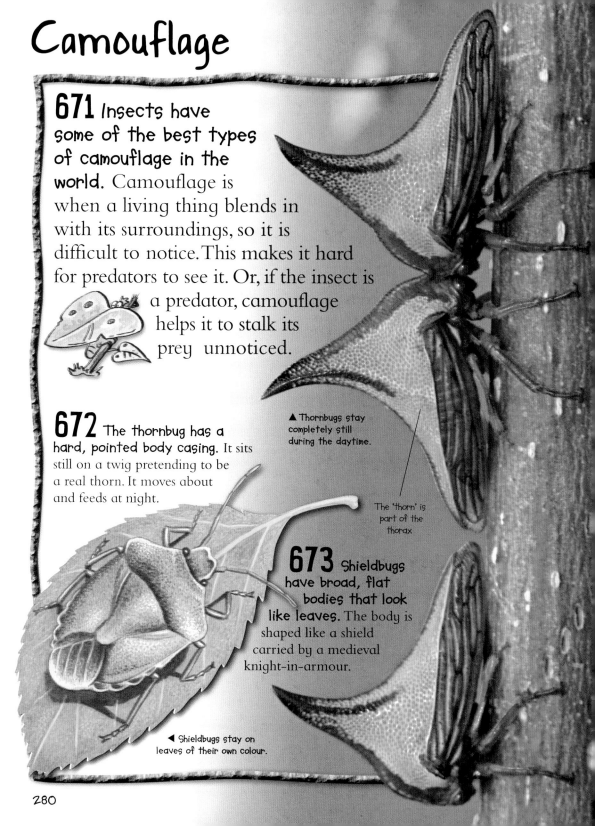

671 **Insects have some of the best types of camouflage in the world.** Camouflage is when a living thing blends in with its surroundings, so it is difficult to notice. This makes it hard for predators to see it. Or, if the insect is a predator, camouflage helps it to stalk its prey unnoticed.

672 **The thornbug has a hard, pointed body casing.** It sits still on a twig pretending to be a real thorn. It moves about and feeds at night.

▲ Thornbugs stay completely still during the daytime.

The 'thorn' is part of the thorax

673 Shieldbugs have broad, flat bodies that look like leaves. The body is shaped like a shield carried by a medieval knight-in-armour.

◄ Shieldbugs stay on leaves of their own colour.

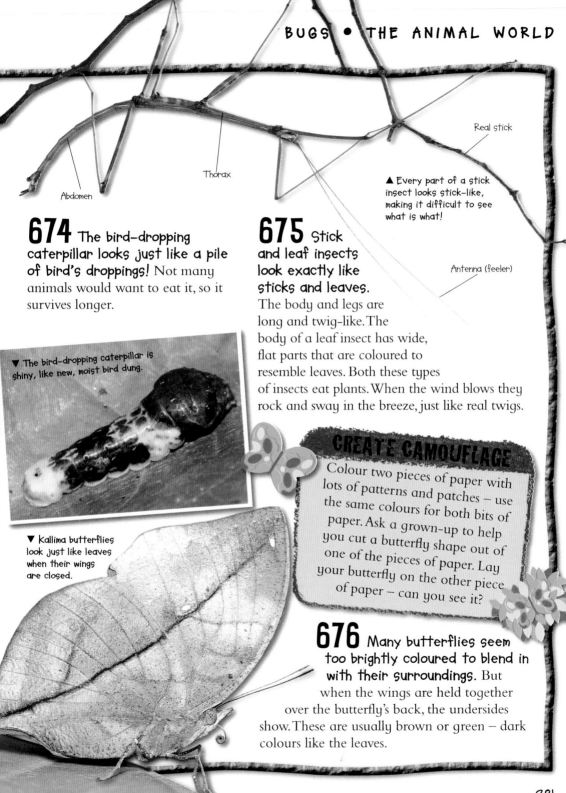

Real stick

Thorax

Abdomen

▲ Every part of a stick insect looks stick-like, making it difficult to see what is what!

Antenna (feeler)

674 The bird–dropping caterpillar looks just like a pile of bird's droppings! Not many animals would want to eat it, so it survives longer.

▼ The bird–dropping caterpillar is shiny, like new, moist bird dung.

▼ Kallima butterflies look just like leaves when their wings are closed.

675 Stick and leaf insects look exactly like sticks and leaves. The body and legs are long and twig-like. The body of a leaf insect has wide, flat parts that are coloured to resemble leaves. Both these types of insects eat plants. When the wind blows they rock and sway in the breeze, just like real twigs.

CREATE CAMOUFLAGE

Colour two pieces of paper with lots of patterns and patches – use the same colours for both bits of paper. Ask a grown-up to help you cut a butterfly shape out of one of the pieces of paper. Lay your butterfly on the other piece of paper – can you see it?

676 Many butterflies seem too brightly coloured to blend in with their surroundings. But when the wings are held together over the butterfly's back, the undersides show. These are usually brown or green – dark colours like the leaves.

Bugs at night

677 **Insects and other bugs are amongst the noisiest nocturnal animals, especially in hot countries.** An evening walk in a rainforest is accompanied by a chorus of clicks, buzzing, humming and chattering. These are some of the sounds made by millions of insects, which are invertebrates – animals without backbones.

▲ Common earwigs are insects that measure 8 to 18 millimetres in length. They are native to Europe, but are found in many countries.

678 **Just like bigger creatures, insects and bugs use sound to communicate with each other at night.** Cockroaches are leathery-skinned insects that are common throughout the world. Most spend their time scuttling silently through the leaf litter and twigs on the forest floor. However, the Madagascan hissing cockraoch can hiss if it's disturbed by pushing air out through its abdomen.

679 **They may look menacing, but earwigs are completely harmless.** By day they hide under leaves or in cracks and crevices. At night they come out to eat rotting plant and animal matter. They have pincers on the ends of their tails, which they use to scare predators away.

◄ Cockroaches can feel movement through their feet, which warns them to dash under cover to avoid predators.

▲ Feathery moth antennae can detect tiny scent particles.

680 Moths have special organs on the front of their heads called antennae. These long, slender or feathery structures detect smells and moths use them to find food and mates. These sensitive organs also help moths find their way in the dark. Moths with damaged antennae can't fly in straight lines – they crash into walls or fly backwards!

▲ Female moon moths produce a chemical that tells males they are ready to mate. Males use their antennae to pick up the scent of the female moths from several hundred metres away.

681 Moths are some of the most elegant and beautiful nocturnal insects. They have decorative patterns that help to camouflage, or hide, them. Members of the tiger moth family are often brightly coloured to tell predators that they are poisonous. Tiger moths also make high-pitched clicks to deter bats, which hunt by sound not sight. Once a bat has tried to eat one nasty-tasting tiger moth, it knows to avoid all clicking moths!

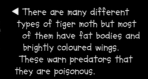

◀ There are many different types of tiger moth but most of them have fat bodies and brightly coloured wings. These warn predators that they are poisonous.

BED-SHEET BUGS!

Find out what nocturnal insects share your habitat.

You will need:

large white sheet   torch   notebook and pencil or camera

On a warm evening, hang a sheet up outside and shine a torch onto it. Wait patiently nearby and soon insects will be attracted to the sheet. Take photos or make sketches of all the bugs you see so you can identify them later. Be careful not to touch them though!

Silky spiders

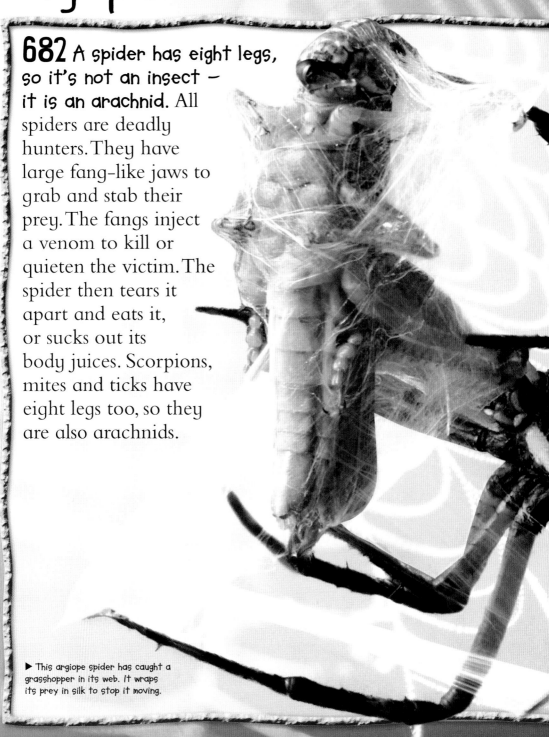

682 A spider has eight legs, so it's not an insect — it is an arachnid. All spiders are deadly hunters. They have large fang-like jaws to grab and stab their prey. The fangs inject a venom to kill or quieten the victim. The spider then tears it apart and eats it, or sucks out its body juices. Scorpions, mites and ticks have eight legs too, so they are also arachnids.

▶ This argiope spider has caught a grasshopper in its web. It wraps its prey in silk to stop it moving.

Several spinnerets produce silk

Spigots produce coarse silk for making webs

Spools produce fine silk for wrapping prey

Front legs wrap silk around prey

683 **All spiders can make thin, fine threads called silk.** These come out of spinnerets at the rear of the spider. About half of the 40,000 kinds of spiders make webs to catch prey. Some spiders make silk bags, called cocoons, to lay their eggs in or create protective 'nursery tents' for their young.

▶ The hardest part of building a web is getting the first thread in place. The spider needs a gust of wind to carry the thread across, so it sticks to a good spot.

① The first thread is horizontal

② The second thread makes a Y-shape

③ More strands, called radials, are added

④ A temporary spiral is put in place

⑤ The final spiral is built more carefully

684 **Some spiders use their silk threads in strange ways.** The spitting spider squirts sticky silk at its victim. The bolas spider creates a fishing line to catch insects flying past. The water spider makes a criss-cross sheet of silk to hold bubbles of air, which it needs in order to breathe underwater.

▼ The spitting spider spits a mixture of venom and 'glue' at its prey.

285

Deadly and dangerous

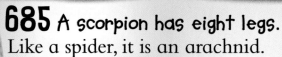

685 A scorpion has eight legs. Like a spider, it is an arachnid. Scorpions live in warm parts of the world. Some are at home in watery rainforests, others like hot deserts. The scorpion has large, crab-like pincers called pedipalps to grab its prey, and powerful jaws like scissors to chop it up.

686 The scorpion has a dangerous venomous sting at the tip of its tail. It can use this to paralyze or kill a victim. The scorpion may also wave its tail at enemies to warn them that unless they go away, it will sting them.

Stinger on last tail part

▶ This scorpion is attacking a grasshopper.

Pedipalp claws grab prey

▶ False scorpions hunt tiny bugs, as small as a full stop.

687 The false scorpion looks like a scorpion with big pincers. It does not have a venomous sting in its tail – it does not even have a tail. It is tiny and could fit into this 'O'! It lives in soil and hunts even smaller creatures.

688 A crab may seem an odd cousin for a spider or scorpion. But the horseshoe or king crab is very unusual. It has eight legs – so it's an arachnid. It also has a large domed shell and strong spiky tail. There were horseshoe crabs in the seas well before dinosaurs roamed the land.

▶ Horseshoe crabs come onto the shore at breeding time.

689 The sun spider or solifuge is another very fierce, spider–like hunter, although it has no venom. Most kinds live in deserts and are known as camel spiders.

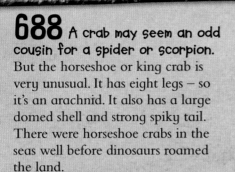

690 Animals don't have to be big to be dangerous. These spiders are all very venomous and their bites can even kill people. This is why you should never mess about with spiders or poke your hands into holes or dark places!

The European black widow has up to 13 red patches on its abdomen

The Australian redback has a body length of about 10 millimetres

New Zealand's katipo is found along seashore dunes

QUIZ

1. Scorpions and spiders belong to which family group?
2. What does a scorpion use its tail for?
3. What is another name for a king crab?

Answers:
1. Arachnids 2. To paralyze the victim 3. Horseshoe crab

691 History is the details of our past. People began to write things down from about 2500 BC. We know a lot of things that happened before 2500 BC, even though nothing was written down, because historians have found remains and artefacts. For example, historians know that the river Nile was important for the ancient Egyptians. The Nile provided water for drinking and for watering crops, and it was also a trade route for the Egyptians.

▼ The Nile supported many activities of ancient Egypt such as trade and farming. It was also an important water source.

Ruling ancient Egypt

692 The rulers of ancient Egypt were called pharaohs. The word 'pharaoh' means great house. The pharaoh was the most important and powerful person in the country. Many people believed he was a god.

693 Ramses II ruled for over 60 years. He was the only pharaoh to carry the title 'the Great' after his name. Ramses was a great builder and a brave soldier. He was also the father of an incredibly large number of children – 96 boys and 60 girls.

Ramses II

▶ Here the pharaoh is holding the symbols of his rule, the hook and flail. Workers used these tools to separate grain from the stalks.

▼ These people are paying tribute to the pharaoh. This means that they have come from the surrounding countries to give him presents and tell him how great he is!

▲ On her wedding day, the bride wore a long linen dress or tunic.

694 Over 30 different dynasties ruled ancient Egypt. A dynasty is a line of rulers from the same family.

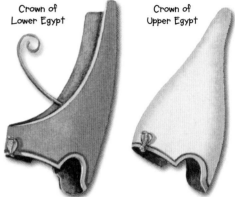

Crown of Lower Egypt

Crown of Upper Egypt

▲ The double crown of Egypt was made up of two crowns, the bucket-shaped red crown of Lower Egypt and the bottle-shaped white crown of Upper Egypt.

695 The pharaoh often married a close female relative, such as his sister or half-sister. In this way, the blood of the royal family remained pure. The title of 'pharaoh' was usually passed on to the eldest son of the pharaoh's most important wife.

696 Officials called viziers helped the pharaoh to govern Egypt. Each ruler appointed two viziers – one each for Upper and Lower Egypt. Viziers were powerful men. Each vizier was in charge of a number of royal overseers. Each overseer was responsible for a particular area of government, for example the army or granaries where the grain was stored. The pharaoh, though, was in charge of everyone.

▲ This vizier is checking the sacks of grain that have been brought in from the harvest while a criminal awaits his punishment. The viziers of ancient Egypt were among the most important people in the country.

Tutankhamun

697 Tutankhamun is one of Egypt's most famous pharaohs. He became king in 1334 BC when he was eight years old. Because he was too young to carry out the important work of ruling Egypt, two of his ministers took charge. They were Ay, chief minister, and Horemheb, head of the army. They made decisions on Tutankhamun's behalf.

◀ This model of Tutankhamun was buried with him in his tomb.

▼ Tutankhamun was buried in three separate coffins that fitted inside each other. This is the middle coffin, which is made of gold and decorated with a gem called lapis lazuli.

698 Tutankhamun was pharaoh for about nine years. He died when he was 17 years old. His body was mummified and buried in a tomb cut into the side of a valley. Many pharaohs were laid to rest in this valley, known as the Valley of the Kings. Tutankhamun was buried with valuables for use in the next life.

699 The tombs in the Valley of the Kings were meant to be secret. However robbers found them, and stole the precious items buried there. They found Tutankhamun's tomb, but were caught before they could do much damage. Years later, when the tomb of Rameses VI was being dug, rubble rolled down the valley and blocked the entrance to Tutankhamun's tomb. After that, it was forgotten about.

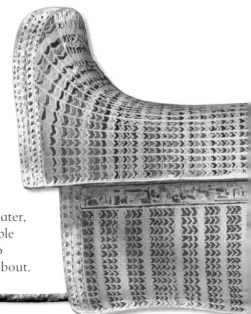

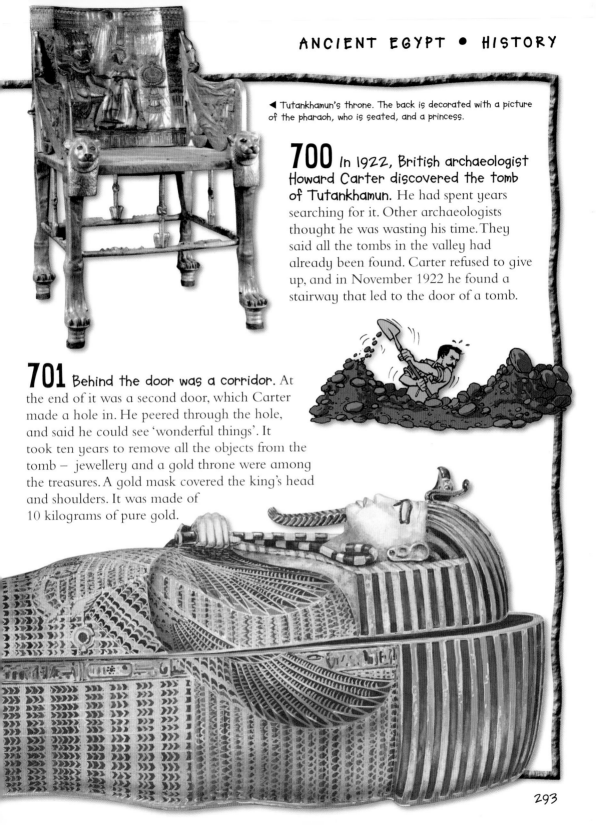

◀ Tutankhamun's throne. The back is decorated with a picture of the pharaoh, who is seated, and a princess.

700 In 1922, British archaeologist Howard Carter discovered the tomb of Tutankhamun. He had spent years searching for it. Other archaeologists thought he was wasting his time. They said all the tombs in the valley had already been found. Carter refused to give up, and in November 1922 he found a stairway that led to the door of a tomb.

701 Behind the door was a corridor. At the end of it was a second door, which Carter made a hole in. He peered through the hole, and said he could see 'wonderful things'. It took ten years to remove all the objects from the tomb — jewellery and a gold throne were among the treasures. A gold mask covered the king's head and shoulders. It was made of 10 kilograms of pure gold.

293

Land of pyramids

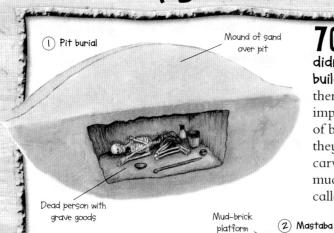

① Pit burial

Mound of sand over pit

Dead person with grave goods

▲ ▶ At first, bodies were buried in pits (1). Later on, the pits were covered with mud-brick platforms, or mastabas (2). Finally, several platforms were put on top of each other to make the first pyramid — the Step Pyramid (3).

703 The ancient Egyptians didn't suddenly decide to start building pyramids. Around 3100 BC there was a change in the way important people were buried. Instead of burying them in holes in the desert, they were buried in underground tombs carved into the rock. A low platform of mud-brick was built over the tomb, called a mastaba.

Mud-brick platform

② Mastaba

Graves below ground surface

702 The word 'pyramid' was introduced to the English language by the ancient Greeks. They saw that Egyptian loaves were a similar shape to Egypt's huge buildings. The Greeks called Egyptian loaves 'pyramides', meaning 'wheat cakes'. In time, this word changed into the English word 'pyramid'.

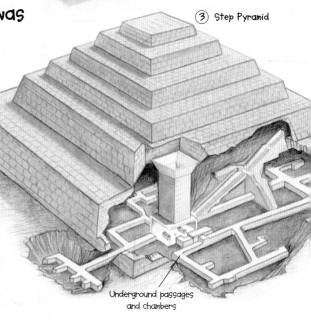

③ Step Pyramid

Underground passages and chambers

704 **Pyramids developed from mastabas.**
The first pyramid was built for Djoser, one of
the first Egyptian pharaohs (kings). It began
as a mastaba, but was built from stone
instead of mud-brick. A second platform was
added on top of the mastaba, followed by a
smaller one on top of that. The mound grew
until it had six platforms. It looked like an
enormous staircase, which is why it is known
as the Step Pyramid.

QUIZ

1. How many steps does the Step Pyramid have?
2. What type of tombs did pyramids grow out of?
3. Who was buried inside the Step Pyramid?
4. Who was the architect of the Step Pyramid?

Answers:
1. Six 2. Mastaba tombs
3. King Djoser 4. Imhotep

705 **The architect Imhotep
built the Step Pyramid.**
He was Djoser's vizier, or
chief minister, and was in
charge of all building
projects. It was his idea to
build Djoser's tomb from
stone, and to create a pyramid.
Imhotep was also a poet, a
priest and a doctor. Many years
after his death he was made into
a god, responsible for wisdom,
writing and medicine.

706 **The Step Pyramid is at
Saqqara – an ancient Egyptian
cemetery.** The pyramid was built around
2650 BC. It is about 60 metres high and its
sides are more than 100 metres in length.
King Djoser was buried inside one of the
chambers that were carved into the solid
rock beneath the pyramid.

▶ The Step Pyramid was a series of
platforms on top of each other. It was
an experiment in building a tall
structure, and it led the way
to later pyramids with
smooth sides.

Building a pyramid

707 The ancient Egyptians built their pyramids on the west bank of the river Nile. This was because the Egyptians linked the west with death, as this was where the sun set. The site had to be far enough away from the river to avoid flooding, but close enough for building materials to be transported to it.

▼ Builders made slots in the bedrock that were filled with water. The water was at the same level in every slot, showing the builders how much rock to remove in order to make the site flat.

708 After a site was chosen, the position of the pyramid was decided. Egyptian pyramids have sides that face north, south, east and west, but it is not clear how this was worked out. People may have used the stars to work out the position of north. Once they knew where north was, it was easy to work out the positions of south, east and west.

709 The site had to be flat, so the pyramid would rise straight up. One idea is that the builders flooded the site with water, and measured down from the surface. By keeping the measurement the same across the site, it showed them how much bedrock had to be cut away to make the site level.

▶ At the stone quarries, teams of men had specific jobs to do. Some split and levered rough blocks away from the bedrock. Others smoothed the sides of the blocks, and then they were ready to transport to the building site.

710 Pyramid workers used simple tools. Mattocks (digging tools) were used to clear the building site, and the rubble was carried away in woven reed baskets. In the stone quarries, stone was cut using mauls (stone hammers), copper chisels, and wedges. Woodworkers cut and shaped wood using copper saws and chisels, drills, hammers and planes.

711 Hundreds of men usually worked in the stone quarries. At busy times there may have been a few thousand. They worked in teams, cutting blocks of limestone and granite. The bedrock was marked with the outlines of blocks, and then the outlines were chiselled away to leave a grid of grooves. Copper wedges were knocked into the grooves to make the bedrock split. Last of all, wooden levers prised the blocks free.

Raising the blocks

712 Moving the heavy blocks was a hard job. Some quarries were close to the building site, but many were far away. The best limestone came from quarries on the east side of the river Nile, and granite came from the south. Barges (large ships), transported these blocks along the river to harbours built close to the pyramid sites.

▼ The river Nile was Egypt's main highway. Boats carried people, animals and goods along its length.

713 Wooden rollers were probably used to move the blocks over land. A block was placed onto a set of rollers, and ropes were tied to it. As men pulled the ropes, the rollers turned and the block moved. After the block moved off the back rollers, they were carried to the front. Slowly, the block moved towards the site.

714 How the blocks reached their final destination is a puzzle. Historians agree that they were dragged up ramps made from hard soil and rubble – but there's disagreement about what shape the ramps were. One idea says there was one ramp that wrapped around the growing pyramid in a spiral shape. Another says there was a straight ramp against one side of the pyramid. A third idea is that there were four ramps, one on each side of the pyramid.

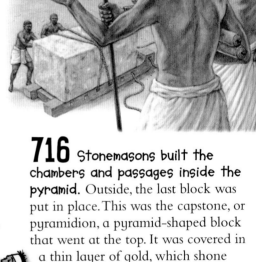

▶ Pharaohs probably inspected their pyramids as they were built. Their crowns showed which part of Egypt they ruled – the White Crown represented Upper Egypt, whereas the Red Crown represented Lower Egypt.

715 Once a block had been moved up the ramp, it was set in place. This was skilled work, and the stone setters had to make sure the blocks fitted neatly together. They used wooden levers to move the blocks around, and by the time one block was in place, another one had been brought up the ramp to be fitted. It was non-stop work.

716 Stonemasons built the chambers and passages inside the pyramid. Outside, the last block was put in place. This was the capstone, or pyramidion, a pyramid-shaped block that went at the top. It was covered in a thin layer of gold, which shone brightly in the sunlight.

ANCIENT ART

Use books and the Internet to find pictures of the beautiful paintings that the Egyptians created on the walls of burial chambers. You could even try to paint some of your own!

717 Finally, the ramps were removed. As the ramps came down, workers set slabs of limestone in place. These gave the sides a smooth finish. Inside, painters decorated the burial chamber walls and ceilings with pictures and magical spells. The pyramid was finished, and was ready to be used as a pharaoh's tomb.

Supreme beings

718 **The ancient Egyptians worshipped more than 1000 different gods and goddesses.** The most important god of all was Ra, the sun god. People believed that he was swallowed up each evening by the sky goddess Nut. During the night Ra travelled through the underworld and was born again each morning.

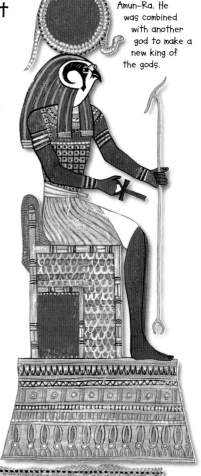

◄ The sun god Ra later became Amun-Ra. He was combined with another god to make a new king of the gods.

719 A god was often shown as an animal, or as half-human, half-animal. Sobek was a god of the river Nile. Crocodiles were kept in pools next to Sobek's temples. Bastet was the goddess of cats, musicians and dancers. The cat was a sacred animal in ancient Egypt. When a pet cat died, the body would be wrapped and laid in a cat-shaped coffin before burial in the city's cat cemetery. The moon god Thoth usually had the head of an ibis, but he was sometimes shown as a baboon. The ancient Egyptians believed that hieroglyphic writing came from Thoth.

▼ Some of the well-known gods that were represented by animals.

Sobek   Bastet   Thoth

720 As god of the dead, Osiris was in charge of the underworld. Ancient Egyptians believed that dead people travelled to the kingdom of the underworld below the Earth. Osiris and his wife Isis were the parents of the god Horus, protector of the pharaoh.

Isis   Osiris   Horus

721 Anubis was in charge of preparing bodies to be mummified. This work was known as embalming. Because jackals were often found near cemeteries, Anubis, who watched over the dead, was given the form of a jackal. Egyptian priests often wore Anubis masks.

Amenhotep IV

722 A pharaoh called Amenhotep IV changed his name to Akhenaten, after the sun god Aten. During his reign he made Aten the king of all the gods.

▶ Anubis preparing a body for mummification.

301

In tombs and temples

723 From about 2150 BC pharaohs were not buried in pyramids, but in tombs in the Valley of the Kings. At that time it was a fairly remote place, surrounded by steep cliffs lying on the west bank of the Nile opposite the city of Thebes. Some of the tombs were cut into the sides of the cliffs, others were built deep underground.

▲ Robbers looted everything from the royal tombs — gold, silver, precious stones, furniture, clothing, pots — sometimes they even stole the dead ruler's body!

724 Like the pyramids, the riches in the royal tombs attracted robbers. The entrance to the Valley of the Kings was guarded, but robbers had broken into every tomb except one within 1000 years. The only one they missed was the tomb of the boy king Tutankhamun, and even this had been partially robbed and re-sealed.

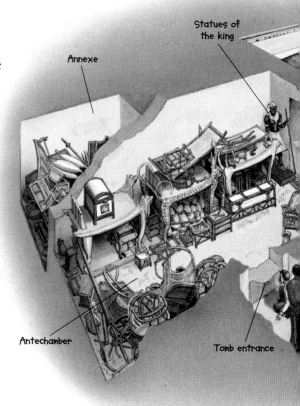

Statues of the king

Annexe

Antechamber

Tomb entrance

▲ The solid gold death mask of Tutankhamun found in the Valley of the Kings. The young king's tomb was discovered, with its contents untouched, about 90 years ago.

725 When Tutankhamun's body was found it was inside a nest of three mummy cases in a sarcophagus (stone coffin). The sarcophagus was inside a set of four wooden shrines big enough to contain a modern car.

I DON'T BELIEVE IT!
Temple visitors had to shave off their hair and eyebrows before they were allowed to enter the sacred buildings.

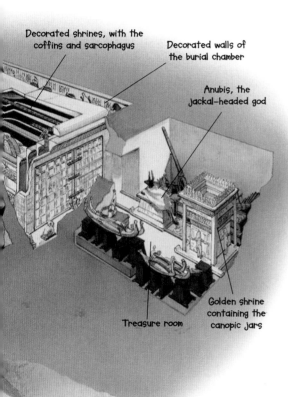

Decorated shrines, with the coffins and sarcophagus

Decorated walls of the burial chamber

Anubis, the jackal-headed god

Golden shrine containing the canopic jars

Treasure room

▲ Arcaeologist Howard Carter, and his sponsor Lord Carnarvon, finally found Tutankhamun's tomb after five years of exploration. Carnarvon died just four months after he first entered the tomb. Some people said he was the victim of Tutankhamun's 'curse' because he had disturbed the pharaoh's body. In fact Carnarvon died from an infected mosquito bite.

726 The ancient Egyptians built fabulous temples to worship their gods. Powerful priests ruled over the temples, and the riches and lands attached to them. Many of the finest temples were dedicated to Amun-Ra, king of the gods.

727 The temple at Abu Simbel, in the south of Egypt, is carved out of sandstone rock. It was built on the orders of Ramses II. The temple was built in such a way that on two days each year (22 February and 22 October) the Sun's first rays shine on the back of the inner room, lighting up statues of the gods.

▲ Four enormous statues of Ramses II, each over 20 metres high, guard the temple entrance at Abu Simbel.

Mummies

▲ Even pet dogs were mummified in ancient Egypt.

728 The most famous mummies were made in ancient Egypt. The Egyptians were skilled embalmers (mummy-makers). Pharaohs (rulers of Egypt) and ordinary people were made into mummies, along with many kinds of animal.

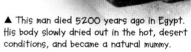

▲ This man died 5200 years ago in Egypt. His body slowly dried out in the hot, desert conditions, and became a natural mummy.

▲ Two people walk through the Field of Reeds, which was the ancient Egyptian name for paradise.

729 Mummies were made because the Egyptians thought that the dead needed their bodies in a new life after death. They believed a person would live forever in paradise, but only if their body was saved. Every Egyptian wanted to travel to paradise after death. This is why they went to such trouble to preserve the bodies of the dead.

730 Ancient Egypt's first mummies were made by nature. When a person died, their body was buried in a pit in the desert sand. The person was buried with objects to use in the next life. Because the sand was hot and dry, the flesh did not rot. Instead, the flesh and skin dried and shrivelled until they were stretched over the bones. The body had been mummified. Egypt's natural mummies date from around 3500 BC.

731 The ancient Egyptians made their first artificial mummies around 3400 BC. The last mummies were made around AD 400. This means the Egyptians were making mummies for 4000 years! They stopped making them because as the Christian religion spread to Egypt, mummy-making came to be seen as a pagan (non-Christian) practice.

▶ Many Egyptian coffins were shaped like a person and beautifully painted and decorated.

732 When an old grave was found, perhaps by robbers who wanted to steal the grave goods, they got a surprise. Instead of digging up a skeleton, they uncovered a dried-up body that still looked like a person! This might have started the ancient Egyptians thinking – could they find a way to preserve bodies themselves?

Home sweet home

733 Egyptian houses were made from mud bricks dried in the sun. Mud was taken from the river Nile, and straw and pebbles were added to make it stronger. The trunks of palm trees supported the flat roofs. The inside walls of houses were covered with plaster, and often painted. Wealthy Egyptians lived in large houses with several storeys. A poorer family might live in a crowded single room.

◄ A mixture of mud, straw and stones was poured into wooden frames, or shaped into bricks and left to harden in the sun.

734 In most Egyptian homes there was a small shrine. Here, members of the family worshipped their household god.

◄ The dwarf god, Bes, was the god of children and the home.

735 Egyptians furnished their homes with wooden stools, chairs, tables, storage chests and carved beds. A low three- or four-legged footstool was one of the most popular items of furniture. Mats of woven reeds covered the floors.

736 Rich families lived in spacious villas in the countryside. A typical villa had a pond filled with fish, a walled garden and an orchard of fruit trees.

▼ Here, two family members are playing a popular board game called senet.

737 **Families cooked their food in a clay oven or over an open fire.** Most kitchens were equipped with a cylinder-shaped oven made from bricks of baked clay. They burned either charcoal or wood as fuel, and cooked food in two-handled pottery saucepans.

738 **Pottery lamps provided the lighting in Egyptian homes.** The container was filled with oil and a wick made of cotton or flax was burned. Houses had very small windows, and sometimes none at all, so there was often little natural light. Small windows kept out the strong sunlight, helping to keep houses cool.

739 **In Egypt it was good to eat with your fingers!** In rich households, servants would even bring jugs of water between courses so that people could rinse their hands.

Clever Egyptians

740 The insides of many Egyptian tombs were decorated with brightly coloured wall paintings. They often depicted scenes from the dead person's life, showing him or her as a healthy young person. The Egyptians believed that these scenes would come to life in the next world.

Sunken relief

► The Egyptians produced raised reliefs by cutting away the background, and sunken reliefs by cutting stone from inside the outline.

Raised relief

742 Egyptian sculptors carved enormous stone statues of their pharaohs and gods. These were often placed outside a tomb or temple to guard the entrance. Scenes, called reliefs, were carved into the walls of temples and tombs. These often showed the person as they were when they were young, enjoying scenes from daily life. This was so that when the god Osiris brought the dead person back to life, the tomb owners would have a good time in the afterlife.

741 The ancient Egyptians had three different calendars: an everyday farming one, an astronomical one, and a lunar (Moon) calendar. The 365-day farming calendar was made up of three seasons of four months. The astronomical calendar was based on observations of the star Sirius, which reappeared each year at the start of the flood season. Priests kept a calendar based on the movements of the Moon which told them when to perform ceremonies for the moon god Khonsu.

▲ The days on this calendar are written in black and red. Black days are ordinary, but the red days are unlucky.

◄ Several artists worked on the tomb paintings. A junior artist drew the outlines of the scene, which were then checked and corrected by a senior artist. Next, painters filled in the outlines in colour.

743 Astronomers recorded their observations of the night skies. The Egyptian calendar was based on the movement of Sirius, the brightest star in the sky. The Egyptians used their knowledge of astronomy to build temples that lined up with certain stars.

I DON'T BELIEVE IT!

Bulbs of garlic were used to ward off snakes and to get rid of tapeworms from people's bodies.

744 Egyptian doctors knew how to set broken bones and treat illnesses such as fevers. They used medicines made from plants such as garlic and juniper to treat sick people. The Egyptians had a good knowledge of the basic workings of the human body.

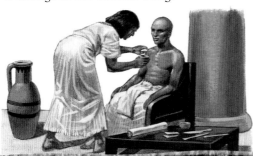

Nilometer

745 The Egyptians used a nilometer to measure the depth of the river Nile. They inserted measuring posts into the riverbed at intervals along the bank so they could check the water levels at the start of each flood season.

From pictures to words

746 **The Egyptians had no paper – they wrote on papyrus.** It was made from the tall papyrus reeds that grew on the banks of the Nile. At first papyrus was sold as long strips, or scrolls, tied with string. Later the Egyptians put the papyrus sheets into books. Papyrus is very long lasting – sheets of papyrus have survived 3000 years to the present day.

Reed brush

Papyrus scroll

Ink

747 **Ink was made by mixing water with soot, charcoal or coloured minerals.** Scribes wrote in ink on papyrus scrolls, using reed brushes with specially shaped ends.

① Cutting

▼ This is the process of making a papyrus sheet.

1. Papyrus was expensive because it took a long time to make. First people had to cut down the papyrus stems, and cut them up into lots of thin strips.

② Laying

2. Then someone laid these strips in rows on a frame to form layers.

3. The papyrus strips were then pressed under weights. This squeezed out the water and squashed the layers together.

4. Finally, when the papyrus was dry, a man with a stone rubbed the surface smooth for writing.

③ Pressing

④ Rubbing

748 The Rosetta Stone was found in 1799 by a French soldier in Egypt. It is a large slab of stone onto which three different kinds of writing have been carved: hieroglyphics, a simpler form of hieroglyphics called demotic, and Greek. All three sets of writing give an account of the coronation of King Ptolemy V. By translating the Greek, scholars could understand the Egyptian writing for the first time.

Rosetta Stone

749 In the 5th century BC a Greek historian called Herodotus wrote about life in ancient Egypt. As he travelled across the country he observed and wrote about people's daily lives, and their religion and customs such as embalming and mummification – he even wrote about cats!

750 The ancient Egyptians used a system of picture writing called hieroglyphics. Each hieroglyph represented an object or a sound. For example, the picture of a lion represented the sound 'l' and a basket represented the word 'lord'. Altogether there were about 700 different hieroglyphs. Scribes wrote them on papyrus scrolls or carved them into stone.

▼ A junior artist's work was checked by a senior artist, who then painted over the work in black paint.

WRITE YOUR NAME IN HIEROGLYPHICS

Below you will see the hieroglyphic alphabet. I have written my name in hieroglyphs. Can you write yours?

J A N E

A B C D E F G H

I J K L M N O P

Q R S T U V W X Y Z

751 The hieroglyphs of a ruler's name were written inside an oval-shaped frame called a cartouche. The pharaoh's cartouche was carved on pillars and temple walls, painted on tomb walls and mummy cases, and written on official documents.

Greece was great

752 **The ancient Greeks were proud of their beautiful country.** There were high snowy mountains, swift rushing streams, thick forests, flowery meadows and narrow, fertile plains beside the sea. Around the coast there were thousands of rocky islands, some small and poor, others large and prosperous.

◀ A carved stone figure of a woman found in the Cyclades Islands. The design is very simple but strong and graceful.

753 **Greek civilization began on the islands.** Some of the first evidence of farming in Greece comes from the Cyclades Islands. Around 6000 BC, people living there began to plant grain and build villages.

754 **They buried their dead in graves filled with treasures.** These included carved marble figures, pottery painted with magic sun symbols and gold and silver jewellery.

▼ This timeline shows some of the important events in the history of ancient Greece.

TIMELINE OF GREECE

c. 40,000 BC
First people in Greece. They are hunters and gatherers

c. 2000–1450 BC
Minoan civilization on the island of Crete

c. 1250 BC
Traditional date of the Trojan War

c. 900–700 BC
Greek civilization grows strong again

c. 6000 BC
First farmers in Greece

c. 1600–1100 BC
Mycenean civilization on mainland Greece

c. 1100–900 BC
A time of decline – kingdoms weaken, writing stops

c. 776 BC
Traditional date of first Olympic Games

◀ This jar, made around 900 BC, is rather dull and plain. It suggests that times were troubled and Greek people had no money to spare for art.

755 **Between 1100–900 BC, the history of Greece is a mystery.** From 2000–1100 BC, powerful kings ruled Greece. They left splendid buildings and objects behind them, and used writing. But between around 1100–900 BC, there were no strong kingdoms, little art, few new buildings – and writing disappeared.

▲ Alexander the Great conquered an empire stretching from Greece to India.

756 **Migrants settled in distant lands.** By around 700 BC, Greece was overcrowded. There were too many people, not enough farmland to grow food and some islands were short of water. Greek families left to set up colonies far away, from southern France to North Africa, Turkey and Bulgaria.

757 **When the neighbours invaded, Greek power collapsed.** After 431 BC, Greek cities were at war and the fighting weakened them. In 338 BC, Philip II of Macedonia (a kingdom north of Greece) invaded with a large army. After Philip died, his son, Alexander the Great, made Greece part of his mighty empire.

c. 700–500 BC
Greeks set up colonies around Mediterranean Sea

c. 480–479 BC
Greece fights invaders from Persia (now Iran)

c. 338 BC
Philip II of Macedonia conquers Greece

c. 147–146 BC
Romans conquer Greece and Macedonia

c. 500–430 BC
Athens leads Greece, creates amazing art, has democratic government

c. 431–404 BC
Wars between Athens and Sparta

c. 336–323 BC
Alexander the Great of Macedonia and Greece conquers a vast empire

Kings and warriors

758 **King Minos ruled an amazing palace city.** The first great Greek civilization grew up at Knossos on the island of Crete. Historians call it 'Minoan' after its legendary king, Minos. Around 2000 BC, Minoan kings built an amazing palace-city, with rooms for 10,000 people. It was decorated with wonderful frescoes (wall paintings), statues and pottery.

▲ A section of the palace at Knossos on the island of Crete. A succession of powerful kings ruled a rich kingdom here.

759 Minoan Greeks honoured a monster. Greek myths describe how a fearsome monster was kept in a labyrinth (underground maze) below the palace. It was called the Minotaur, and it was half-man, half-bull.

▲ Greek legends told how the young hero Theseus bravely entered the labyrinth and killed the Minotaur.

QUIZ

1. What was the Minotaur?
2. What was the labyrinth?
3. Where was Knossos?

Answers:
1. A monster – half-man, half-bull 2. A maze underneath the Minoan royal palace 3. On the Greek island of Crete

Oule = Hello

Khaire = Goodbye

▶ This golden mask was found in one of the royal tombs at Mycenae. It covered the face of a king who died around 1500 BC.

760 Invaders brought the Greek language. Between around 2100–1700 BC, warriors from the north arrived in mainland Greece. They brought new words with them and their language was copied by everyone else living in Greece.

▼ Works of art found at Knossos include many images of huge, fierce bulls with athletes leaping between their horns in a deadly religious ritual.

761 Mycenae was ruled by warrior kings. Around 1600 BC new kings took control of Minoan lands from forts on the Greek mainland. The greatest fort was at Mycenae, in the far south of Greece. Mycenaean kings sent traders to Egypt and the Near East to exchange Greek pottery and olive oil for gold, tin and amber. They used their wealth to pay for huge tombs in which they were buried.

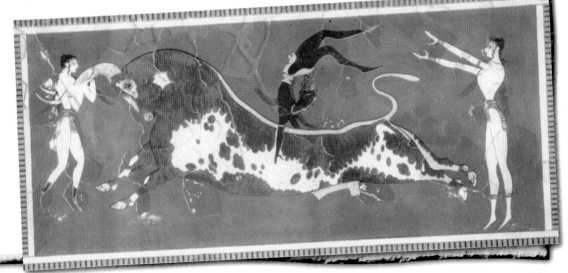

City-states

762 The power of Mycenaean kings collapsed around 1200 BC. By 700 BC, Greece had been divided into 300 city-states, which were cities and the land around them. Some city-states were ruled by kings, some by tyrants (men who governed by force) and some by oligarchs (small groups of rich, powerful men).

▶ Merchant ships carried goods from all around the Mediterranean Sea to sell in Greek markets. They could only travel in the summer, as winter seas were too stormy.

763 Most city-states grew rich by buying and selling. The agora (market-place) was the centre of many cities. Goods on sale included farm produce such as grain, wine and olive oil, salt from the sea, pottery, woollen blankets, sheepskin cloaks, leather sandals and slaves.

764 Top craftsmen made fine goods for sale. Cities were home to many expert craftsmen. They ran small workshops next to their homes, or worked as slaves in factories owned by rich businessmen. Greek craftworkers were famous for producing fine pottery, stone-carvings, weapons, armour and jewellery.

765 Coins displayed city wealth and pride. They were invented in the Near East around 600 BC. Their use soon spread to Greece, and each city-state issued its own designs, stamped out of real silver. Coins were often decorated with images of gods and goddesses, heroes, monsters and favourite local animals.

▶ The design on the top coin shows the head of Alexander the Great. The other is decorated with an owl, the symbol of Athens' guardian goddess, Athena.

766 Cities were defended by strong stone walls. City-states were proud, independent and quarrelsome. They were often at war with their rivals, and were also in constant danger of attack from neighbouring nations, especially Persia (now Iran). To protect their homes, temples, workshops, market-places and harbours, citizens built strong wooden gates and high stone walls.

◀▲ The walls and gates guarding the city of Mycenae were made of huge stone slabs. The gate had a huge sculpture of two lions above it.

▶ Many Greek ships were wrecked together with their cargoes. Some have survived on the seabed for over 2000 years and are studied by divers today.

QUIZ

1. What was a city-state?
2. What was the centre of many cities?
3. What were coins made of?
4. How did the Greeks defend their cities?

Answers:
1. A city and the land around it
2. The agora (market-place) 3. Real silver 4. With strong wooden gates and high stone walls

Mighty Athens

767 **Athens was the greatest city in Greece.** Between 510–431 BC, it was the leading Greek city-state. Athens owned some of the best farmland, a port with a fine harbour, fabulous silver mines and a well-trained citizen army. All these made it rich, strong and confident.

▶ A steep winding road leads up to the Parthenon temple from the city far below. On festival days, processions of citizens lead prize animals along it to sacrifice to the goddess Athena.

768 **The Acropolis ('high city') was a holy hill and ancient fortress that overlooked Athens.** Many fine buildings stood there, including the magnificent Parthenon temple. Built between 447 BC and 432 BC, it housed a 15-metre-high gold and marble statue of Athena, the city's guardian goddess.

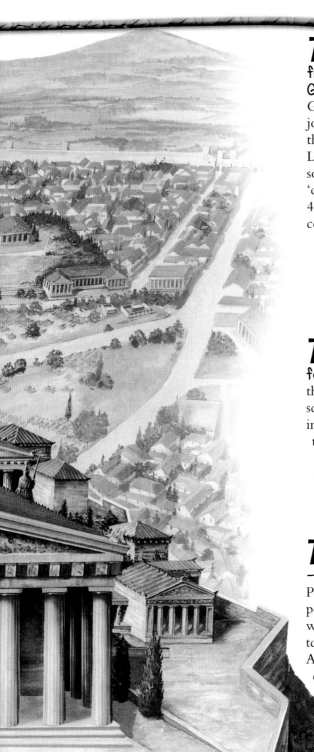

769 In 490 and 480 BC, armies from Persia (now Iran) invaded Greece. They were defeated, but Greek city-states felt threatened. They joined together in a League against the Persians. Athens took charge of the League, built a splendid navy and sent soldiers and government officials to 'advise' other city-states. By around 454 BC, Athens had taken control of most of Greece.

770 Athenian city leaders paid for fine works of art. They invited the best artists, architects, sculptors, scientists and scholars to live and work in their city, and gave money to build temples, monuments and public buildings. They vowed to make their city 'an education to Greece'.

771 Athenians are famous today – after more than 2000 years. Pericles was a great general and political leader. Socrates and Plato were philosophers and teachers who taught how to think and question. Aristotle was a scientist who pioneered a new way of studying by carefully observing and recording evidence.

Family life

772 Families were very important. A person's wealth, rank and occupation all depended on their family circumstances, as did the part they played in community life. Some families were very active in politics and had powerful friends – and enemies.

773 Fathers were the heads of families. They had power over everyone in their households – wives, children and slaves. However, families also worked as a team to find food, make a safe, comfortable home and train their children in all the skills they would need in adult life.

Bedrooms were upstairs

Pottery tiles

Mud-brick walls covered with plaster

Slaves cooked in the kitchen

Prayers were said around the altar each morning

774 All Greek parents longed for a son. Boys passed on the family name to the next generation and they could protect family property and run businesses or farms. However, girls had to be fed and housed at the family's expense, before they left to get married.

▲ Greek houses were designed to provide security and privacy. They had high, windowless outer walls and a hidden inner courtyard, which only the inhabitants and trusted visitors could see.

775 **Most girls married very young, aged around 13 years.** Their husbands, who were several years older, were chosen by their fathers for political or business reasons. A marriage linked two familes together. Romantic love was not important in marriage – the Greeks thought it was dangerous!

▼ Weddings took place at dusk. The bride was driven to the bridegroom's family home, accompanied by guests carrying flaming wooden torches.

776 **Women did not have the same rights as men.** Many women had strong opinions about city and community life. A few were also well-educated and interested in new ideas. However, according to the law, women could not vote, make a public speech or take any part in politics.

777 **Funerals were important family occasions.** Wives and daughters spent most of their lives at home. However, they were allowed to attend family funerals. All family members said prayers together and made offerings to the gods in memory of the dead person.

Clothes and fashion

778 Greek clothes were just draped around the body. They were loose and flowing, for comfort in the hot summer months. For extra warmth in winter, both men and women draped a thick woolly himation (cloak) over their shoulders.

779 Each piece of cloth used to make a garment was specially made. It had to be the right length and width to fit the wearer. All cloth was handwoven, usually by women in their homes. Cool, smooth linen was the favourite cloth for summer. In winter, Greeks preferred cosy wool. Very rich people wore fine clothes of silk imported from India.

▶ Men's clothing was designed for action. Young men wore short tunics so they could work – and fight – easily. Older men's robes were longer.

◀ Women's clothing was modest and draped the body from top to toe. Respectable women covered their heads and faces with a veil when they went outside the house.

MAKE A GREEK CHITON

You will need:
length of cloth twice as wide as your outstretched arms and half your height
safety pins   belt or length of cord

1. Fold the cloth in half.
2. Fasten two edges of the cloth together with safety pins, leaving a gap of about 30 cm in the middle.
3. Pull the cloth over your head so that the safety pins sit on your shoulders.
4. Fasten the belt or cord around your waist. Pull some of the cloth over the belt so that the cloth is level with your knees.

780 Women – and men – took care of their skin. To keep their skin smooth and supple, men and women rubbed themselves all over with olive oil. Rich women also used sunshades or face powder to achieve a fashionably pale complexion. They did not want to look sun-tanned – that was for farm workers, slaves – and men!

Before 500 BC

500–300 BC

After 300 BC

▲ Before 500 BC, long, natural hairstyles were popular. Between 500–300 BC, women tied their hair up and held it in place with ribbons or scarves. After 300 BC, curled styles and jewelled hair ornaments were popular and men shaved off their beards.

781 Curls were very fashionable. Women grew their hair long and tied it up with ribbons or headbands, leaving long curls trailing over their shoulders. Men, except for Spartan warriors, had short curly hair. Male and female slaves had their hair cropped very short – this was a shameful sign.

782 The Greeks liked to look good and admired fit, slim, healthy bodies. Women were praised for their grace and beauty. Young men were admired for their strong figures, and often went without clothes when training for war or taking part in sports competitions. Top athletes became celebrities, and were asked by artists to pose for them as models.

783 Sponges, showers and swimming helped the Greeks keep clean. Most houses did not have piped water. So people washed themselves by standing under waterfalls, swimming in streams or squeezing a big sponge full of water over their heads, like a shower.

◀ Athletes and their trainer (left) pictured on a Greek vase.

Gods and goddesses

784 To the Greeks, the world was full of dangers and disasters that they could not understand or control. There were also many good things, such as love, joy, music and beauty, that were wonderful but mysterious. The Greeks thought of all these unknown forces as gods and goddesses who shaped human life and ruled the world.

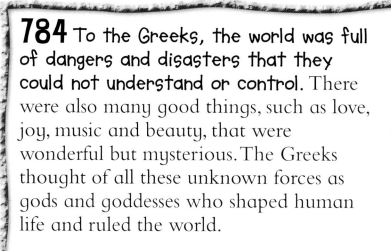

▶ This statue of the goddess Aphrodite was carved from white marble — a very smooth, delicate stone. It was designed to portray the goddess' perfect beauty. Sadly, it has been badly damaged over the centuries.

▶ Poseidon was god of the sea and storms. He also sent terrifying earthquakes to punish people — or cities — that offended him.

785 Gods and goddesses were pictured as superhuman creatures. They were strong and very beautiful. However, like humans, gods and goddesses also had weaknesses. Aphrodite was thoughtless, Hera was jealous, Apollo and his sister Artemis were cruel, and Ares was bad-tempered.

▲ Odysseus and his shipmates were surrounded by the Sirens — beautiful half-women, half-bird monsters. They sang sweet songs, calling sailors towards dangerous rocks where their ships were wrecked.

786 The Greeks believed in magic spirits and monsters. These included Gorgons who turned men to stone, and Sirens – bird-women whose song lured sailors to their doom. They also believed in witchcraft and curses and tried to fight against them. People painted magic eyes on the prows of their ships to keep a look-out for evil.

787 Individuals were often anxious to see what the future would bring. They believed that oracles (holy messengers) could see the future. The most famous oracles were at Delphi, where a drugged priestess answered questions, and at Dodona, where the leaves of sacred trees whispered words from the gods.

▶ Herakles was a hero – a man who became a god. He performed amazing feats of strength and fought against many monsters. This statue shows him killing a centaur, half-man, half-horse.

788 Poets and dramatists retold myths and legends about the gods. Some stories were explanations of natural events – thunder was the god Zeus shaking his fist in anger. Others explored bad thoughts and feelings shared by gods and humans, such as greed and disloyalty.

325

War on land and sea

789 As teenagers, all Greek male citizens were trained to fight. They had to be ready to defend their city whenever danger threatened. City-states also employed men as bodyguards and mercenary troops with special skills.

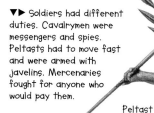

▼▶ Soldiers had different duties. Cavalrymen were messengers and spies. Peltasts had to move fast and were armed with javelins. Mercenaries fought for anyone who would pay them.

Peltast

Cavalry

Hoplite

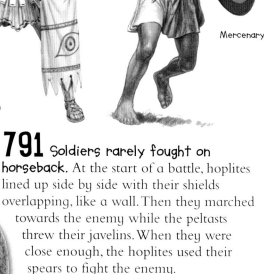

Mercenary

790 Each soldier paid for his own weapons and armour. Most soldiers were hoplites (soldiers who fought on foot). Their most important weapons were swords and spears. Poor men could not afford swords or armour. Their only weapons were slings for shooting stones and simple wooden spears.

791 Soldiers rarely fought on horseback. At the start of a battle, hoplites lined up side by side with their shields overlapping, like a wall. Then they marched towards the enemy while the peltasts threw their javelins. When they were close enough, the hoplites used their spears to fight the enemy.

◀ A Corinthian-style helmet. Soldiers tried to protect themselves from injury with bronze helmets, breastplates, greaves (shin guards) and round wooden shields.

I DON'T BELIEVE IT!

Ancient Greek soldiers rarely rode horses — because stirrups had not yet been invented. Without stirrups to support him, a soldier on horseback who hurled a spear or stabbed with a sword was likely to fall off backwards!

▼ Greek ships were made of wood. If they were holed below the waterline they sank very quickly.

792 City-states paid for fleets of fast, fearsome wooden warships, called triremes. Each ship had a crew of about 170 oarsmen who sat in three sets of seats, one above the other. They rowed the ship as fast as they could towards enemy vessels, hoping that the sharp, pointed ram at its prow would smash or sink them. The most famous naval battle in Greece was fought at Salamis, near Athens, in 480 BC, when the Greeks defeated the Persians.

Hoplites and phalanxes

793 **Hoplites were armoured infantry.** From about 700 BC Greek infantry (foot soldiers) were equipped with a shield, helmet, spear and sword. They were called 'hoplites' ('armoured men'). Each hoplite used his own weapons and armour.

794 **Hoplites fought in formations called phalanxes.** When going into battle, hoplites stood shoulder to shoulder so that their shields overlapped, and pointed their spears forwards over the shields. A phalanx was made up of six or more ranks of hoplites, one behind the other.

795 **A Greek who lost his shield was a coward.** The shield carried by hoplites was over one metre across and made of wood and bronze. It was very heavy, and anyone trying to run away from an enemy would throw it away, so men who lost their shields in battle were often accused of cowardice.

▶ The success of Greek soldiers in battle depended on them keeping tightly in formation so that enemy soldiers could not get past the line of shields.

I DON'T BELIEVE IT!

Spartan hoplites were so tough that they reckoned they could win any battle, even if they were outnumbered by as many as five to one!

796 Greek spears had a 'lizard stabber'. Hoplite spears had a bronze spike at the bottom end. This was used to stick the spear upright into the ground and was called a 'sauroter', meaning 'lizard stabber'.

797 The best helmets were made from a single sheet of metal. Skilled metalworkers in the Greek city of Corinth invented a way to make a helmet by beating a single sheet of bronze into shape. This produced a helmet that was much stronger than one made of several pieces of metal. The helmets were called 'Corinthian'.

Temples and festivals

798 **In Greece and the lands where the Greeks settled, we can still see the remains of huge, beautiful temples.** They were built as holy homes for gods and goddesses. Each city-state had its own guardian god and many temples housed a huge, lifelike statue of him or her. People hoped that the god's spirit might visit them and live in the statue for a while.

▶ This gigantic statue of the goddess Athena was 15 metres high and was made of gold and ivory. It stood inside her finest temple, the Parthenon in Athens. In her right hand, Athena holds Nike, the goddess of victory.

799 As well as visiting a temple, people hoped – or feared – that they might meet a god or goddess in a forest or on a mountain top. It was thought that all the gods met at Mount Olympus to feast, love, quarrel and make plans. Another high peak, Mount Parnassus, was sacred to the Muses – nine graceful goddesses who guided the arts, such as music and drama.

▲ The summit of the tallest mountain in Greece, Mount Olympus (1951 metres), was often hidden in clouds. It was remote, dangerous and mysterious – a suitable home for the mighty gods.

▼ The first temples were made of wood and shaped like ordinary houses. By around AD 600, temples were built of stone.

c. 800 BC tree trunks hold up the roof. Small inner room.

800 People offered prayers and sacrifices (gifts) to their gods and goddesses. Gifts might be just a few drops of wine or a valuable live animal. The meat of the sacrifice was cooked and shared among the worshippers and the bones and skin were burned on the altar. People thought that smoke carried their prayers up to the gods.

c. 600 BC tree trunks replaced by stone columns. More rooms inside.

801 City–states held festivals to honour their guardian gods. There would be a procession towards the city's main temple or to a shrine (holy place). At temples, crowds watched priests and priestesses making special sacrifices. At shrines, citizens might take part in secret rituals. Afterwards there could be music and drama or sports contests.

c. 440 BC temples are huge, with rows of columns and carved decorations.

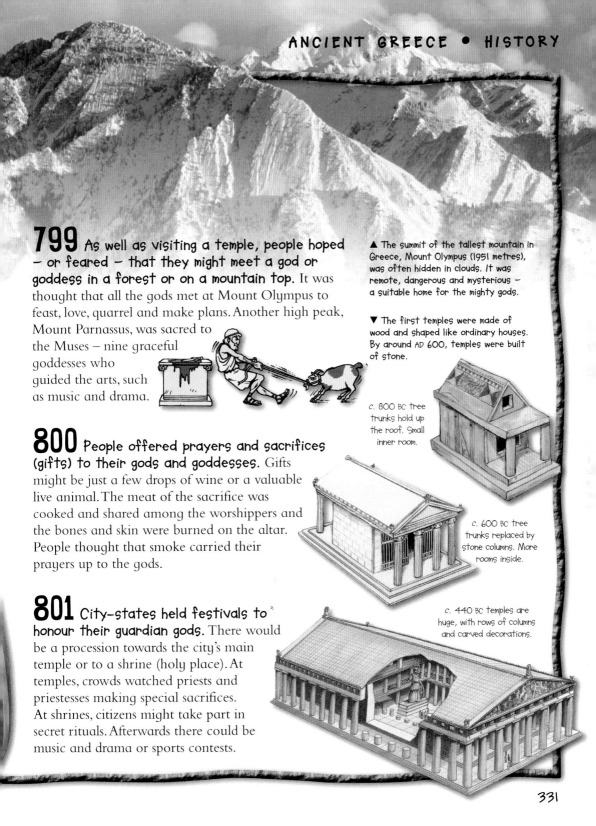

Olympic Games

802 **The Olympic Games began as a festival to honour Zeus.** Over the centuries, it grew into the greatest sports event in the Greek world. A huge festival complex was built at Olympia with a temple, sports tracks, seats for 40,000 spectators, a campsite and rooms for visitors and a field full of stalls selling food and drink.

▶ Victory! The Greeks believed that winners were chosen by the gods. The first known Olympic Games was held in 776 BC, though the festival may have begun years earlier.

803 Every four years athletes travelled from all over Greece to take part in the Olympic Games. They had to obey strict rules – respect for Zeus, no fights among competitors and no weapons anywhere near the sports tracks. In return they claimed protection – the holy Olympic Peace. Anyone who attacked them on their journeys was severely punished.

QUIZ

1. When were the first Olympic Games held?
2. Could women take part in the Olympic Games?
3. What did winning athletes wear on their heads?

Answers:
1. 776 BC, though the festival may have begun years earlier 2. No. There was a separate women's games held 3. Crowns of holy laurel leaves

804 The most popular events were running, long jump, wrestling and boxing. Spectators might also watch chariot races, athletes throwing the discus and javelin or weightlifting contests. The most prestigious event was the 200-metre sprint. There was also a dangerous fighting contest called *pankration* (total power).

▲ Boxers did not wear gloves. Instead they wrapped their hands in bandages.

805 Many events featured weapons or skills that were needed in war. One of the most gruelling competitions was a race wearing heavy battle armour. The main Olympic Games were for men only – women could not take part. There was a separate women's games held at Olympia on different years from the men's competitions.

▲ Throwing the discus was a test of strength and balance. It was also useful training for war.

▲ Swimmer Michael Phelps sets a new world record at the Beijing Olympics, 2008. The modern Olympics is modelled on the ancient games and since 1896 has remained the world's greatest sports festival.

806 Athletes who won Olympic contests were honoured as heroes. They were crowned with wreaths of holy laurel leaves and given valuable prizes of olive oil, fine clothes and pottery. Poets composed songs in their praise and their home city-states often rewarded them with free food and lodgings for life!

▶ A crown of laurel leaves was given to winning athletes as a sign of their god-like strength and speed.

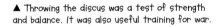

Plays and poems

807 Greek drama originated at religious festivals. In the earliest rituals, priests and priestesses sometimes played the part of gods or goddesses. They acted out stories told about them or famous local heroes. Over the years, these ancient rituals changed into a new art form – drama.

808 Drama became so popular that many city-states built splendid new open-air theatres. Greek theatres were built in a half-circle shape with tiers (raised rows) of seats looking down over an open space for performers. Most seats were filled by men – women were banned from many plays.

▶ The theatre at Epidaurus, in southern Greece, is one of the largest built by the ancient Greeks. It had seats for over 10,000 spectators.

809
All the parts in a play were performed by men. They wore masks, wigs and elaborate costumes to look like women or magic spirits and monsters. Some theatres had ladders and cranes so that actors playing gods could appear to fly or sit among the clouds.

810
In some city-states, especially Athens, drama remained an important part of several religious festivals. Writers competed for prizes for the best new plays. They wrote serious plays called tragedies and lively comedies. Some plays lasted all day long. Others had extra 'satyr plays' added on. These were short, funny pieces.

▶ Actors wore masks to show which character they were playing. Bright-coloured masks were for cheerful characters and dark-coloured masks were more gloomy. Some masks were double-sided so that the actors could change parts quickly.

811
Plays were written like poetry. The main actors were always accompanied by singers and dancers. Poems were also recited to music. Tunes were sad for tragic poems or rousing for those about war. Poets performed at men's dinner parties and in rich families' homes. Public storytellers entertained crowds by singing poems in the streets.

Barbarian – or monster – with wild, shaggy hair

Angry young man

Huge, funnel-shaped mouths helped the actors' words reach the audience

Masks with beards and bald heads were for actors playing old men

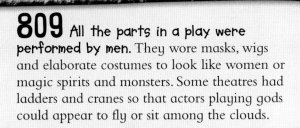

335

The centre of an empire

812 Over a million people lived in Rome.
By around AD 300, Rome was the largest
city in the world. There were citizens
who could vote and serve in the army,
and there were non-citizens who did not
have these rights. The government was
run by nobles and knights who were
usually very rich. Plebeians, or
ordinary people, were usually
fairly poor but were citizens
of Rome. Slaves were not
citizens. They were not free
to leave their owners and
had no rights.

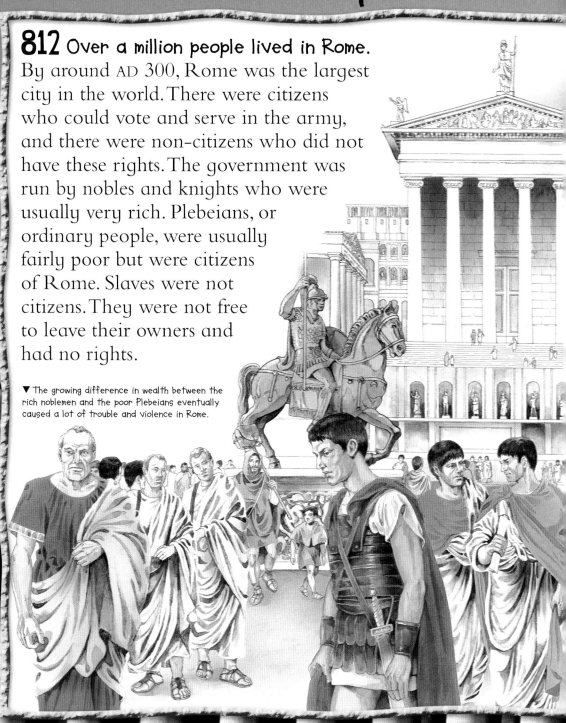

▼ The growing difference in wealth between the
rich noblemen and the poor Plebeians eventually
caused a lot of trouble and violence in Rome.

813 The Forum was the government district in the centre of Rome. People went there to meet their friends and business colleagues, discuss politics, and to listen to famous orators who made speeches in the open air. The Forum was mainly a market-place, surrounded by government buildings such as offices and law-courts.

814 The Romans were great water engineers. They designed aqueducts, raised channels to carry water from streams in faraway hills and mountains to the city. The richest Roman homes were supplied with constant running water carried in lead pipes. Ordinary people had to drink from public fountains.

Aqueduct

816 Rome relied on its drains. The city was so crowded that good drains were essential. Otherwise, the citizens could have caught diseases from sewage and died. The largest sewer, called the 'cloaca maxima', was so high and so wide that a horse and cart could drive through it.

815 Rome was a well-protected city. It was surrounded by 50 kilometres of strong stone walls to keep out attackers. All visitors had to enter the city through one of its 37 gates, which were guarded by soldiers and watchmen.

Roman soldier

I DON'T BELIEVE IT!
Roman engineers also designed public lavatories. These lavatories were convenient, but not private. Users sat on rows of seats, side by side!

City life

817 **The Romans built the world's first high-rise apartments.** Most of the people who lived in Ostia, a busy port close to Rome, had jobs connected with trade, such as shipbuilders and money-changers. They lived in blocks of flats known as 'insulae'. A typical block was three or four storeys high, with up to a hundred small, dirty, crowded rooms.

818 **Rich Romans had more than one home.** Rome was stuffy, dirty and smelly, especially in summer. Wealthy Roman families liked to get away from the city to cleaner, more peaceful surroundings. They purchased a house (a 'villa urbana') just outside the city, or a big house surrounded by farmland (a 'villa rustica') in the countryside far away from Rome.

▲ On the ground floor of an *insula* were shops, and on the first floor were flats and apartments for families. The poorest families lived in single rooms on the top floor.

▼ Pools were also used to collect and store rainwater for cooking or washing.

819 Many Roman homes had a pool, but it was not used for swimming! Pools were built for decoration, in the central courtyards of large Roman homes. They were surrounded by plants and statues. Some pools had a fountain; others had mosaics – pictures made of tiny coloured stones or squares of glass – covering the floor.

MAKE A PAPER MOSAIC

You will need:
large sheet of paper   scissors   pencil   glue
scraps of coloured and textured paper

Draw the outlines of your design on a large sheet of paper. Plan which colours to use for different parts of the mosaic.

Cut the paper scraps into small squares, all roughly the same size. The simplest way to do this is to cut strips, then snip the strips into squares.

Stick the paper squares onto the large sheet of paper following the outlines of your design.

820 **Fortunate families had hot feet.** Homes belonging to wealthy families had underfloor central heating. Blasts of hot air, warmed by a wood-burning furnace, circulated in channels built beneath the floor. The furnace was kept burning by slaves who chopped wood and stoked the fire.

▼ For the rich, a heating system made cold winters much more bearable.

Space in walls for hot air to circulate

Fire for heating

Space under the floor for hot air

821 **Rome had its own fire brigade.** The 7000 firemen were freed slaves, who had all been specially trained. Ordinary families could not afford central heating, so they warmed their rooms with fires in big clay pots which often set the house alight.

Roman style

822 **Most Roman clothes were made without sewing.** Roman men and women wore loose-fitting robes, made of long strips of cloth. They were draped round the body, and held in place by pins, brooches or belts. Most women wore several layers – a thin shift, a 'tunica', a long, sleeveless dress called a 'stola', and a thick cloak called a 'palla'. Men wore a knee-length tunic, a 'colobium', with a semi-circular cloak called a 'toga' over the top.

Gold brooch

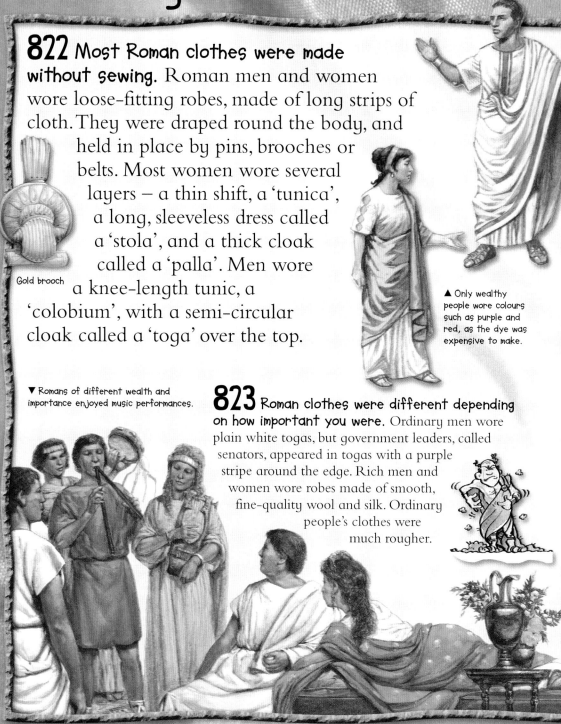

▲ Only wealthy people wore colours such as purple and red, as the dye was expensive to make.

▼ Romans of different wealth and importance enjoyed music performances.

823 **Roman clothes were different depending on how important you were.** Ordinary men wore plain white togas, but government leaders, called senators, appeared in togas with a purple stripe around the edge. Rich men and women wore robes made of smooth, fine-quality wool and silk. Ordinary people's clothes were much rougher.

824 Clothes told the world who you were. People from many different cultures and races lived in lands ruled by the Romans. They wore many different styles of clothes. For example, men from Egypt wore wigs and short linen kilts. Celtic women from northern Europe wore long, woollen shawls, woven in brightly coloured checks. Celtic men wore trousers.

▼ Sandals known as 'crepidae' were worn by men and women all year round.

▼ These Roman sandals have metal studs in the soles to make sure that they don't wear down too quickly.

TOGA TIME!

Ask an adult for a blanket or sheet. White is best, like the Romans.

Drape the sheet over your left shoulder. Now pass the rest behind your back.

Pull the sheet across your front, so that you're wrapped up in it.

Finally, drape the last end over your right hand and there you have it, a Roman toga!

825 Roman boots were made for walking! Roman soldiers and travellers wore lace-up boots with thick leather soles studded with iron nails. Other Roman footwear included 'socci', loose-fitting slippers to wear indoors. Farmers wore shoes made of a single piece of ox-hide wrapped round the foot, called 'carbatinae'. There were also 'crepidae', comfortable lace-up sandals with open toes.

Bath time

826 The Romans went to the public baths in order to relax. These huge buildings were more than a place to get clean. They were also fitness centres and places to meet friends. Visitors could take part in sports, such as wrestling, do exercises, have a massage or a haircut. They could buy scented oils and perfumes, read a book, eat a snack or admire works of art in the baths' own sculpture gallery.

◄ There were public baths in most districts of Rome. They were built by Roman emperors or rich families as a gift to the citizens. The finest were the baths of Caracalla (opened around AD 215), which had room for 1600 bathers at a time.

▶ Roman bathing involved five different stages that took place in separate areas of the baths.

827 Men and women could not bathe together. Women usually went to the baths in the mornings, while most men were at work. Men went to the baths in the afternoons.

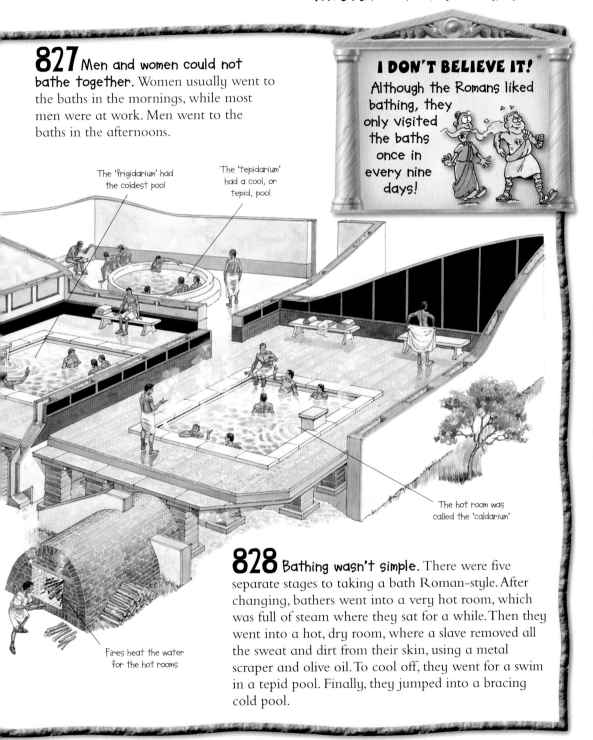

I DON'T BELIEVE IT!
Although the Romans liked bathing, they only visited the baths once in every nine days!

The 'frigidarium' had the coldest pool

The 'tepidarium' had a cool, or tepid, pool

The hot room was called the 'caldarium'

Fires heat the water for the hot rooms

828 Bathing wasn't simple. There were five separate stages to taking a bath Roman-style. After changing, bathers went into a very hot room, which was full of steam where they sat for a while. Then they went into a hot, dry room, where a slave removed all the sweat and dirt from their skin, using a metal scraper and olive oil. To cool off, they went for a swim in a tepid pool. Finally, they jumped into a bracing cold pool.

Ruling Rome

829 **Rome used to be ruled by kings.** According to legend, the first king was Romulus, who came to power in 753 BC. Six more kings ruled after him, but they were unjust and cruel. The last king, Tarquin the Proud, was overthrown in 509 BC. After that, Rome became a republic, a state without a king. Every year the people chose two senior lawyers called consuls to head the government. Many other officials were elected, or chosen by the people, too. The republic lasted for over 400 years.

▼ Senators were men from leading citizen families who had served the Roman republic as judges or state officials. They made new laws and discussed government plans.

▲ Roman coin showing Emperor Constantine.

830 **In 47 BC a successful general called Julius Caesar declared himself dictator.** This meant that he wanted to rule on his own for life. Many people feared that he was trying to end the republic, and rule like the old kings. Caesar was murdered in 44 BC by a group of his political enemies. After this, there were many years of civil war.

Julius Caesar

831 **In 27 BC an army general called Octavian seized power in Rome.** He declared himself 'First Citizen', and said he would bring back peace and good government to Rome. He ended the civil war, and introduced many strong new laws. But he also changed the Roman government forever. He took a new name, 'Augustus', and became the first emperor of Rome.

Octavian

◀ Roman courts were busy places. There was a public gallery where people could watch cases. People who were accused of crime and refused to go to court could be made to attend by force. Lawyers called advocatus spoke on their behalf.

832 The Romans were proud of their laws. Everyone in Rome, from the emperor to the poorest beggar, was expected to obey the law. The first rules of the Roman legal system were recorded in 450 BC in a document called the Twelve Tables. Roman laws were strict but fair. Everyone was considered innocent until they had been proved guilty in an open trial. The Roman system forms the basis of many legal systems today.

I DON'T BELIEVE IT!
Some Roman emperors were mad and dangerous. Emperor Nero was said to have laughed and played music while watching a terrible fire that destroyed a large part of Rome.

In the army

833 Being a soldier was a good career, if you did not get killed! Roman soldiers were well paid and well cared for. The empire needed troops to defend its land against enemy attack. A man who fought in the Roman army received a thorough training in battle skills. If he showed promise, he might be promoted and receive extra pay. When he retired after 20 or 25 years of service, he was given money or land to help him start a business.

▲ Roman troops defended the empire from attack, they were well paid but it was a dangerous job.

I DON'T BELIEVE IT!

Roman soldiers guarding the cold northern frontiers of Britain kept warm by wearing short woollen trousers, such as underpants, beneath their tunics!

834 The Roman army contained citizens and 'helpers'. Roman citizens joined the regular army, which was organized into legions of around 5000 men. Men who were not citizens could also fight for Rome. They were known as auxiliaries, or helpers, and were organized in special legions of their own.

836 **The army advanced 30 kilometres every day.** When they were hurrying to put down a rebellion, or moving from fort to fort, Roman soldiers travelled quickly, on foot. Troops marched along straight, well-made army roads. On the march, each soldier had to carry a heavy pack. It contained weapons, armour, tools for building a camp, cooking pots, dried food and spare clothes.

837 **Soldiers worshipped their own special god.** At forts and army camps, Roman soldiers built temples where they honoured Mithras, their own god. They believed he protected them, and gave them life after death.

835 **Soldiers needed many skills.** In enemy territory, soldiers had to find or make everything they needed to survive. When they first arrived they built camps of tents, but soon afterwards they built permanent forts defended by strong walls. Each legion contained men with a wide range of skills, such as cooks, builders, carpenters, doctors, blacksmiths and engineers – but they all had to fight!

Barracks, where soldiers slept

Protective wall

Gate

Exercise yard

Roman legions

▲ A Roman legion marches out of a border fortress supervised by the legate, who commands the legion.

838 **Armoured infantry formed legions.** The main fighting formation of the Roman army was the legion. Most were equipped with body armour, a helmet, a large rectangular shield, a sword and a throwing spear.

839 Roman armour was made of metal strips. At the height of the Roman Empire, around AD 50 to AD 250, legionaries wore armour called *lorica segmentata*. It was made up of strips of metal that were bent to fit the body, and held together by straps and buckles.

▶ The armour of a legionary was made up of several pieces, each of which could be replaced if it was damaged.

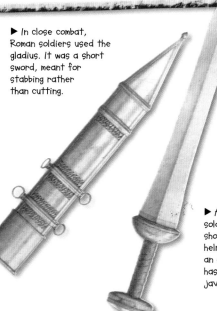

▶ In close combat, Roman soldiers used the gladius. It was a short sword, meant for stabbing rather than cutting.

840 Roman swords were copied from the Spanish. After 200 BC, Roman soldiers carried swords with straight blades and sharp points. They were copied from swords used by Spanish soldiers who had defeated the Romans in battle.

▶ An auxiliary soldier wearing a short mail tunic and helmet, and carrying an oval shield. He has a gladius and javelin as weapons.

841 Roman auxiliaries wore cheaper armour. Every Roman legion included soldiers called auxiliaries (soldiers from places other than Rome). These units had to provide their own armour, often wearing tunics covered with mail or scale armour, which was made up of lots of small metal plates.

842 Roman shields could form a 'tortoise'. One tactic used by the Romans was called the 'testudo', or 'tortoise'. Soldiers formed short lines close together, holding their shields so they interlocked on all sides and overhead, just like the shell of a tortoise. In this formation they could advance on an enemy, safe from spears or arrows.

The fall of Rome

843 **Roman infantry later abandoned armour.** By around AD 350, Roman legions preferred to fight by moving quickly around the battlefield. They stopped wearing heavy armour and relied upon large shields and metal helmets for protection.

844 **Later Roman armies also used mercenary archers.** Roman commanders found that archers were useful for attacking barbarian tribesmen. Few Romans were skilled at archery, so the Romans hired soldiers from other countries (mercenaries) to fight as archers in the Roman army.

845 **Roman shields were brightly coloured.** Each unit in the late Roman army had its own design of shield. Some were decorated with pictures of eagles, scorpions or dolphins, while others had lightning bolts or spirals.

◀ Late Roman shields were brightly decorated with impressive designs, but were also very important as a form of defence in battle.

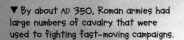

▼ By about AD 350, Roman armies had large numbers of cavalry that were used to fighting fast-moving campaigns.

846 The eagle was a sacred standard. Each Roman legion had an eagle standard, the *aquila* – a bronze eagle covered in gold leaf mounted on top of a pole about 3 metres long. The *aquila* was thought to be sacred, and it was a great humiliation if it was captured by the enemy.

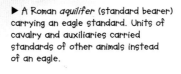

▶ A Roman *aquilifer* (standard bearer) carrying an eagle standard. Units of cavalry and auxiliaries carried standards of other animals instead of an eagle.

847 Later Roman cavalry had enormous shields. One later group of Roman mounted soldiers was the *scutati*. These men wore coats of mail, and carried enormous shields with which they were expected to defend themselves and their horses. They would gallop towards the enemy army, throw javelins and then ride away before the enemy could strike back.

I DON'T BELIEVE IT!

Alaric the Goth and his men looted Rome in AD 410. Alaric was famously known to carry a sword with a handle made of solid gold.

The first gladiators

848 **The first gladiators were not from Rome.** The Romans did not invent the idea of gladiators. The idea of men fighting in an arena probably came to Rome from the region of Etruria. But the first proper gladiators probably came from Campania, an area of Italy south of Rome.

▲ The first gladiators probably came from Campania, in the south, and more fought in this area than in Rome.

849 **The first Roman gladiators fought in 264 BC.** Six slaves were set to fight each other with swords, but they were not allowed to wear any armour. The fights did not last for long before one of the slaves in each pair was killed.

▶ The gladius was the standard weapon used by early gladiators. It was kept in a sheath called a scabbard.

850 The first gladiatorial fights were always part of a funeral. The name for a gladiatorial show, a munus, means a duty owed to the dead. The first fights were held at the funerals of politicians and noblemen, who ordered the games in their wills.

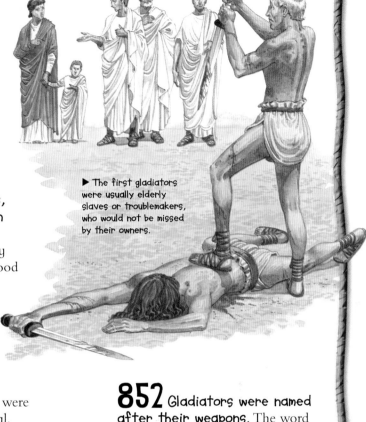

▶ The first gladiators were usually elderly slaves or troublemakers, who would not be missed by their owners.

851 In early funeral games, food was more important than gladiators. The Romans used funerals to show off how wealthy and important they were. Free food and drink were laid out at the funeral for any Roman citizen who wanted to come along. Gifts of money, jewellery and clothing were also handed out. The family of the person being buried would wear their finest clothes. The first gladiator fights were just one part of the whole funeral.

Scabbard

Gladius

852 Gladiators were named after their weapons. The word gladiator means 'a man who uses a gladius'. The gladius was a type of short, stabbing sword that was used by Roman soldiers. It was about 40 centimetres long and had a very sharp point. It was generally used for slashing, not for cutting. Not all gladiators used the gladius, but the name was used for all fighters in the arena.

The mighty Colosseum

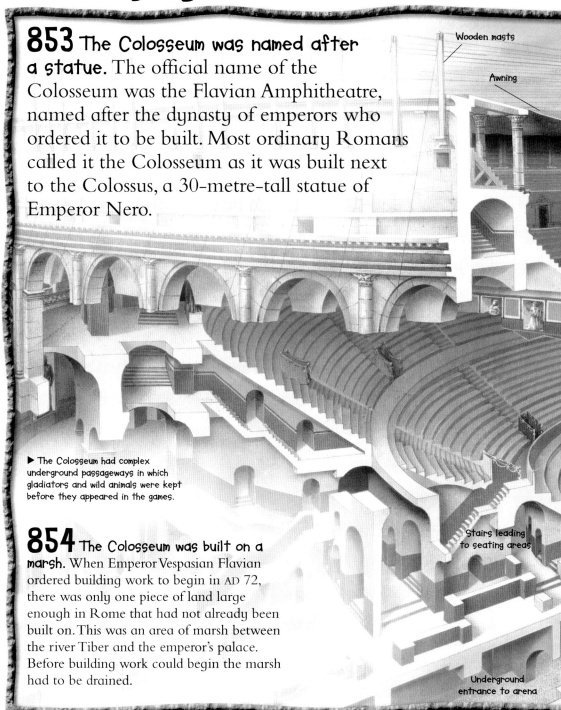

853 **The Colosseum was named after a statue.** The official name of the Colosseum was the Flavian Amphitheatre, named after the dynasty of emperors who ordered it to be built. Most ordinary Romans called it the Colosseum as it was built next to the Colossus, a 30-metre-tall statue of Emperor Nero.

Wooden masts

Awning

▶ The Colosseum had complex underground passageways in which gladiators and wild animals were kept before they appeared in the games.

Stairs leading to seating areas

854 **The Colosseum was built on a marsh.** When Emperor Vespasian Flavian ordered building work to begin in AD 72, there was only one piece of land large enough in Rome that had not already been built on. This was an area of marsh between the river Tiber and the emperor's palace. Before building work could begin the marsh had to be drained.

Underground entrance to arena

855 The Colosseum could seat 50,000 spectators. The huge seating area was divided into over 80 sections. Each section had a door and flight of steps that led to the outside of the Colosseum. The standing room at the top was reserved for slaves and may have held another 4000 people.

856 The Colosseum was probably the largest building in the world. The outer walls stood 46 metres tall and covered an area 194 metres long by 160 metres wide. The walls were covered in stone, but the structure was made of brick or concrete.

857 The first games in the Colosseum lasted 100 days. The Colosseum was finished in AD 80, during the reign of Emperor Titus. He wanted to show that he was the most generous man ever to live in Rome, so he organized gladiatorial games to last for 100 days. Thousands of gladiators and animals fought in these games.

Tiered seating

Trapdoors

Arena floor

Network of corridors and machinery beneath arena floor

The first castles

858 **The first castles in Europe were mostly built from wood on top of a hill.** Sometimes castle builders piled up soil to make the hill artificially. On top of the hill, called a motte, stood a wooden tower, or keep. This was the central part of the castle and the easiest part to defend.

▼ This is a motte and bailey castle. The Normans from France introduced this kind of castle in the 1000s, and it soon became popular across Europe.

◄ Castles and forts have been built all over the world since the earliest times. This is the fortified town of Great Zimbabwe, located in modern day Zimbabwe. The oldest part dates from the 700s.

► By the 1500s the Japanese were building strong, permanent castles of their own. Castles were often built with different layers to fire on the enemy from different heights.

859 At the bottom of the motte was a courtyard called a bailey. It was usually surrounded by a wooden fence. Castle builders dug a deep ditch, called a moat, all around the outside of the motte and bailey. They often filled the moat with water. Moats were designed to stop attackers reaching the castle walls.

◀ For extra protection, a wooden fence was often built around the top of the motte. The top of each wooden plank was shaped into a point to make it harder for the enemy to climb over.

I DON'T BELIEVE IT!
The builders of the early wooden castles covered the walls with wet leather – to stop them from burning down.

860 Wooden castles were not very strong – and they caught fire easily. From around 1100 onwards, people began to build castles in stone. A stone castle gave better protection against attack, fire and cold rainy weather.

▶ Sometimes an extra wall was built on the inside of the strong outer wall. Archers could stand on the inner wall and fire down onto the outer wall if it was captured.

Gatehouse

Inner defensive wall

Outer defensive wall

Keep

Turret

357

Who's who in the castle

861 A castle was the home of an important and powerful person, such as a king, a lord or a knight. The lord of the castle controlled the castle itself, as well as the lands and people around it. The lady of the castle was in charge of the day-to-day running of the castle. She controlled the kitchens and gave the servants their orders for feasts and banquets.

▶ Lord and lady of the manor

862 The constable was in charge of defending the castle. He was usually a fierce and ruthless man. He trained his soldiers to guard the castle properly and organized the rota of guards and watchmen. The constable was in charge of the whole castle when the lord was away.

863 Many servants lived and worked inside the castle, looking after the lord and his family. They cooked, cleaned, served at the table, worked as maids and servants and ran errands. A man called the steward was in charge of all the servants.

Servants   Steward   Cooks

864 Inside the castle walls were many workshops where goods were made and repaired. The castle blacksmith was kept busy making shoes for all the horses. The armourer made weapons and armour.

Blacksmith   Armourer

▶ The master of the horse had to look after the lord's horses.

865 Local villagers would shelter in the castle when their lands were under attack. They were not allowed to shelter inside the keep itself, so they stayed inside the bailey with their families and all their animals.

Early knights

866 **The first knights wore mail armour.** Around the year 1000, most body armour in Europe was made of mail. This was flexible to wear and could stop a sword blow with ease. Such armour was expensive to make so only richer men could afford to wear it.

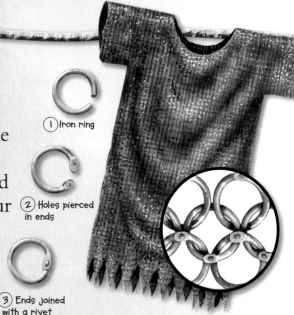

① Iron ring

② Holes pierced in ends

③ Ends joined with a rivet

▲ Mail armour was made by linking together hundreds of small iron rings. The rings could be linked in a number of different ways, just like knitting a jumper.

867 **Shields were decorated to identify their owners.** From about 1150, knights wore helmets that covered their faces for extra protection. Around the same time, they began to paint heraldic designs (coats of arms) on their shields so that they could recognize each other in battle.

868 **Early knights sometimes used leather armour.** Mail armour was effective, but heavy and expensive, so some knights wore armour made of boiled, hardened leather. This was lighter and easier to wear, and was still some defence against attack.

◄ A knight in about 1100. He wears a shirt and trousers made of mail and a helmet shaped from a sheet of steel. His shield is made of wood.

869 **Plate armour gave better protection than mail.** By about 1300, new types of arrows and swords had developed to pierce mail armour. This led to the development of plate armour, made of sheets of steel shaped to fit the body, which arrows and swords could not easily penetrate.

870 **The mace could smash armour to pieces.** The most effective of the crushing weapons developed to destroy plate armour, the mace had a big metal head on a long shaft. A blow from a mace crushed plate armour, breaking the bones of the person wearing it.

The armour around the stomach and groin had to be flexible enough to allow bending and twisting movements

The most complicated section of plate armour was the gauntlet that covered the hands. It might contain 30 pieces of metal

The legs and feet were protected by armour that covered the limbs entirely

▶ A suit of plate armour made in Europe in the early 14th century.

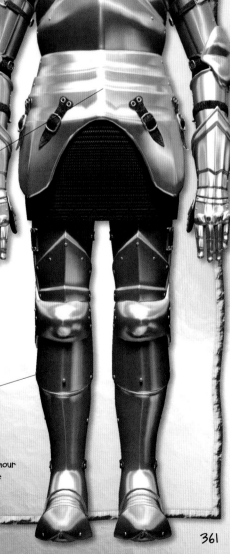

QUIZ

1. Why did knights paint coats of arms on their shields?
2. How was leather armour treated to make it tough?
3. Which was the most effective crushing weapon?

Answers:
1. So that they could recognize each other in battle 2. It was boiled 3. The mace

Later knights

871 **Armoured knights were the most important troops.** Knights had the best arms and armour and were the most experienced men in any army, so they were often put in command.

872 Knights sometimes fought on foot, instead of on horseback. English knights fought on foot after about 1300. This enabled them to hold a position more securely and co-operate more effectively with other soldiers.

▶ The bascinet helmet had a visor that could be lifted so the wearer could see and breathe.

I DON'T BELIEVE IT!

At the Battle of Agincourt in France in 1415, the English killed 10,000 Frenchmen, but only about 100 Englishmen lost their lives.

873 Horse armour made of metal and leather was introduced to protect horses. By about 1300, knights began to dress their horses in various sorts of armour. Horses without armour could be killed or injured by enemy arrows or spears, leaving the knight open to attack. Men with armoured horses were put in the front rank during battle.

▶ Horse armour was shaped to fit the horse's head and neck, then was left loose to dangle down over the legs.

874 The flail was a difficult weapon to use. It consisted of a big metal ball studded with spikes and attached to a chain on a handle. It could inflict terrible injuries, but also swing back unexpectedly, so only men who practised with it for hours each day could use it properly.

▲ The flail was often used by knights who fought on foot.

875 Each man had his place in battle. Before each battle, the commander would position his men to ensure that the abilities of each were put to best use. The men with the best armour were placed where the enemy was expected to attack, while archers were positioned on the flank (left or right side) where they could shoot across the battlefield. Lightly armoured men were held in the rear, ready to chase enemy soldiers if they began to retreat.

Colours and coats of arms

876 When a knight went into battle in full armour wearing a helmet with a visor, no one could recognize him. This problem was solved by putting a different set of coloured symbols on each knight's shield. These sets of symbols became known as coats of arms, and each family had its own personal design. No other family was allowed to use that design.

◀ Heraldry, the system of using coats of arms, became a very complex system of signs and symbols. Schools of heraldry were set up to sort out disputes over coats of arms.

877 Only certain colours and styles of design could be used to create a coat of arms. The colours allowed were red, blue, black, green, purple, silver and gold. The arms also indicated the wearer's position in his family. So, a second son showed a crescent symbol, and a seventh son displayed a rose.

878 On the battlefield, each nobleman had his own banner around which his knights and other soldiers could meet. The nobleman's colours and coat of arms were displayed on the banner. Banners decorated with coats of arms also made a colourful display at tournaments and parades.

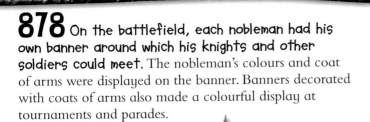

◀ The banner of a nobleman was a very important symbol during battle. If the person holding the banner was killed in battle, someone had to pick the banner up and raise it straight away.

879 Messengers called heralds carried messages between knights during battle. They had to be able to recognize each individual knight quickly. After coats of arms were introduced, the heralds became experts at identifying them. The system of using coats of arms became known as heraldry.

▲ After a battle, it was the sad job of a herald to walk around the battlefield and identify the dead by their coats of arms.

DESIGN YOUR OWN COAT OF ARMS

Would you like your own personal coat of arms? You can design one by following the basic rules of heraldry explained on these pages. You will need the seven paint colours listed opposite, a paintbrush, a fine-tipped black felt pen, a ruler and some thick white paper. Good luck!

Practice for battle

880 In a tournament, knights divided into two sides and fought each other as if in a proper battle. Tournaments were good practice for the real thing – war. The idea for these mock battles, called tourneys, probably started in France in the 12th century.

▼ Jousting knights charged at each other at top speed. Each one tried to knock his opponent off his horse with a blow from a long wooden lance.

▲ Edward I of England was a keen supporter of tournaments and jousts. He banned spectators from carrying weapons themselves because this caused too much trouble among the watching crowds.

881 Tournaments took place under strict rules. There were safe areas where knights could rest without being attacked by the other side. Knights were not meant to kill their opponents but they often did. Several kings became so angry at losing their best knights that all tournaments were banned unless the king had given his permission.

I DON'T BELIEVE IT!
Some knights cheated in jousts by wearing special armour that was fixed onto the horse's saddle!

884 Sometimes the knights carried on fighting on the ground with their swords. The problem was that this was as dangerous as a tourney!

882 Jousting was introduced because so many knights were being killed or wounded during tournaments. More than 60 knights were killed in a single tourney in Cologne, Germany. Jousting was a fight between two knights on horseback. Each knight tried to win by knocking the other off his horse. Knights were protected by armour, and their lances were not sharp.

885 A joust gave a knight the chance to prove himself in front of the woman he loved. Jousts were very social events watched by ladies of the court as well as ordinary people. Knights could show off their skills and bravery to impress the spectators.

883 A knight's code of chivalry did not allow him to win a tournament by cheating. It was better to lose with honour than to win in disgrace.

Under attack

886 An attacking enemy had to break through a castle's defences to get inside its walls. One method was to break down the castle gates with giant battering rams. Attackers and defenders also used siege engines to hurl boulders at each other.

887 A siege is when an enemy surrounds a castle and stops all supplies from reaching the people inside. The idea is to starve the castle occupants until they surrender or die.

888 A riskier way of trying to get inside a castle was to climb over the walls. Attackers either used ladders or moved wooden towers with men hidden inside them into position beside the walls.

889 Giant catapults were sometimes used to fire stones or burning pieces of wood inside the castle. The Romans were some of the first people to use catapults in warfare.

▶ Attackers could also dig a tunnel under a wall or a tower. They would then light a fire that burnt away the supports of the tunnel. The tunnel collapsed, and brought down the building above.

▲ This siege engine was called a trebuchet. It had a long wooden arm with a heavy weight at one end and a sling at the other. A heavy stone was placed inside the sling. As the weight dropped, the stone was hurled towards the castle walls, sometimes travelling as far as 300 metres.

I DON'T BELIEVE IT!
The ropes used to wind up siege catapults were made from plaits of human hair!

890 The enemy sometimes succeeded in tunnelling beneath the castle walls. They surprised the defenders when they appeared inside the castle itself.

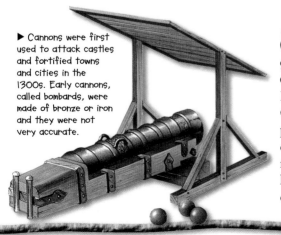

▶ Cannons were first used to attack castles and fortified towns and cities in the 1300s. Early cannons, called bombards, were made of bronze or iron and they were not very accurate.

891 The invention of cannons and gunpowder brought the building of castle strongholds almost to an end. It marked the end of warrior knights too. Castle walls could not stand up to the powerful cannonballs that exploded against them. Guns and cannons were now used on the battlefield, so armies no longer needed the services of brave armoured knights on horseback.

Defending a castle

892 When the enemy was spotted approaching a castle, its defenders first pulled up the castle drawbridge. They also lowered an iron grate, called a portcullis, to form an extra barrier behind the drawbridge.

893 The castle archers fired their arrows through narrow slits in the thick castle walls. They also fired through the gaps in the battlements.

▶ Soldiers could use a longbow while the enemy was still a long way away.

▶ Crossbows were far slower to aim and fire than longbows.

894 In the middle of the night, a raiding party might leave a besieged castle to surprise the enemy camped outside. The raiders would move along secret passages and climb out through hidden gates or doorways.

895 Defenders poured boiling-hot water onto the heads of the enemy as they tried to climb the castle walls. Quicklime was also poured over the enemy soldiers, making their skin burn.

▶ Water was poured onto the enemy's heads through holes in the stonework of the battlements.

QUIZ

1. What weapons did archers use?

2. What was pulled up when an enemy was spotted?

3. What was another name for the iron gate at a castle entrance?

4. Why were battlements so helpful in defending a castle?

Answers:
1. Crossbows and longbows 2. The castle drawbridge 3. Portcullis 4. They hid the defenders from view

896 Heavy stones and other missiles often rained down from the battlements onto the enemy below. Hidden from view by the high battlements, the defenders stood on wooden platforms to throw the missiles.

Index

Index

Index

Index

Index

Index

Acknowledgements

All artworks are from the Miles Kelly Artwork Bank

The publishers would like to thank the following sources for the use of their photographs:
(t = top, b = bottom, l = left, r = right, c = centre, bg = background)

Front cover Shutterstock (c) DM7, (tr) Benjamin Albiach Galan, (tl) Somchai Som (bl) TravelMediaProductions;
Spine Shutterstock (t) Lukas Gojda; **Back cover** Shutterstock (cr) ifong, (bl) George W. Bailey

Alamy
48(b) nagelestock.com; 54(bl) Prisma Bildagentur AG; 57(br) Avalon/World Pictures; 63(b) Minden Pictures; 70(br) Kevin Schafer;
71(tr) JTB MEDIA CREATION, Inc.; 72 Jeremy Horner; 86(bl) Mike Goldwater; 94–95(bg) MARKA; 317(br) Charles Stirling
(Diving); 334(bg) mauritius images GmbH

Diomedia
205(b) imageBROKER RM; 209(br) imageBROKER RM/Philip Perry, (bl) imageBROKER RM/Malcolm Schuyl

Dreamstime
104(b) Theo Gottwald; 105(r) Adam Gryko; 122(b) Alan Heartfield ; 133(tr) Kati1313; 145(tr) Galina Barskaya; 192(fish) Olga
Khoroshunova; 284(bg) Cathy Keifer

Ecoscene
79(bl) Nick Hawkes

FLPA
58(bg) Phil McLean; 59(tr) Michael & Patricia Fogden/Minden Pictures; 196(bg) Elliott Neep; 200(cl) Chris Stenger/Minden
Pictures; 201(t) ImageBroker/Imagebroker; 204(bg) Jurgen & Christine Sohns; 211(b) Michael Quinton; 212(c) Mark Newman;
233(bl) Roger Tidman; 235(br) Shem Compion; 246(bg) Tui De Roy; 257(bl) Emanuele Biggi; 258(t) Bruno Cavignaux;
261(br) Mark Moffett

Fotolia
36(bl) QiangBa DanZhen; 50 Cornelius; 55(tl) Albo; 93(bl) schaltwerk; 96(t) Steve Estvanik; 100(b) Sharpshot; 110(br) Chris
Fourie; 129(cl) Alexander Y; 141(cr) Andres Rodriguez; 192(reptile) Paul Murphy; 238(c) Grigory Kubatyan; 244(cl) James
Warren; 250(br) Ami Beyer; 255(c) Eric Gevaert; 257(tl) Shane Kennedy; 283(bc) Audrey Eun; 286(bg) noyiil

Getty Images
44(tr) David Samuel Robbins; 46(tr) AFP; 51(bg) Bloomberg; 55(r) Pablo Corral V/Corbis/VCG; 62(t) Tim Davis/Corbis/VCG;
64(b) Robert Glusic; 65(t) Paul A. Souders; 71(br) Paul Chesley; 92(tl) Bettmann; 94 Viviane Moos/Corbis Historical;
97(b) Per-Anders Pettersson; 101(b) Laguna Design; 184(bl) Layne Kennedy; 185(b) Colin Keates; 331(t) Richard Cummins

iStock
42(tl) titine974/iStock/Getty; 45 Froggery/iStock/Getty; 57(tl) pkruger; 78 MvH/iStock/Getty; 80(c) DanBrandenburg/iStock/
Getty; 83(b) dswebb; 89(t) WiganPier/iStock/Getty; 90(br) micheldenijs/iStock/Getty; 95(t) egdigital, (b) Sportstock;
97(b) dejan750; 204(tr) markrhiggins; 206(bg) derwood05; 208(t) GlobalP; 213(br) Thomasaurus; 267(t) CathyKeifer;
282(bl) DavidHCoder; 325(br) Danilo Ascione; 326(bc) Keith Binns; 333(tl) Brianna May, (br) redmal

NASA
10(tl) & 12(bg) & 20(c) NASA-JPL; 11(cl) Goddard Space Flight Center Scientific Visualization Studio/NASA, (tr) & 23(tl) & 25(tl)
& 27(tr) & 73(l), (r) & 86(tr) NASA; 17(c) T.Rector (University of Alaska Anchorage); 19(tr) NASA-GSFC, (br) Greatest Images of
NASA (NASA-HQ-GRIN); 20(c) NASA-STScl; 25(bg) Dick Clark; 120(bc) NASA/JPL-Caltech/University of Arizona; 121(bg) Adam
Block, Mt. Lemmon SkyCenter, U. Arizona

Nature Picture Library
199(br) Nature Production; 219(bg) Jabruson; 234(bg) Rolf Nussbaumer; 266(tr) Meul/ARCO; 269(b) Marco Uliana;
271(c) Visuals Unlimited; 280 John Cancalosi

Photoshot
197(bl) Mike Lane/Woodfall; 210(b) NHPA; 253(tr) NHPA; 256(bl) NHPA

Acknowledgements

Reuters
81(br) Str Old

Rex
87(t) Sipa Press/REX/Shutterstock; 333(bl) KPA/Zuma

Robert Harding
81 Scott Warren

Shutterstock
22(tr) Eky Studio, (br) Karin Wassmer; 23(bg) Manamana; 29(tr) godrick; 33(bl) Dudarev Mikhail; 35(b) Sam Dcruz; 37(b) Celso Diniz; 44(b) Aleix Ventayol Farrés; 49 Paolo Gianti; 52(bl) Vadim Petrakov; 53(bl) Willem Tims; 59(bl) Steve Bower; 65(br) evenfh; 76(bc) Alexandr Zyryanov; 82(t) Roypix; 84 Justin Hobson; 98–99(bg) ssguy; 102(tr) Pavel Vakhrushev, (bl) Ivonne Wierink; 102–103(bg) DeymosHR; 103(t) w shane dougherty; 106–107(bg) vadim kozlovsky; 108(bl) dslaven, (cr) Smileus; 108–109(bg) Gunnar Pippel; 109(c) Ray Hub; 115(bl) Hywit Dimyadi; 116(c) ifong; 116–117(bg) archibald; 118(bg) Jaggat Rashidi; 119(t) miker; 122–123(bg) casejustin; 124(bl) Lilya Espinosa; 125(bl) Stanislav Fridkin; 131(cr) Lawrence Wee; 136–137(bg) Sebastian Kaulitzki; 139(tr) beerkoff; 141(cl) Paul Matthew Photography; 143(tl) Elena Elisseeva; 147(tr) Sebastien Burel; 190(bg) Igor Janicek; 192(amphibian) Audrey Snider-Bell, (invertebrate) Richard Waters, (bird) Steve Byland; 193(br) Rita Januskeviciute; 194(tr) Pan Xunbin; 195(bl) wim claes, (t) van Kuzmin; 197(br) Cathy Keifer; 198(tl) Geoffrey Kuchera, (bl) Dirk Ercken, (c) Audrey Snider-Bell; 201(cr) StevenRussellSmithPhotos; 202(bl) Incredible Arctic, (ct) BMJ, (tr) Smileus; 203(bl) Incredible Arctic; 214(tc) Shannon Workman; 215(bc) Shane Gross; 230(bg) Targn Pleiades, (l) Florian Andronache, (cl) & (cr) Eduardo Rivero, (r) Clinton Moffat; 231 BMJ; 232(bl) ktsdesign; 233(t) AndreAnita; 234(bl) Richard Fitzer; 235(tl) zimmytws; 236(tr) tntphototravis; 237(b) Stuart G Porter; 247(bg) Rich Carey; 249(bl) Glenn Young; 256(bg) Brian Lasenby; 259(bl) AdStock RF; 262(c) cbpix; 264(br) Volkov Alexey; 265(bg) Tan Hung Meng; 267(bc) aabeele; 268(bl) jps, (c) Marco Uliana; 270(bg) Smit; 272(tr) Sue Robinson; 273(tr) Dirk Ercken; 274 fotoslaz; 275(br) Steve Byland; 276(bg) Jorge Moro; 277(cl) monbibi, (br) dabjola, (tr) Nick Stubbs, (cl) Meul, J./Arco Images GmbH, (bl) Henrik Larsson; 278(tr) Csati; 281(t) IrinaK, (cl) Matt Jeppson, (bl) Lovely Bird; 286(bl) Cosmin Manci; 287(t) blewisphotography; 200–201(bg) Anna Om; 363(b) Alice Day

Science Photo Library
28(bg) Mark Garlick; 79(c) Peter Menzel; 89(b) NOAA

Still Pictures
88 C A.Ishokon-UNEP

Superstock
248(bg) Animals Animals

Topfoto
37(br) Topham Picturepoint; 292 CM Dixon/HIP; 293(tl) Topham Picturepoint; 304–305(c) CM Dixon/HIP